TACITUS,

15.20–23, 33–45

Tacitus, *Annals*, 15.20–23, 33–45

Latin Text, Study Aids with Vocabulary, and Commentary

Mathew Owen and
Ingo Gildenhard

http://www.openbookpublishers.com

Digital material and resources associated with this volume are available on our website at: http://www.openbookpublishers.com/isbn/9781783740000

ISBN Hardback: 978-1-78374-001-7
ISBN Paperback: 978-1-78374-000-0
ISBN Digital (PDF): 978-1-78374-002-4
ISBN Digital ebook (epub): 978-1-78374-003-1
ISBN Digital ebook (mobi): 978-1-78374-004-8

DOI: 10.11647/OBP.0035

Cover image: Bust of Nero, the Capitoline Museum, Rome (2009) © Joe Geranio (CC-BY-SA-3.0), Wikimedia.org.

All paper used by Open Book Publishers is SFI (Sustainable Forestry Initiative), and PEFC (Programme for the Endorsement of Forest Certification Schemes) Certified.

Printed in the United Kingdom and United States by Lightning Source for Open Book Publishers (Cambridge, UK).

Contents

1. Preface and acknowledgements

The selective sampling of Latin authors that the study of set texts at A-level involves poses four principal challenges to the commentators. As we see it, our task is to: (i) facilitate the reading or translation of the assigned passage; (ii) explicate its style and subject matter; (iii) encourage appreciation of the extract on the syllabus as part of wider wholes – such as a work (in our case the *Annals*), an *oeuvre* (here that of Tacitus), historical settings (Neronian and Trajanic Rome), or a configuration of power (the principate); and (iv) stimulate comparative thinking about the world we encounter in the assigned piece of Latin literature and our own. The features of this textbook try to go some way towards meeting this multiple challenge:

To speed up comprehension of the Latin, we have given a fairly extensive running vocabulary for each chapter of the text, printed on the facing page. We have not indicated whether or not any particular word is included in any 'need to know' list; and we are sure that most students will not require as much help as we give. Still, it seemed prudent to err on the side of caution. We have not provided 'plug in' formulas in the vocabulary list: but we have tried to explain all difficult grammar and syntax in the commentary. In addition, the questions on the grammar and the syntax that follow each chapter of the Latin text are designed, not least, to flag up unusual or difficult constructions for special attention. Apart from explicating grammar and syntax, the commentary also includes stylistic and thematic observations, with a special emphasis on how form reinforces, indeed generates, meaning. We would like to encourage students to read beyond the set text and have accordingly cited parallel passages from elsewhere in the *Annals* or from alternative sources, either in Latin and English or, when the source is in Greek, in English only. Unless otherwise indicated, we give the text and translation (more or less modified) according to the editions in the Loeb Classical Library. Our introduction places Tacitus and the set text within wider historical parameters, drawing on recent – and, frequently, revisionist – scholarship on imperial Rome: it is meant to provoke, as well as to inform. Finally, for each chapter of the Latin text we have included a 'Stylistic Appreciation' assignment and a 'Discussion Point': here we flag up issues and questions, often with a contemporary angle, that lend themselves to open-ended debate, in the classroom and beyond.

* * *

We would like to thank the team at Open Book Publishers, and in particular Alessandra Tosi, for accepting this volume for publication, speeding it through production – and choosing the perfect reader for the original manuscript: connoisseurs of John Henderson's peerless critical insight will again find much to enjoy in the following pages (acknowledged and unacknowledged), and we are tremendously grateful for his continuing patronage of, and input into, this series.

2. Introduction

DOI: 10.11647/OBP.0035.01

At the outset of his *Annals*, which was his last work, published around AD 118, Tacitus states that he wrote *sine ira et studio* ('without anger or zeal'), that is, in an objective and dispassionate frame of mind devoted to an uninflected portrayal of historical truth. The announcement is part of his self-fashioning as a muckraker above partisan emotions who chronicles the sad story of early imperial Rome: the decline and fall of the Julio-Claudian dynasty (AD 14–68) in the *Annals* and the civil war chaos of the year of the four emperors (AD 69) followed by the rise and fall of the Flavian dynasty (AD 69–96) in the (earlier) *Histories*. But his narrative is far from a blow-by-blow account of Roman imperial history, and Tacitus is an author as committed as they come – a literary artist of unsparing originality who fashions his absorbing subject matter into a dark, defiant, and deadpan sensationalist vision of 'a world in pieces', which he articulates, indeed enacts, in his idiosyncratic Latinity.[1] To read this Latin and to come to terms with its author is not easy: 'No one else ever wrote Latin like Tacitus, who deserves his reputation as the most difficult of Latin authors.'[2]

This introduction is designed to help you get some purchase on Tacitus and his texts.[3] We will begin with some basic facts, not least to establish Tacitus as a successful 'careerist' within the political system of the principate who rose to the top of imperial government *and stayed there* even through upheavals at the centre of power and dynastic changes (1). A few comments on the configuration of power in imperial Rome follow, with a focus on how emperors stabilized and sustained their rule (2). In our survey of Tacitus' *oeuvre*, brief remarks on his so-called *opera minora* (his 'smaller' – a better label would be 'early' – works) precede more extensive consideration of his two great works of historiography: the *Histories* and,

---

1   Henderson (1998).
2   Woodman (2004) xxi.
3   We are not trying to compete with general introductions to Tacitus and his works, of which there are plenty. We particularly recommend Ash (2006) and the two recent companions to Tacitus edited by Woodman (2009a) and Pagán (2012). See also, more generally, the companions to (Greek and) Roman historiography edited by Marincola (2007) and Feldherr (2009).

in particular, the *Annals*. Here issues of genre – of the interrelation of content and form – will be to the fore (3). We then look at some of the more distinctive features of Tacitus' prose style, with the aim of illustrating how he deploys language as an instrument of thought (4). The final two sections are dedicated to the two principal figures of the set text: the emperor Nero (and his propensity for murder and spectacle) (5); and the senator Thrasea Paetus, who belonged to the so-called 'Stoic opposition' (6). None of the sections offers anything close to an exhaustive discussion of the respective topic: all we can hope to provide are some pointers on how to think with (and against) Tacitus and the material you will encounter in the set text.

2.1 Tacitus: life and career

Cornelius Tacitus was born in the early years of Nero's reign *c.* AD 56/58, most likely in Narbonese or Cisalpine Gaul (modern southern France or northwestern Italy). He died around AD 118/120.[4] His father is generally assumed to have been the Roman knight whom the Elder Pliny (AD 23 – 79) identifies in his *Natural History* (7.76) as 'the procurator of Belgica and the two Germanies.' We do not know for sure that Tacitus' first name (*praenomen*) was Publius, though some scholars consider it to be 'practically certain.'[5] His *nomen gentile* Cornelius may derive from the fact that his non-Roman paternal ancestors received citizenship in late-republican times 'through the sponsorship of a Roman office-holder called Cornelius.'[6] Our knowledge of his life and public career is also rather sketchy, but detailed enough for a basic outline. If we place the information we have or can surmise from his works on an imperial timeline, the following picture emerges:

Dates	Reigning Emperor	Tacitus
54 – 68	Nero	Born *c.* 56
68 – 69 (January)	Galba	
69 (January – April)	Otho	
69 (April – 22 December)	Vitellius	

---

4   This paragraph is based on Birley (2000) and Martin and Woodman (2012).
5   Birley (2000) 231 n. 4 with reference to Oliver (1977).
6   Birley (2000) 233–34.

69 – 79	Vespasian	In Rome from 75 onwards (if not earlier) 77/78: marriage to Julia Agricola, daughter of Gnaeus Julius Agricola (dates: 40–93; governor of Britain 77–85)
79 – 81	Titus	80s (or even earlier): Membership in the priestly college of the *Quindecimviri sacris faciundis* *c.* 81: *Quaestor Augusti* (or *Caesaris*)?
81 – 96	Domitian	88: Praetor 89–93: Absence from Rome, perhaps on official appointments
96 – 98	Nerva	97: Suffect consul (after the death of Verginius Rufus) 98: Publication of the *Agricola* and the *Germania*
98 – 117	Trajan	*c.* 101/2: Publication of the *Dialogus* ? *c.* 109–10: Publication of the *Histories* 112–13: Proconsulship of Asia
117 – 138	Hadrian	Died not before 118, *c.* 120? ? Shortly before: Publication of the *Annals*

Overall, we are looking at an impressive career both in Rome and in provincial government, which he entered at an early age and sustained throughout his life. As Birley notes with respect to one of his earliest appointments: 'His membership of the *XVviri*, prestigious enough at any stage in a man's career, had come early. Often senators did not get into this élite priestly college or one of the other three of equal status until after being consul. Further, in 88 the *XVviri* had a particularly important role: supervising the Secular Games.'[7] Tacitus managed

---

7 Birley (2000) 234. Tacitus himself records his involvement at *Annals* 11.11.1: *Isdem consulibus ludi saeculares octingentesimo post Romam conditam, quarto et sexagesimo quam*

to remain active in public life through several regime changes: he seems to have done equally well under emperors he excoriates in his writings (in particular Domitian) and under emperors he deems worthy of praise (Nerva, Trajan). This raises an interesting, and potentially awkward, question, well articulated by A. J. Woodman: 'Tacitus' smooth progression from office to office – and in particular his relatively early acquisition of a major priesthood and his culminating proconsulship of Asia – bespeak of someone who was more than happy to take advantage of the political opportunities which the system had to offer and whose debt to the emperors listed in the preface to the *Histories* [on which see below] was not inconsiderable. It is thus all the more curious that, as usually interpreted, his treatment of the early empire in the *Annals* represents a general indictment of the system from which he had derived such personal benefit.'[8] Curious indeed. Does Tacitus just indict specific emperors? Or certain dynasties? Or the entire system of the principate? Or only variants thereof? And why? The scholarly verdict is divided...

2.2 Tacitus' times: the political system of the principate

It is easy to think of Roman emperors as omnipotent rulers who could do (and did) whatever struck their fancy. The truth is more complex – and arguably more interesting (if less sensational). The duration and success of an emperor's reign depended not least on the way he interacted with a range of individuals and groups, which needed 'to accept' him:[9]

Augustus ediderat, spectati sunt. utriusque principis rationes praetermitto, satis narratas libris quibus res imperatoris Domitiani composui. nam is quoque edidit ludos saecularis iisque intentius adfui sacerdotio quindecimvirali praeditus ac tunc praetor; quod non iactantia refero sed quia collegio quindecimvirum antiquitus ea cura et magistratus potissimum exequebantur officia caerimoniarum. [Under the same consulate (= 47 AD), eight hundred years from the foundation of Rome, sixty-four from their presentation by Augustus, came a performance of the Secular Games. The calculations employed by the two princes I omit, as they have been sufficiently explained in the books which I have devoted to the reign of Domitian (= the closing books, now lost, of the *Histories*). For he too exhibited Secular Games, and, as the holder of a quindecimviral priesthood and as praetor at the time, I followed them with more than usual care: a fact which I recall not in vanity, but because from of old this responsibility has rested with the Fifteen, and because it was to magistrates in especial that the task fell of discharging the duties connected with the religious ceremonies.]

8   Woodman (2004) xi.
9   Noreña (2011) 7. His conception of imperial Rome owes much to Paul Veyne (1976) and, in particular, Egon Flaig (1992) (2010).

It would be misleading... to conceptualize the emperor as an omnipotent monarch capable of dominating his far-flung empire. The structural limitations to the practical power of Roman emperors were simply too great. Aristocratic competitors could be very dangerous, especially those in command of legions stationed in the periphery. From such potential pretenders to the throne the threat of usurpation could never be extinguished entirely. Less acute but more constant pressure came from those groups within Roman imperial society that were capable of meaningful collective action in the public sphere. Especially significant were the senate, the *plebs urbana* of Rome, and the legionary armies. With these influential collectivities the emperor was in constant dialogue, both real and symbolic, interacting with each in a highly prescribed manner calculated to elicit the public displays of consensus, or 'acceptance', upon which imperial legitimacy ultimately rested.[10]

In addition to the social groups identified by Noreña, we should recognize the imperial family and the court, its personnel, and its social dynamics as major factors in how power worked during the principate. Relatives with 'dynastic' credentials joined ambitious aristocrats as potential pretenders to the throne.[11] (Nero kills off in cold blood one such, Junius Torquatus Silanus, in our set text: see *Annals* 15.35 and Section 5 below.) The daily proximity to the emperor turned female figures of the court (mothers, wives, mistresses) into potential power brokers but also potential victims of imperial whim: Agrippina and Poppaea are prime examples of *both* in Tacitus' Nero-narrative. The same is true of the emperor's closest advisors and high-ranking members of his staff, frequently highly skilled (and highly loyal) freedmen. Senatorial sources tend to look askance at such – from a republican point of view – 'interlopers' in the Roman field of power. Neither women nor freedmen shared in political decision-making in republican times, but now could wield greater influence than many a distinguished senator, simply because they had easy access to, and the ear of, the emperor. The same goes for the prefect of the Praetorian Guard, the bodyguard of the emperor and the most significant military presence in the city of Rome.

---

10   The distinction between 'real' and 'symbolic' Noreña draws here is perhaps unhelpful – since symbolic interactions were very real as well. Presumably, though, he means to distinguish between interactions that happened face-to-face or had a material dimension and those that happened via symbolic gestures or other media of communication (coins, religious worship etc.). Some forms of interaction, such as the donative to the soldiers on special occasions, had both a material and a symbolic value.

11   The Roman principate was not a hereditary monarchy: the potential for usurpation defined the political system, even though succession frequently followed dynastic principles. See further Bert Lott (2012).

What made being a Roman emperor so difficult was the fact that each constituency brought a different set of expectations to bear on their *princeps*:[12] the ideal emperor of the army was never going to be the ideal emperor of the senate was never going to be the ideal emperor of the people. Moreover, the groups were in latent rivalry with one another for access to the emperor and for his attention, which caused potential problems in those settings – such as public games – when he interacted with several simultaneously: gestures of special proximity or favour towards the plebs, for instance, might miff the ruling élite (and vice versa). Finally, the groupings themselves were not necessarily homogeneous. At the opening of *Annals* 16, for instance, Tacitus reports in disgust that the urban plebs reacted to Nero's public performance as cithara player with enthusiasm and delight, yet goes on to note with grim satisfaction that this (from his point of view) shameful disgrace of imperial dignity scandalized and saddened those common people who had travelled to the city from remote places in the countryside where the values of old Italy were still alive.[13]

The relation between the emperor and the senatorial *ordo*, i.e. the politically active members of the élite, was especially fraught, and for various reasons. In comparison with republican times, the aristocracy was particularly affected by the 'massive and unprecedented relocation of power and authority in the Roman world' brought about by 'the advent... of the imperial regime we call the principate.'[14] Élite Romans experienced – and had to cope with and negotiate – 'concrete social and cultural dislocations ... in the face of the emperor's power – for example, a reduction of the opportunities and rewards for displaying military prowess, and a perceived aggravation of certain problems associated with flattery.'[15] They now occupied a paradoxical position in the field of power. On the one hand, they remained rulers of the world: emperor and senators governed the empire together (with the emperor having exclusive control over the army), in close interaction with local élites. (The interaction of centre and periphery is one of the main topics of the first few chapters of the set text.) On the other hand, they were subordinate to the *princeps* and had to accommodate his existence – not least because the emperor put a cap on senatorial rivalry, preventing the senate from dissolving into suicidal infighting and kicking off civil war. For

---

12   We owe appreciation of this point to discussions with Ulrich Gotter.
13   *Annals* 16.4–5.
14   Roller (2001) 6.
15   Roller (2001) 11.

the Roman aristocracy remained a highly competitive body: senators who pursued a public career vied for prestigious appointments, acted as patrons for others with like ambitions, and desired glory. In contrast to republican times, however, success and effectivness in these roles and undertakings depended in large part on being in favour (or at least not on bad terms) with the emperor – though, as we shall see in Section 6, defying the emperor could also yield a type of fame.

The mutual reliance of *princeps* and ruling élite in governing the empire and the fact that inner-aristocratic competition over posts and honors now inevitably revolved around the figure of the *princeps* promoted novel forms of behaviour among the senators. Rituals of consensus, in which senators demonstrated their proximity and loyalty to the *princeps*, became important; senators vied with each other for recognition by the emperor; some tried to get ahead by charging others with disloyalty: the figure of the informer (*delator*) who broke with group-solidarity and tried to get others charged with treason (*maiestas*) – an extreme form of aristocratic rivalry to acquire a position of influence close to the *princeps* – populates Tacitus' historical narratives;[16] others endeavoured to make a name for themselves by pursuing a collision course with the emperor – often much to the chagrin of their senatorial peers (see Section 6 below on Thrasea Paetus). Observers with a literary bent (such as Tacitus or Pliny) are often as scathing about their fellow-senators as they are about the behaviour of specific emperors, evaluating senatorial conduct on a moralizing scale that ranges from servility on the one hand to a defiant embrace of republican *libertas* on the other: 'The instances of servile behaviour that Tacitus chronicles are legion, and all readers will have their favourites; any selection that is not copious is false to the tone of his writing.'[17] This is for sure an accurate description of what Tacitus does in his narrative, but we shouldn't assume that his categorical grid of *servitus* vs. *libertas* yields an accurate interpretation of senatorial conduct in imperial Rome – however tempting this may be. As Egon Flaig asks, (as he means it) rhetorically: 'Were the 600 highest ranking persons of an enormous empire of 60-80 million inhabitants really slaves at heart?'[18]

For members of the senatorial aristocracy, the emperor would ideally conform to the image of the *civilis princeps* – a ruler in other words who

---

16   See e.g. Lintott (2001–2003) (including discussion of the republican background) and Rutledge (2001).

17   Oakley (2012a) 188.

18   Flaig (1992) 123 n. 98.

aligned his forms of interaction with the senate according to proto-republican norms and values: freedom of speech; strict limits to *adulatio*; recognition of the value of republican office which emperor and other aristocrats could hold or aspire to, especially the consulship; investment in a private status – as if an ordinary citizen – in dress and appearance. From an emperor's point of view, balancing ritual elevation with ritual humility – to be part of the society, not above society – was entirely functional: 'An emperor whom ritual and ceremonial raised above the level of human society, whose power was represented symbolically as deriving from "outside", from the gods, owed nothing to the internal structure of the society he ruled. To act, by contrast, as a member of that society, as the peer of its most elevated members, was (symbolically) to associate autocratic power with the social structure. Civility both reinforced the social hierarchy by demonstrating imperial respect for it, and strengthened the autocracy by linking it with the social structure.'[19] Not all emperors felt necessarily obliged to try to confirm to this image (their reigns often came to an abrupt end...); and as we shall see in Section 5 below, different emperors had different notions of what 'civility' consisted in.

Consideration of the underlying 'structure' of the imperial system also helps to put our sources into perspective – enabling us to read them as highly rhetorical and personally and politically committed views on, rather than entirely accurate representations of, historical realities. Just taking our imperial sources at face value results in the kind of history one gets in the (highly engrossing and actively emetic) BBC-series *Horrible Histories*, where the 'Rotten Romans' feature prominently – and Nero gets the final riff in the 'Roman Emperor's Song – Who's Bad?', topping the pops against classic competition: the apparently certifiable sociopaths Caligula (emperor 37–41), Elagabalus (218–222), and Commodus (180–192).[20] But the composition of literature by members of the ruling élite was never a neutral activity; rather, it was itself implicated in the imperial configuration of power, in the jostling for position, in exercises of self-promotion: Pliny, Tacitus, and Suetonius wrote (mainly) for fellow aristocrats about a shared world dominated by the emperor – and used their works to define their own status, position, and prestige within it.

Rhetorical myth-making is rampant in Roman historical writing. Most notoriously, our sources show an avowed interest in portraying emperors who for one reason or other fell out of favour as mentally deranged. In many

---

19   Wallace-Hadrill (1982) 47.
20   http://www.youtube.com/watch?v=w-Nh-zSMzqo. For an equivalent in adult entertainment check out History Channel's *Caligula: 1400 Days of Terror*.

a text, early imperial Rome comes across as a society ruled over by lunatics besotted with power and keen to act on every depraved instinct. Tacitus contributed his share to our image of Roman emperors as evil freaks. Over the last few decades, however, scholarship has increasingly started to question this picture, arguing that your favourite salacious anecdote about imperial Rome (such as Caligula appointing his horse to the consulship) may just be too good to be true – and is in fact a distorting rumour put into circulation posthumously by individuals and groups much invested in blackening the reputation of the deceased emperor.[21] Could it be that our sources are so hostile to certain emperors not because they were deranged – but that they look deranged because our sources are so hostile?

This possibility may come as a let-down. But it shouldn't: critical debunking of historiographical myth-making is in itself an exciting exercise that opens insights into a foreign culture. Fascination shifts from history to the 'making' of history, from the allure of alleged facts to the power of historical fabrications. The question as to why these sensationalizing stories have emerged and been able to colonize our imagination so effectively is arguably just as interesting as trying to put an emperor on the psychiatric couch on the basis of insufficient and distorted evidence. What went down in imperial Rome was not just the power of the sword but the power of the word, especially when it came to shaping (or disfiguring) posthumous reputations.

2.3 Tacitus' *oeuvre*: *opera minora* and *maiora*

From the very beginning of Roman historiography in the late third century BC political achievement and authoritative prose about historical events or figures had gone hand-in-hand. The composition of historical narratives in a range of genres was very much the domain of senators. As Ronald Syme puts it:[22]

> In the beginning, history was written by senators (first a Fabius, and Cato was the first to use the Latin language); it remained for a long time the monopoly of the governing order; and it kept the firm imprint of its origins ever after. The senator came to his task in mature years, with a proper knowledge of men and government, a sharp and merciless insight. Taking up the pen, he fought again the old battles of Forum and Curia. Exacerbated by failure or not mollified by worldly success, he asserted a personal claim to glory and survival; and, if he wrote in retirement from affairs, it was not always with tranquillity of mind.

---

21 For rehabilitation of Caligula see Winterling (2003/2011); for 'Nero the Hero' Champlin (2003). See also *Caligula with Mary Beard* on BBC2 (available on-line).

22 Syme (1970) 1–2.

It is thus telling that Tacitus' literary career begins in earnest only after he had reached the pinnacle of public life: the *Agricola* or *De vita et moribus Iulii Agricolae* appeared in the year after he held the consulship (AD 98). His literary debut also coincided with a major upheaval at the centre of power. AD 96 saw the end of the Flavian dynasty through the assassination of Domitian and the crowning of Nerva as emperor at the age of 65, after years of loyal service under Nero and the Flavians. Pressure from the Praetorian Guard and the army more generally soon compelled Nerva to adopt Trajan as his eventual successor, and Tacitus' first literary activities fall within this period of transition and change, which he himself marks out as a watershed in politics and culture. In fact, he explicitly links the demise of Domitian (and his oppressive regime) to the renaissance of creative efforts in the literary sphere.[23] His writings in and of themselves thus advertise the current system of government as a good one (or at least an improvement over what had come before) and signal Tacitus' (new) political allegiances. (Much of the bad press that has come down to us on the last Flavian comes from writers in the reign of Trajan – Pliny, Tacitus, Suetonius, above all – keen to paint the past in black and the present in white, thereby promoting both the reigning emperors and themselves.)

The *Agricola* is difficult to classify in generic terms. *Prima facie*, it is a 'biography' of his father-in-law Gnaeus Julius Agricola; but it also sports striking affinities with various forms of historiographical writing, not least the works of Sallust (the last 'republican' historiographer) or, in its year-by-year account of Agricola's governorship of Britain, annalistic history. It also includes a brief ethnographic excursion on the British (10–12). But arguably the most striking features are the three chapters of prologue (1–3) and epilogue (44–46) that Tacitus devotes almost exclusively to an attack on the principate of Domitian, which had just come to a violent end.[24] The historical material, the overall outlook, and the timing of the publication all reek of a republican ethos.

Tacitus' next work builds on the ethnographic pilot paragraphs in the *Agricola*. His *Germania* or *De origine et situ Germanorum* is an ethnographic treatise on the German tribes, which he uses as a mirror to reflect on contemporary Rome.[25] Soon thereafter Tacitus published the so-called *Dialogus* (*Dialogus de oratoribus*),

---

23   See *Agricola* 2, where Tacitus envisions all the pursuits (such as the writing of history) that were traditionally located in aristocratic *otium* exiled from Rome during the reign of Domitian.

24   See further Ash (2006) 20 and, for a close reading of the preface, Woodman (2012).

25   There was a sinister side to the treatise's history of reception as it inspired many a German nationalist after it was rediscovered in the Renaissance: see Krebs (2012).

in which he employed yet another genre (the dialogue) to explore whether or not the quality of public oratory had deteriorated under the principate – a traditional preoccupation going back to Cicero who already diagnosed the rise of autocracy as fatal for high-quality speech in the civic domain owing to a disappearance of freedom of expression. These three works are often labelled Tacitus' *opera minora*, his 'minor works.' They are all 'historical' in one way or another and thus set the stage for the two major pieces of historiography: the *Histories* and the *Annals*.

The Histories

The opening paragraph of the *Histories* contains the most detailed self-positioning of Tacitus as a writer of history and is worth a detailed look. Already the opening sentence – *Initium mihi operis Servius Galba iterum Titus Vinius consules erunt*: 'I begin my work with the second consulship of Servius Galba, when Titus Vinius was his colleague' – is jaw-dropping. What makes it so, is not so much what's in it but what isn't. At the beginning of AD 69, when Tacitus begins his *Histories*, Galba was not just consul for the second time – he was also emperor! As Nero's successor he had already been in power since 6 June 68. Tacitus, however, blithely glosses over this not entirely insignificant fact, preferring instead to give a historiographical shout-out to Galba in his role as 'republican' high magistrate. This programmatic keynote sets the tone for the rest of the work – and the remainder of the opening paragraph (*Histories* 1.1):[26]

> nam post conditam urbem octingentos et viginti prioris aevi annos multi auctores rettulerunt, dum res populi Romani memorabantur pari eloquentia ac libertate: postquam bellatum apud Actium atque omnem potentiam ad unum conferri pacis interfuit, magna illa ingenia cessere; simul veritas pluribus modis infracta, primum inscitia rei publicae ut alienae, mox libidine adsentandi aut rursus odio adversus dominantis: ita neutris cura posteritatis inter infensos vel obnoxios. sed ambitionem scriptoris facile averseris, obtrectatio et livor pronis auribus accipiuntur; quippe adulationi foedum crimen servitutis, malignitati falsa species libertatis inest. mihi Galba Otho Vitellius nec beneficio nec iniuria cogniti. dignitatem nostram a Vespasiano inchoatam, a Tito auctam, a Domitiano longius provectam non abnuerim: sed incorruptam fidem professis neque amore quisquam et sine odio dicendus est. quod si vita suppeditet, principatum divi Nervae

---

26 We cite the text and translation by C. H. Moore in the Loeb Classical Library (Cambridge, Mass., 1925).

et imperium Traiani, uberiorem securioremque materiam, senectuti seposui, rara temporum felicitate ubi sentire quae velis et quae sentias dicere licet.

[Many historians have treated of the earlier period of eight hundred and twenty years from the founding of Rome, and while dealing with the Republic they have written with equal eloquence and freedom. But after the battle of Actium, when the interests of peace required that all power should be concentrated in the hands of one man, writers of like ability disappeared; and at the same time historical truth was impaired in many ways: first, because men were ignorant of politics as being not any concern of theirs; later, because of their passionate desire to flatter; or again, because of their hatred of their masters. So between the hostility of the one class and the servility of the other, posterity was disregarded. But while men quickly turn from a historian who curries favour, they listen with ready ears to calumny and spite; for flattery is subject to the shameful charge of servility, but malignity makes a false show of independence. In my own case I had no acquaintance with Galba, Otho, or Vitellius, through either kindness or injury at their hands. I cannot deny that my political career owed its beginning to Vespasian; that Titus advanced it; and that Domitian carried it further; but those who profess inviolable fidelity to truth must write of no man with affection or with hatred. Yet if my life were to last, I have reserved for my old age the history of the deified Nerva's reign and of Trajan's rule, a richer and less perilous subject, because of the rare good fortune of an age in which we may feel what we wish and may say what we feel.]

Tacitus here takes us on a flash journey through Roman history, from the foundations of Rome way back when down to his own times, with Actium and Augustus, AD 69 (the year of the four emperors), and the Flavian dynasty as major pit stops. Onto this chronological skeleton, Tacitus hangs systematic comments on the (changing) political regimes, which he matches to the (changing) outlook of Latin historiography. His basic thesis of an inextricable link between the political environment and the quality of writing it sponsors raises some awkward questions about his own literary efforts. Tacitus confronts this challenge head-on by scripting a mini-autobiography into his opening salvo that outlines his political career and his approach to historical writing. If we extrapolate the information Tacitus has packed into his opening paragraph and present it in the form of a table we get the following:

Period	Regime/emperor in charge	Characteristics	The quality of historiography and historiographers	Tacitus (54/56 – c. 120)	Tacitus' historiographical writings
751–31 BC [founding of Rome – Actium]	res populi Romani *	libertas, eloquentia, veritas	Very high: cf. magna ingenia	Before his birth	
30 BC – 68 AD [Augustus – Nero]	Julio-Claudian dynasty	- veritas infracta - libido adsentandi - odium adversus dominantes	Rather low, falling into two flawed types: one motivated by hatred; the other by subservience: neither cares for posterity ambitio scriptoris (a turn-off) obtrectatio et livor (lurid fascination)	Before his birth; childhood	(to be covered later, in the Annals)
69 AD [The year of the four emperors]	Galba, Otho, Vitellius; Vespasian	?	?	mihi Galba Otho Vitellius nec beneficio nec iniuria cogniti;	Histories 1–3

* Unlike the opening of the Annals (for which see below), Tacitus here glosses over the fact that initially Rome was ruled by kings, in the process playing down the traditional assumption that primeval monarchy was simply 'natural'.

Period	Regime/ emperor in charge	Characteristics	The quality of historiography and historiographers	Tacitus (54/56 – c. 120)	Tacitus' historiographical writings
69 – 96 [Vespasian – Domitian]	Flavian dynasty: Vespasian (69–79) Titus (79–81) Domitian (81–96)	?	?	Stellar public career (cf. *dignitas nostra*); this won't compromise his commitment to *incorrupta fides* & absence of *amor* and *odium* in his writings	*Hist.* 4 (21 December 69 – 1 January 70), beginning of 5 (70); the rest of the work is lost, but covered events till the death of Domitian
96 –	'Adopted emperors': Nerva (96–98), Trajan (98–117), Hadrian (117–138)	*uberior securiorque materia; rara temporum felicitas;* freedom of thought and speech	Tacitus seems to imply that the political situation enables: *veritas* *libertas* *eloquentia* This would seem to entail that Tacitus could be a *magnum ingenium* in the republican mould	? What was/ is his status/ career under Nerva and Trajan? Looking towards the future: retirement (*senectus*)	Writing about this period a task for retirement

In his history of Rome and Roman historiography, Tacitus posits two key watersheds: 31 BC and AD 96. This generates a tripartite scheme. In republican times, the political set-up produced and enabled outstanding authors. By contrast, the period from Actium until the death of Domitian, dominated as it was by the Julio-Claudian and Flavian dynasties, was not conducive to literary talents: contemporary accounts are marred by various flaws to do with the wider political milieu. With the rise to power of a new type of *princeps* committed to republican norms in the wake of Domitian, could historiography, too, regain its former heights and produce an account of the previous epoch that avoids the inevitable deficiencies of contemporary voices? Without being too explicit about it, Tacitus seems to be answering this question in the affirmative: only now, under Trajan, so he seems to be saying, has the time come for writing the history of the earlier emperors, thereby advertising the job he is minded to take on himself.

Tacitus approaches his task in inverse chronological order: in the *Histories*, he revisits the year of the four emperors and the rise and fall of the Flavian dynasty (AD 69 –96); in the subsequent *Annals*, he covers the period from the death of the first to the death of the last of the Julio-Claudian emperors, that is, Augustus to Nero.

The Annals

As in the *Histories*, Tacitus uses the opening sentence of the *Annals* for a grand sweep through Roman history from the very beginning down to imperial times (*Annals* 1.1):

> Urbem Romam a principio reges habuere; libertatem et consulatum L. Brutus instituit. dictaturae ad tempus sumebantur; neque decemviralis potestas ultra biennium, neque tribunorum militum consulare ius diu valuit. non Cinnae, non Sullae longa dominatio; et Pompei Crassique potentia cito in Caesarem, Lepidi atque Antonii arma in Augustum cessere, qui cuncta discordiis civilibus fessa nomine principis sub imperium accepit. sed veteris populi Romani prospera vel adversa claris scriptoribus memorata sunt; temporibusque Augusti dicendis non defuere decora ingenia, donec gliscente adulatione deterrerentur. Tiberii Gaique et Claudii ac Neronis res florentibus ipsis ob metum falsae, postquam occiderant, recentibus odiis compositae sunt. inde consilium mihi pauca de Augusto et extrema tradere, mox Tiberii principatum et cetera, sine ira et studio, quorum causas procul habeo.
>
> [Rome at the outset was a city state under the government of kings: liberty and the consulate were institutions of Lucius Brutus. Dictatorships were always

a temporary expedient: the decemviral office was dead within two years, nor was the consular authority of the military tribunes long-lived. Neither Cinna nor Sulla created a lasting despotism: Pompey and Crassus quickly forfeited their power to Caesar, and Lepidus and Antony their swords to Augustus, who, under the title 'princeps', gathered beneath his empire a world outworn by civil conflicts. But, while the glories and disasters of the old Roman commonwealth have been chronicled by famous writers, and intellects of distinction were not lacking to tell the tale of the Augustan age, until the rising tide of sycophancy deterred them, the histories of Tiberius and Caligula, of Claudius and Nero, were falsified through cowardice while they flourished, and composed, when they fell, under the influence of still rankling hatreds. Hence my design, to treat a small part (the concluding one) of Augustus' reign, then the principate of Tiberius and its sequel, without anger and without partiality, from the motives of which I stand sufficiently removed.]

And, as in the *Histories*, he stakes a claim to superiority over previous accounts: his history of the Julio-Claudian dynasty, written in retrospect, surpasses earlier, contemporary sources in veracity by virtue of his dispassionate handling of the subject matter. In the one manuscript that preserved the opening books of the *Annals* the text is presented under the title *Ab excessu divi Augusti*. Our conventional label *Annals* has therefore 'no ancient authority', but it is nevertheless 'a happy choice in that it reminds the reader that Tacitus, most original of Roman historians, wrote within the traditional framework of year-by-year narrative' (more *annal*ysis on this to come in a moment).[27] In fact, at one point Tacitus himself refers to 'the *Annals*' as 'his annals' (*Annals* 4.32.1):[28]

Pleraque eorum quae rettuli quaeque referam parva forsitan et levia memoratu videri non nescius sum: sed nemo annalis nostros cum scriptura eorum contenderit qui veteres populi Romani res composuere.

[I am not unaware that very many of the events I have reported, and shall report, may perhaps seem little things, trifles too slight for record; but no parallel can be drawn between these annals of mine and the work of the men who composed the affairs of the Roman people of old.]

What *are* annals? This type of historiography, which originated in the second centry BC, gets its name from its policy of year-by-year recording (*annus* = year).[29] Notable features include dating of the years with reference

---

27   Martin (1981) 104.
28   Much like Livy 43.13.2: *meos annales*.
29   See Gotter and Luraghi (2003).

to the two high magistrates who entered into office at the beginning of the year ('when x and y were consuls...' is the most conspicuous annalistic tag) and attention to signs of interaction between the *res publica* and the supernatural sphere (such as prodigies). As such, the genre came with certain formal expectations and under the principate carried a potentially built-in political ideology: it was a distinctively republican mode of writing.

Tacitus felt by no means bound to a strictly chronological presentation of his material. There is evidence that he even re-ordered material across year-boundaries – in violation of his own principle *suum quaeque in annum referre* (4.71: 'to record each event in its year of occurrence'). And within the year, he operates freely to generate special effects, not least through the striking juxtaposition of distinctive narrative blocks. The set text offers a superb example: Nero's decision not to proceed with his plan to visit the East and in particular Egypt (15.36) segues seamlessly into an orgy that turns Rome *into* Egyptian Alexandria (15.37), which is followed abruptly by the Great Fire of Rome (15.38) as if moral chaos entails physical destruction.[30] The sequence owes itself to Tacitus' selection and arrangement of the material, and the order in which he narrates these events hints at – even if it does not expressly articulate – an interpretation of Nero's world and the historical forces at work therein.

Yet, however much he was free-lancing generically, his commitment to annalistic history remains fundamental to the politics of his prose – and literary originality.[31] One could argue that Tacitus generated a new generic hybrid – 'imperial annals' – insofar as he superimposed an annalistic structure on imperial history, thereby integrating a republican way of ordering time with another ordering principle, the reigns of individual emperors.[32] To write imperial history in annalistic form was a choice that

---

30 Woodman (1992).
31 Ginsberg (1981) 100: 'Tacitus has rejected traditional annalistic history, but he has not rejected its form. There is a good reason. The annalistic form was traditionally associated with the republican past, and Tacitus wanted to evoke that past, if only to deny its application to the present. ... In rejecting traditional annalistic history, Tacitus rejects also an interpretation of history.'
32 Griffin (2009) 182: 'The structure of the *Annals* as a whole combines an annalistic principle, which applies to the smaller organisation within each book, and a regnal principle, which groups the books according to the reigns of emperors and which ensures that the reigns of Tiberius and Claudius (and doubtless of Caligula) each close with the end of a book.' As Griffin goes on to show, the relative dominance of the two principles throughout the narrative varies from emperor to emperor – one of the formal means by which Tacitus generates meaning.

ensured a paradoxical tension in the very make-up of his text. Or, in the words of John Henderson:[33]

> The annalistic form of 'our *Annals*' (4.32) binds the work to the politics of the *res publica*, consular figureheads leading a yearly change of the guard to link human with solar time. *Annals* are the voice of the tribune, the censor, the consul, of *that* Rome, they can speak no other language. It was not possible to write *Annals* before (in the myth of *respublica libera*) Brutus expelled the Tarquins. ... What Tacitus documents under the flag of dispassion (so: laments, protests, contemns?) is collapsed into the reigns of emperors, as Livian history of Rome *Ab urbe condita* is ousted by Tacitean history of the Caesars' re-foundation *Ab excessu divi Augusti*.

Only parts of the *Annals*, which, on the most plausible reconstruction, originally added up to 18 Books, have survived. Here is what we have (and what we haven't):

Book	Years Covered	Emperor(s)
1	14 – 15	Augustus, Tiberius
2	16 – 19	Tiberius
3	20 – 22	Tiberius
4	23 – 28	Tiberius
5	29	Tiberius
6	31 – 37	Tiberius
[Lost: 7 – 10	37 – 47	Caligula, early years of Claudius]
11	47 – 48 (first part)	Claudius
12	48 (rest) – 54 (first part)	Claudius; book ends with Nero's ascent to the throne
13	54 (rest) – 58	Nero
14	59 – 62 (first part)	Nero
15	62 (rest) – 65 (first part)	Nero
16 (breaks off in ch. 35 with the death of Thrasea Paetus)	65 (rest) – 66 (first part)	Nero
[Lost ? 17 – 18	? 66 (rest) – 68 (till the death of Nero) ?	Nero]

---

33   Henderson (1998) 257–58.

One conspicuous aspect of the *Annals* that the table illustrates nicely is a change in policy after the Tiberius-narrative in how Tacitus distributed his material across books. Throughout his account of Tiberius' reign, a new book coincides with a new year and hence new consuls – in traditionally annalistic fashion. In the Claudius- and Nero-narratives, Tacitus abandons this practice. As a result the beginnings and ends of books – always marked moments – foreground imperial themes. Consider:

End of Book 11: execution of Claudius' wife Messalina

Beginning of Book 12: choice of Agrippina (Nero's mother) as new wife

End of Book 12: death of Claudius and Nero's ascent to the throne

Beginning of Book 13: murder of Junius Silanus

End of Book 13: the death – and revival (!) – of the *arbor ruminalis*, the tree that 830 years ago gave shadow to Romulus and Remus when they were babies[34]

Beginning of Book 14: Annalistic opening ('under the consulship of Gaius Vipstanus and C. Fonteius', i.e. AD 59), followed by the failed and successful murder of Agrippina[35]

End of Book 14: Exile and murder of Nero's first wife Octavia; preview of the conspiracy of Piso

Beginning of Book 15: War in the East

End of Book 15: Honours for Nero in the wake of the conspiracy of Piso

Beginning of Book 16: the 'treasure of Dido' (a hare-brained idea to solve a financial crisis)

---

34 Spot the odd one out (*Annals* 13.58): *Eodem anno Ruminalem arborem in comitio, quae octingentos et triginta ante annos Remi Romulique infantiam texerat, mortuis ramalibus et arescente trunco deminutam prodigii loco habitum est, donec in novos fetus reviresceret* ('In the same year, the Ruminal tree in the Comitium, which 830 years earlier had sheltered Remus and Romulus in their infancy, through the death of its boughs and the withering of its stem reached a stage of decrepitude which was regarded as a portent – until it revived with fresh shoots'). A portent such as the withering of a sacred tree may well have been entered in the annalistic record – but also if it then consumes itself? Is Tacitus pulling our leg here, with an unexpected, yet deconstructive, gesture to a formal device of annalistic writing?

35 This return to a coincidence of beginning of the year and beginning of the book also receives instant and ironic qualification: right after the dating, Tacitus drops the acid remark that the length of his reign (*vetustate imperii* – a dark-humoured hyperbole that mockingly asserts the dominance of the imperial principle) had finally rendered Nero sufficiently audacious to go through with the long-plotted matricide.

2.4 Tacitus' style (as an instrument of thought)[36]

Tacitus is one of the great prose stylists to write in Latin. Indeed, to be able to read him in the original is held by some to be in itself sufficient justification 'to believe that learning Latin is worthwhile.'[37] But readers of Tacitus weaned on Ciceronian Latin are in for a disquieting experience. While it is important to bear in mind F. R. D. Goodyear's point that Tacitean style is protean (both across his *oeuvre* and within a single work) and his writings constitute an 'endless experiment with his medium, the discontent with and reshaping of what had been achieved before, the obsessive restlessness of a stylist never satisfied that he had reached perfection', it is nevertheless possible to identify some pervasive features that are also amply on display in the set text.[38]

(a) Where Cicero aims for fullness of expression (*copia verborum*), the name of Tacitus' game is brevity (*brevitas*), not least in how he deploys ellipsis and asyndeton. As Ronald Syme puts it, 'The omission of words and connectives goes to ruthless extremes for the sake of speed, concentration, and antithesis; and stages in a sequence of thought or action are suppressed, baffling translation (but not hard to understand).'[39]

(b) Whereas Cicero's diction tends to be conservative, Tacitus delights in the unusual lexical choice.[40]

(c) Cicero takes pride in balance and symmetry; Tacitus goes for disjunctive *varietas*. His 'studied avoidance of syntactical balance and the pursuit of asymmetry' is in evidence throughout the set text and noted in the commentary.[41]

(d) One particular Tacitean technique of throwing syntactical symmetry off-balance is to unsettle 'the relationship and respective weight of main clauses and subordinate clauses.'[42] As Ronald Martin put it: '[Tacitus] makes use, far more than any other Latin writer, of sentences in which the main clause is completed early and the

---

36 Our discussion in this section draws above all on Martin (1981), Henderson (1998), O'Gorman (2000), and Oakley (2009b).
37 Woodman (2009b) 14.
38 Goodyear (2012) 369.
39 Syme (1958) 347.
40 Martin (1981) 214–15.
41 Martin (1981) 220.
42 O'Gorman (2000) 3.

centre of gravity is displaced to appended, syntactically subordinate, elements.'[43] The first sentence of the set text (15.20.1) is an excellent case in point.

(e) More generally, Cicero and Tacitus differ in their deployment of irony – which advances to something of a master-trope in Tacitus. O'Gorman defines irony as 'a mode of speaking which establishes an unquantifiable distinction between a statement and "its" meaning' and adds an important clarification: 'A crude definition of an ironic statement would define the meaning as *opposite to* what is said, but it is better to conceive of the meaning of an ironic statement as *different from* what is said, not exclusively or even necessarily its opposite.'[44] She aptly calls on Cicero, who equates irony with dissimulation (*de Oratore*/ *On the Ideal Orator* 2.269):[45]

> Urbana etiam dissimulatio est, cum alia dicuntur ac sentias, non illo genere, de quo ante dixi, cum contraria dicas, ut Lamiae Crassus, sed cum toto genere orationis severe ludas, cum aliter sentias ac loquare.

> Irony, that is, saying something different from what you think, is also elegant and witty. I don't mean the kind I mentioned earlier, saying the exact opposite (as Crassus did to Lamia), but being mock-serious in your whole manner of speaking, while thinking something different from what you are saying.

As O'Gorman puts it: 'Irony depends upon the divergence in sense between utterance (*quae dicuntur*) and the unsaid (*quae sentias*). But the nature of the unsaid is indeterminable; all we know about it is that it is *aliud* – *other than* what is uttered.'[46] In the case of irony in Cicero's orations, however, it is often rather obvious what Cicero thinks, even if it is not what he says: an orator, after all, relies on his eloquence to produce tangible results (a verdict of innocence or guilt, a decision on a matter of policy) and therefore must communicate what he means. Also, for an ironic utterance to be witty, both meanings, the stated and the implied, must resonate simultaneously. In contrast, Tacitus' use of irony is more opaque. And indeed he often leaves it unstated of what precisely he means – even if we realize

---

43   Martin (1981) 221.
44   O'Gorman (2000) 11.
45   O'Gorman (2000) 11; we give the translation of J. M. May and J. Wisse, *Cicero On the Ideal Orator (De Oratore)*, New York and Oxford 2001.
46   O'Gorman (2000) 11.

that authoritative irony is in play: in his works, irony is not a local phenomenon, applied for special effect – it is an ubiquitous feature of his narrative and authorial voice, the counterpart to his claim to be in ruthless pursuit of the truth. In Cicero, irony is an occasional figure of speech; in Tacitus, it is a pervasive mode of critique.

This leads to a more general consideration: as with his resourceful manipulation of genre, style in Tacitus is a formal instrument of thought – an essential aspect of how he defines his authorial voice. His style ought to be embraced as a means and a medium of political commentary.[47] It enacts his interpretation of history: it is as dark, difficult, and fractured as the world in pieces he sets out to describe. If the empire struck, Tacitus strikes back – often with a dark sense of humour, manifesting itself in 'arch wit, appalled satire, sleazy innuendo, surreal coincidence …'[48]

In part, Tacitus thereby addresses the problem of authenticity. How do you develop an authentic voice on subject matter suffused with fraud and deceit? How do you avoid your own authorial project, your own rhetoric becoming subsumed by the imperial vices you set out to chronicle and expose? One way is to deploy irony to shift and hide. As a result, coming up with the definitive interpretation of Tacitus is a bit like trying to find a stable position in quicksand. Or, as Henderson puts it, 'he'll never be caught with his rhetorical trousers down, his work is ironized beyond anything so crude. Instead, his text writes in "anti-language", held always just beyond reach of secure reading, recuperative comprehension, not a "story" but a deadly serious challenge to think out, re-think and be out-thought by "the consular historian".'[49]

2.5 Tacitus' Nero-narrative: Rocky-Horror-Picture Show and Broadway on the Tiber

Tacitus' portrayal of Nero is in some respects more restrained than those of other contemporary sources. Examples from the set text include his selective Taci-turn-ity in reporting Nero's alleged sex crimes and his

---

47 See O'Gorman (2000) 2: 'The formal structures of Tacitus' prose embody a political judgement of the principate. Tacitean style can be seen as the manifestation in narrative of a particular historical understanding, one which is integrally linked to a senatorial view of the principate.'

48 John Henderson, *per litteras.*

49 Henderson (1998) 260–61.

judiciously aporetic stance on whether the emperor was responsible for setting Rome afire. But his Nero, too, is a murderous pervert with disgusting inclinations (such as a penchant for Greek culture...) and a prolific contributor to imperial *Grand Guignol* (as the French call theatre that specializes in naturalistic horror shows) – to begin with, unwittingly so. Here is the first sentence of the Nero-narrative (*Annals* 13.1.1–2):

> Prima novo principatu mors Iunii Silani proconsulis Asiae ignaro Nerone per dolum Agrippinae paratur, non quia ingenii violentia exitium inritaverat, segnis et dominationibus aliis fastiditus, adeo ut C. Caesar pecudem auream eum appellare solitus sit: verum Agrippina fratri eius L. Silano necem molita ultorem metuebat, crebra vulgi fama anteponendum esse vixdum pueritiam egresso Neroni et imperium per scelus adepto virum aetate composita insontem, nobilem et, quod tunc spectaretur, e Caesarum posteris: quippe et Silanus divi Augusti abnepos erat. haec causa necis.

> [The first death under the new principate, that of Junius Silanus, proconsul of Asia, was brought to pass, without Nero's knowledge, by treachery on the part of Agrippina. It was not that he had provoked his doom by violence of temper, lethargic as he was, and so completely disdained by former despotisms that Gaius Caesar [sc. Caligula] usually styled him 'the golden sheep'; but Agrippina, who had procured the death of his brother Lucius Silanus, feared him as a possible avenger, since it was a generally expressed opinion of the multitude that Nero, barely emerged from boyhood and holding the empire in consequence of a crime, should take second place to a man of settled years, innocent character, and noble family, who – a point to be regarded in those days – was counted among the descendents of the Caesars: for Silanus, like Nero, was the son of a great-grandchild of Augustus. This was the cause of death...]

The imperial principle is evidently in play here: the book doesn't start with the new year and the new consuls, but with a new series of imperial murders. As such it looks back to the beginning of the Tiberius narrative – and forward to the set text:[50] later on in his reign, the grown-up Nero takes care of business himself and kills off another Junius Silanus without the help of his mother (by then herself a murder victim) because he was a potential pretender to the throne, having similar dynastic credentials. The incident is part of the set text: see 15.37. More generally, Tacitus makes it abundantly clear that all of Nero's reign lives up to its ominous beginnings,

---

50 See *Annals* 1.6.1 (on the beginning of Tiberius' reign as princeps): *primum facinus novi principatus fuit Postumi Agrippae caedes* ('The opening crime of the new principate was the murder of Agrippa Postumus').

as the youthful emperor starts to ring the changes on murder. A (very) selective survey may include reference to his 'fratricide', insofar as Nero does away with his stepbrother Britannicus, the son of his predecessor Claudius and third wife Messalina (Agrippina, the mother of Nero, was Claudius' fourth spouse).[51] Matricide follows, the gruesome slaughter of Agrippina.[52] Nero's two wives Octavia and Poppaea Sabina (implicated in the murder of her predecessor) fall victim to, respectively, deliberate and accidental 'uxoricide', the latter combined with 'foeticide': Poppaea was pregnant at the time when Nero, in a fit of anger, kicked her to death.[53] The set text concludes with the unsuccessful attempt at the 'senicide' of Seneca, a failure made up for in the wake of the Pisonian conspiracy.[54] The surviving portion of the *Annals* ends with a killing spree (or wave of suicides) that includes the death of Thrasea Paetus.[55] In addition, ancient sources – though not necessarily Tacitus – charge Nero with 'urbicide', that is, the killing of the city of Rome in the great fire (*Ann.* 15.38–4, part of the set text).

But Subrius Flavus, one of the conspirators around Piso, singles out not only matricide and arson as his reason for treason, but a third factor of a rather different nature: Nero's attempt to turn Rome into an ancient variant of Broadway, with the emperor himself getting top billing.[56] This was part of a more general embrace of public spectacle moralists like Tacitus considered frivolous and Greek: Nero's reign is marked by a heavy investment in festivals (including his own, the *Neronia*); games, not least chariot-races; the whole culture of *mousike* (including poetry competitions and singing to the lyre); and the building of Greek cultural institutions such as *gymnasia*. Towards the end of his life, he even took his talents abroad, first to Southern Italy (a step covered in the set text: see 15.33), then with a trip to Greece (AD 66–67, i.e. not covered in the surviving portion of the *Annals*). Relying on Tacitus and other sources, Ted Champlin argues that 'Nero's progression from private to public performance, and from amateur to professional, develops in three distinct stages' both for music and charioteering:[57]

---

51 *Ann.* 13.15–17.
52 *Ann.* 14.1–9.
53 *Ann.* 14.60–64; 16.6.
54 *Ann.* 15.45; 15.60–64.
55 *Ann.* 16.14–35.
56 *Ann.* 15.67.
57 Champlin (2003) 76.

Stage 1: AD 54–58	Rigorous programme of training in music; attention to circus entertainment and religious attendance at the games
Stage 2: AD 59–63	Singing before the people on stage at his private Juvenalia; racing before a private audience in a specially built circus
Stage 3: AD 64–68	Performance of music and racing in public

The theme runs throughout Tacitus' Nero-narrative, from 13.3 (where we catch the youthful Nero exercising his singing and charioteering) to, presumably, his death in the lost portion of the *Annals*. Suetonius reports that Nero's final words were '*qualis artifex pereo*' ('What an artist dies in me!').[58] In Tacitus, an avowed Hellenophobe, Nero's artistic inclinations receive an exceedingly bad press.[59] But once placed in context, matters are not that simple. Ted Champlin has recently challenged the once orthodox view that Nero's sponsorship of, and participation in, these activities was a total turn-off:[60]

> Despite the moral strictures of the authors who report Nero's actions, the social context must be seen as an ambiguous one, and public attitudes as deeply ambivalent. Many of his people surely disapproved of their emperor's games and the damage done to his imperial dignity, but many more just as surely applauded him. His actions sprang from patterns of behavior familiar in contemporary noblemen and approved by ancient precedent, and his people encouraged him. Killing relatives and rivals, real or imaginary, was cold political reality; performing in public may have been a fantasy, but it was one shared by a large part of Roman society. Whether it could be seen as part of the supreme imperial virtue, *civilitas*, is a matter for debate.

From this point of view, Nero's cultivation of his showbiz talents and his desire to turn himself into the biggest star of the imperial entertainment

---

58 Suetonius, *Nero* 49.
59 See Syme (1958) 515–16, in a chapter on 'Tacitus and the Greeks'.
60 Champlin (2003) 68, with page 286 n. 38 where he defines *civilitas*, civility, as 'the ability of the emperor to act as an ordinary citizen, or at least as an ordinary Roman nobleman.' See also page 291 n. 85: 'From the beginning of the reign he had allowed the people to watch him exercise in the Campus Martius; he often declaimed in public; and he had read his own poems not only at home but in the theatre "to such universal joy" that a supplication to the gods was decreed and the poems themselves were inscribed in letters of gold and dedicated to Jupiter Capitolinus: Suetonius 11. 2. These were the actions of an affable emperor, the *civilis princeps*.'

industry were not meant to offend, but to act out one version of the ideal *princeps*. In part, as Champlin goes on to show, Nero succeeded – which accounts for his enormous popularity with certain segments of the population long after his death. One group he did not manage to win over were certain authors of the Trajanic age (Pliny, Tacitus, Suetonius), who are largely responsible for fixing Nero's image in historiography – and thus for posterity (including us...). They are all scathing about Nero's stage-performances and investment in spectacles as a way of defining his public image. In his *Panegyricus*, a speech of praise composed for the emperor Trajan, Pliny the Younger notes the contrast between Nero's and Trajan's style of imperial leadership as follows (46.4–5):

> Idem ergo populus ille, aliquando scaenici imperatoris spectator et plausor, nunc in pantomimis quoque aversatur et damnat effeminatas artes, et indecora saeculo studia. ex quo manifestum est principum disciplinam capere etiam vulgus, cum rem si ab uno fiat severissimam fecerint omnes.

> [And so the same populace which once watched and applauded the performances of an actor-emperor (sc. Nero) has now even turned against the pantomimes and damns their effeminate art as a pursuit unworthy of our age. This shows that even the vulgar crowd can take a lesson from its rulers, since a reform so sweeping, if once started by an individual, can spread to all.]

2.6 Thrasea Paetus and the so-called 'Stoic opposition'

The first figure we encounter in the set text is not the emperor Nero but a senator by the name of Thrasea Paetus (or Paetus Thrasea). He had an illustrious political career, rising to the rank of consul in AD 56 (early in Nero's reign), even though he frequently embarked on a course of collision with the emperor. Within the literary world of the *Annals*, he is a character of structural significance. His appearances (and absences) are always well-timed and strategic: 'Though he [sc. Thrasea Paetus] had been suffect consul in A.D. 56, he does not appear on the pages of Tacitus till two years later. Indeed Tacitus carefully controls his appearances to produce a consistent pattern of one who continuously sought, not always without success, to uphold *libertas senatoria*.'[61] One striking example of

---

61   Martin (1969) 139. See also Syme (1958) II 557.

this policy involves his presence in the first few chapters of the set text (15.20–22), which form the tail end of Tacitus' account of AD 62. As such, his direct speech here correlates with his appearance (including a direct speech) at the beginning of Tacitus' account of the same year (14.48–49). These paragraphs cover the trial of Antistius and form a 'twin' to 15.20–22. The passage is lengthy, but, quite apart from its structural significance, also offers acute insights into the relationship between senate and emperor and into the character of Thrasea Paetus. It is thus worth citing in full (14.48–49):

(48) P. Mario L. Afinio consulibus Antistius praetor, quem in tribunatu plebis licenter egisse memoravi probrosa adversus principem carmina factitavit vulgavitque celebri convivio, dum apud Ostorium Scapulam epulatur. exim a Cossutiano Capitone, qui nuper senatorium ordinem precibus Tigellini soceri sui receperat, maiestatis delatus est. tum primum revocata ea lex, credebaturque haud perinde exitium Antistio quam imperatori gloriam quaeri, ut condemnatum a senatu intercessione tribunicia morti eximeret. et cum Ostorius nihil audivisse pro testimonio dixisset, adversis testibus creditum; censuitque Iunius Marullus consul designatus adimendam reo praeturam necandumque more maiorum. ceteris inde adsentientibus, Paetus Thrasea, multo cum honore Caesaris et acerrime increpito Antistio, non quidquid nocens reus pati mereretur, id egregio sub principe et nulla necessitate obstricto senatui statuendum disseruit: carnificem et laqueum pridem abolita, et esse poenas legibus constitutas, quibus sine iudicum saevitia et temporum infamia supplicia decernerentur. quin in insula publicatis bonis, quo longius sontem vitam traxisset, eo privatim miseriorem et publicae clementiae maximum exemplum futurum.

(49) Libertas Thraseae servitium aliorum rupit, et postquam discessionem consul permiserat, pedibus in sententiam eius iere, paucis exceptis, in quibus adulatione promptissimus fuit A. Vitellius, optimum quemque iurgio lacessens et respondenti reticens, ut pavida ingenia solent. at consules, perficere decretum senatus non ausi, de consensu scripsere Caesari. ille inter pudorem et iram cunctatus, postremo rescripsit: nulla iniuria provocatum Antistium gravissimas in principem contumelias dixisse; earum ultionem a patribus postulatam, et pro magnitudine delicti poenam statui par fuisse. ceterum se, qui severitatem decernentium impediturus fuerit, moderationem non prohibere: statuerent ut vellent; datam et absolvendi licentiam. his atque talibus recitatis et offensione manifesta, non ideo aut consules mutavere relationem aut Thrasea decessit sententia ceterive quae probaverant deseruere, pars, ne principem obiecisse invidiae viderentur, plures numero tuti, Thrasea sueta firmitudine animi et ne gloria intercideret.

[(48) In the consulate of Publius Marius and Lucius Afinius, the praetor Antistius, whose reckless conduct in his plebeian tribuneship I have already mentioned, composed a number of scandalous verses on the *princeps*, and made them public at a well-attended banquet of Ostorius Scapula, with whom he was dining. He was thereupon accused of treason by Cossutianus Capito, who, by the intervention of his father-in-law Tigellinus, had lately recovered his senatorial rank. This was the first revival of the statute; and it was believed that what was sought was not so much death for Antistius as glory for the emperor, whose tribunician veto was to snatch him from death after he had been condemned by the senate. Although Ostorius had stated in evidence that he had heard nothing, the witnesses for the prosecution were believed; and the consul designate, Junius Marullus, moved for the accused to be stripped of his praetorship and put to death according to ancient custom. The other senators were approving the motion, when Thrasea Paetus, with a great show of respect for Caesar and a most vigorous attack on Antistius, argued that it did not follow that the penalty a guilty defendant deserved to suffer was the one that ought to be decided upon, under an outstanding *princeps* and by a senate not fettered by any sort of compulsion. The executioner and the noose had long since been abolished; and there were punishments established by laws under which punitive measures could be decreed without implicating the judges in brutality or the age in infamy. In fact, on an island, with his property confiscated, the longer he dragged out his criminal existence, the deeper would be his personal misery, and he would also furnish an excellent example of public clemency.'

(49) The autonomy of Thrasea broke the servility of others, and, after the consul had authorized a vote, everyone supported his opinion, except a few dissenters, among whom Aulus Vitellius [sc. the future emperor] was the most active sycophant, who levelled his abuse at the very best, and, as is the wont of cowardly natures, lapsed into silence if anyone replied. The consuls, however, not daring to put the senatorial decree into practice, wrote to Caesar about the general consensus of opinion. He, after some vacillation between shame and anger, finally wrote back that 'Antistius, unprovoked by any injury, had uttered to the most intolerable insults against the *princeps*. For those insults retribution had been demanded from the senators; and it would have been appropriate to fix a penalty matching the gravity of the offence. Still, as he had in mind to check undue severity in their verdict, he would not interfere with their moderation; they must decide as they wished – they had been given liberty even to acquit.' These words, and others like it, were read out, and his resentment was plain to see. The consuls, however, did not change the motion on that account; Thrasea did not withdraw his proposal; nor did the remaining members withdraw their support for what they had approved; one part, lest they should seem to have placed the emperor in an invidious position; a majority, because there was safety in their numbers; Thrasea, through his usual firmness of spirit, and a desire not to lose any of his glory.]

The passage offers excellent insights into the fraught relations between senate and *princeps,* achieving two things in one: (i) it illustrates some of the (unwritten) social scripts that both parties could follow to ensure more or less smooth interactions on sensitive issues; (ii) and it shows what happens when one stubborn character like Thrasea Paetus refuses to play by the rules. Let's have a look at the script that everyone tacitly followed before Thrasea's intervention. It would have involved a death sentence passed by the senators followed by a pardon from the emperor. If this scenario had played itself out, everybody would have benefited. First, the defendant: he would have received a slap on the wrist, but not lost his head. Second, the senate: trials of treason put this body in a difficult position. Irrespective of the merits of the case, their actions in such matters were themselves open to critical scrutiny: mild treatment of the defendant could be interpreted as manifesting latent sympathies with the culprit, whereas (overly) harsh punishment, while being a sign of outraged loyalty, could be interpreted as kow-towing to a tyrant. But when it was understood that senatorial severity was a first step in a dialectic that set the *princeps* up for an act of mercy, senators had good reasons for leaning towards passing a harsh verdict since they knew it would not be executed – while also pleasing the emperor. Third, the *princeps*: Nero hoped for a verdict of guilty and a capital sentence as an opportunity to display his mild disposition by pardoning the defendant despite his evident guilt – a scenario in which he would get the best of both worlds: a firm show of senatorial loyalty, plus personal credit for behaving like a *civilis princeps.*

Tacitus' narrative makes it clear that everyone involved played according to this script – until Thrasea Paetus decided to interfere. Then chaos ensued. The senators were put on the spot. As soon as the capital sentence ceases to be unanimous, as soon as alternatives are available, they find themselves in a double bind. Once a milder option is on the table, they lose face if they remain in favour of the death penalty; but voting in favour of the milder proposal – they know – will incur the displeasure of the *princeps.* The dilemma is rendered more uncomfortable by the fact that individual senators could exploit the opportunity to score points for themselves. In this case, Aulus Vitellius opposed Thrasea Paetus, in the full knowledge of endorsing the alternative favoured by the *princeps* – and (one assumes) in the hope of being rewarded for this show of loyalty. Viewed like this, what Tacitus calls senatorial servility (*servitium*) emerges as pragmatism and common sense, and what he calls the independence (*libertas*) of Thrasea Paetus as a rather irritating act of self-promotion that leaves everybody else worse off.

Let's look at the fall-out: by arguing for a more lenient sentencing by the senate Thrasea Paetus pre-empts the role that Nero expected to play himself. (Reading his speech intertextually with Caesar's position in the senatorial debate over the fate of the Catilinarian conspirators as reported by Cicero (in his fourth speech against Catiline) and Sallust (in his *Bellum Catilinae*) heightens the affront: it implies that Paetus is here play-acting as emperor by imitating the founding figure of the Julio-Claudian dynasty.)[62] The senate (including the consuls who had proposed the death penalty) are forced to change tack. The *princeps* is deprived of his opportunity to show mercy and grudgingly concedes what he would have gladly imposed. Aulus Vitellius aggravates the divisions within the senate for personal gain (just like Thrasea). Everyone is insecure and anxious once the *princeps* has been upset. The episode thus illustrates Tacitus' earlier critical comment on Thrasea's adversarial stance towards the *princeps*, when he notes that Thrasea's ostentatious departure from a senate-meeting as protest against excessive adulation of the emperor 'caused danger for himself without initiating freedom for the rest' (*Annals* 14.12.1: *sibi causam periculi fecit, ceteris libertatis initium non praebuit*).

Within the senate, then, Thrasea's refusal to play along in what was ultimately a carefully orchestrated social drama that enabled senators and emperor to negotiate their positions vis-à-vis one another, was bound to prove divisive: it forced all other senators to adopt a much more exposed stance on the matter. From the point of view of the retrospective historiographer, of course, Thrasea's intervention was a godsend: it provided Tacitus with the opportunity to assess the character of the senate as a whole and of specific individuals on a spectrum of possibilities, ranging from 'unscrupulous opportunist' to 'servile' to 'principled and independent.' At the same time, it is important to note that Tacitus enables his readers to appreciate how disruptive a figure Thrasea Paetus was. He could, for instance, easily have enhanced Thrasea's apparent heroism by suppressing the information that Nero planned to pardon the accused in any case: this would have made it much more difficult for his readers to recognize the social script that was playing itself out before Thrasea

---

62   The phrase *multo cum honore Caesaris* (49) is studiously ambiguous: Caesar could be Nero – or Julius Caesar.

interfered. Moreover, he identifies Thrasea's desire for glory as the primary motivating factor behind his intervention. This entails a tension between a principled commitment to republican norms (such as a *libertas*) and the self-seeking desire to inscribe oneself in the memory of the Roman people (*gloria*) – at whatever cost.[63]

It is worth linking this discussion to Tacitus' biography – and authorial preferences. The type of the 'principled troublemaker' or, to use a more positive label, 'martyr of republican *libertas*' is a recurrent figure in Tacitus' *oeuvre*, with Thrasea Paetus, who was invited to commit suicide under Nero, and his son-in-law Helvidius Priscus, who met the same fate under Vespasian, leading the way. Their seemingly upright conduct and apparent adherence to a set of old-fashioned norms and values, their courage, and defiance to death, make for excellent foils for bad emperors.[64] But Tacitus' own position vis-à-vis this kind of senatorial peer was decidedly ambivalent – and unsurprisingly so. Both he himself and his father-in-law Agricola had stellar careers under 'bad' emperors. It is therefore not without interest that Tacitus in the *Agricola* explicitly contrasts the futile, self-serving desire for immortality through heroic suicide that motivated the martyrs with the commitment to civic duties and service to the *res publica* that underwrote the public career of his father-in-law (*Agricola* 42.3–4):

> proprium humani ingenii est odisse quem laeseris: Domitiani vero natura praeceps in iram, et quo obscurior, eo inrevocabilior, moderatione tamen prudentiaque Agricolae leniebatur, quia non contumacia neque inani iactatione libertatis famam fatumque provocabat. sciant, quibus moris est inlicita mirari, posse etiam sub malis principibus magnos viros esse, obsequiumque ac modestiam, si industria ac vigor adsint, eo laudis excedere, quo plerique per abrupta sed in nullum rei publicae usum ambitiosa morte inclaruerunt.

> [It is characteristic of human nature to hate whom you have harmed: but the natural disposition of Domitian, quick to anger, and the more inscrutable the more implacable, was nonetheless mollified by the moderation and circumspection of Agricola, because he was not trying to call forth fame and death with obstinacy and empty boasts of freedom. Let those, whose habit it is to admire what is forbidden, know that even under bad emperors there can be great men; and that obedience and unassuming conduct, as long as

---

63   Sailor (2008) 20: 'One telling feature of Tacitus' treatment of Thrasea and Helvidius, then, is an understated but perceptible emphasis on their strong interest in glory.'

64   See Sailor (2008) 17: 'what gave these men their glamour was their apparent solidarity with the cause of senatorial dignity and significance: to show adherence to a set of values shared by their peers, they had held their own lives cheap.'

they are coupled with effort and initiative, can attain the same degree of praise that many more achieve through perilous courses of action and self-promoting deaths that are of no use to the commonwealth.]

In this passage, at least, Tacitus seems to recommend a middle course between suicide and servility, well captured by D. Sailor: 'a life that bears unmistakable signs of autonomy, signs that suffice for acquiring prestige, but that nonetheless do not lead inevitably to an encounter with the regime's violence. Being killed by the regime was... the lone incontestable proof that you had not surrendered your autonomy to the *princeps'* domination and that you did not recognize the legitimacy of his coercive powers. But there were also alternative "careers" that argued, though less conclusively, for the possibility of both staying alive and securing real distinction for considerable autonomy.'[65] And this may explain why his portrayal of figures like Thrasea in his later historiographical works, while overall positive, also hints at the dysfunctional aspects of their personalities.

---

65   Sailor (2008) 29–30.

3. Latin text with study questions and vocabulary aid

DOI: 10.11647/OBP.0035.02

[20]

1 Exim Claudius Timarchus Cretensis reus agitur, ceteris criminibus ut solent praevalidi provincialium et opibus nimiis ad iniurias minorum elati: una vox eius usque ad contumeliam senatus penetraverat, quod dictitasset in sua potestate situm an pro consulibus qui Cretam obtinuissent grates agerentur. **2** quam occasionem Paetus Thrasea ad bonum publicum vertens, postquam de reo censuerat provincia Creta depellendum, haec addidit: **3** 'usu probatum est, patres conscripti, leges egregias, exempla honesta apud bonos ex delictis aliorum gigni. sic oratorum licentia Cinciam rogationem, candidatorum ambitus Iulias leges, magistratuum avaritia Calpurnia scita pepererunt; nam culpa quam poena tempore prior, emendari quam peccare posterius est. **4** ergo adversus novam provincialium superbiam dignum fide constantiaque Romana capiamus consilium, quo tutelae sociorum nihil derogetur, nobis opinio decedat, qualis quisque habeatur, alibi quam in civium iudicio esse.

20.1:
- What type of genitive is *provincialium*?
- Why is *dictitasset* in the subjunctive?
- Parse *grates*.
- The sentence contrasts (i) *ceteris criminibus* with *una vox* and (ii) *ad iniuriam minorum* with *usque ad contumeliam senatus*: what do these contrasts tell us about how Tacitus viewed the attitude of the senate towards provincial administration?

20.2:
- Explain the syntax of *depellendum*.
- What type of ablative is *provincia Creta*?
- Who is Paetus Thrasea? What do his names *mean*? Where else in the *Annals* does Tacitus mention him?

20.3:
- What are the legislative measures, which Thrasea refers to with *Cincia rogatio, Iuliae leges*, and *Calpurnia scita*? (And what is the difference between *rogatio, leges*, and *scita*?)
- Analyse the design of *nam culpa quam poena tempore prior, emendari quam peccare posterius est.*

20.4:
- Explain the mood of *capiamus*.

Stylistic Appreciation: Looking at this chapter and in particular Tacitus' use of language, consider how he injects a moralising excitement and republican sentiments into his account of the trial of Timarchus.

Discussion Point: What did it take in ancient Rome for a public figure to be counted among 'the good' (*boni*)? What does it take now? Do you agree with Thrasea's assertion that among good men the delinquencies committed by others will entail excellent laws and precedents of honourable conduct? If so, can you think of examples from recent history as evidence? If not, can you think of counter-examples?

exim	then
Cretensis, -e	Cretan (*from Crete*)
reus agor, agi, actus sum	I stand trial
praevalidus, -a, -um	most powerful
provincialis, -is, m.	provincial (*resident of one of Rome's provinces*)
minores, -um, m.pl.	inferiors, lessers
elatus, -a, -um	(*here*) buoyed up, exalted
contumelia, -ae, f.	insult
penetro, -are, -avi, -atum	I reach
dictito, -are, -avi, -atum	I say frequently
situs, -a, -um	located, placed
an	whether
proconsul, -ulis, m.	proconsul (*rank of Roman governor*)
Creta, -ae, f.	Crete
obtineo, -ere, -ui, -tentum	(*here*) I hold, govern
grates ago, -ere, egi, actum	I give thanks
reus, -i, m.	defendant
censeo, -ere, -ui, censum	I propose
depello, -ere, -puli, -pulsum	I banish
usus, -us, m.	(*here*) experience
probo, -are, -avi, -atum	I prove (*here, impersonal passive*)
patres conscripti, m.pl.	senators (*formal mode of address*)
egregius, -a, -um	excellent
honestus, -a, -um	honourable
delictum, -i, n.	misdeed
gigno, -ere, genui, genitum	I produce
licentia, -ae, f.	corruption
rogatio, -onis, f.	legal bill
candidatus, -i, m.	electoral candidate
ambitus, -us, m.	bribery
magistratus, -us, m.	magistrate
avaritia, -ae, f.	greed
scitum, -i, n.	decree
pario, -ere, peperi, partum	I bring about, produce
culpa, -ae, f.	wrongdoing
emendo, -are, -avi, -atum	I reform (*here, pass. infin.* = 'being reformed')
pecco, -are, -avi, -atum	I commit an offence
constantia, -ae, f.	steadfastness
tutela, -ae, f.	protection
derogo, -are, -avi, -atum	I remove, subtract from
opinio, -onis, f.	idea
decedo, -ere, -cessi, -cessum	(*here*) I disappear, cease to exist
habeo, -ere, habui, habitum	(*here*) I consider, value
alibi quam	anywhere other than
iudicium, -ii, n.	judgment

[21]

1 Olim quidem non modo praetor aut consul sed privati etiam mittebantur qui provincias viserent et quid de cuiusque obsequio videretur referrent; trepidabantque gentes de aestimatione singulorum: at nunc colimus externos et adulamur, et quo modo ad nutum alicuius grates, ita promptius accusatio decernitur. **2** decernaturque et maneat provincialibus potentiam suam tali modo ostentandi: sed laus falsa et precibus expressa perinde cohibeatur quam malitia, quam crudelitas. **3** plura saepe peccantur, dum demeremur quam dum offendimus. quaedam immo virtutes odio sunt, severitas obstinata, invictus adversum gratiam animus. **4** inde initia magistratuum nostrorum meliora ferme et finis inclinat, dum in modum candidatorum suffragia conquirimus: quae si arceantur, aequabilius atque constantius provinciae regentur. nam ut metu repetundarum infracta avaritia est, ita vetita gratiarum actione ambitio cohibebitur.'

21.1:
- *privati*: to what does this refer?
- Explain the mood of *viserent* and *referrent*.
- Discuss the contrast Thrasea draws between *olim* and *nunc*: what has changed?

21.2:
- Explain the mood of *decernatur*, *maneat*, and *cohibeatur*.
- What type of verb is *ostento* (whence *ostentandi*)?
- Why does Thrasea regard dishonest praise (*laus falsa*) as worse than malice (*malitia*) and cruelty (*crudelitas*)? Do you agree?

21.3:
- Explain the syntax and analyse the design of *severitas obstinata, invictus adversum gratiam animus*.

21.4:
- *aequabilius atque constantius*: the phrase recalls a passage in Sallust (cited in the commentary). Briefly discuss the effect of this literary echo.
- Explain the significance of the moods and tenses of *regentur* and *cohibebitur*.

Stylistic Appreciation: Look back over the entirety of Thrasea's speech (*usu ... cohibebitur*, 20.3 – 21.4). How does Tacitus make this a powerful piece of persuasive oratory?

Discussion Point: Is Thrasea right that some virtues inspire hatred? Can you think of instances when this point has been made, or ought to have been made, to our leaders today? What do you make of Thrasea's scorn for those who seek popularity 'like electoral candidates'? What does it tell us about Thrasea? He seems to link the pursuit of popular approval with instability and poor governance: does he have a point? (You could consider this from a modern perspective, or from that of first-century Rome at the head of an empire.)

privatus, -i, m.	private citizen
viso, -ere, visi, visum	I visit
obsequium, -ii, n.	obedience, loyalty
trepido, -are, -avi, -atum (de)	I tremble (at)
aestimatio, -onis, f.	judgment
singulus, -i, m.	individual
colo, -ere, colui, cultum	I court, pander to
externus, -i, m.	foreigner
adulor, -ari, -atus sum	I flatter
nutus, -us, m.	nod
grates, -ium f. pl.	votes of thanks
ostento, -are, -avi, -atum	I demonstrate, show off
prex, precis, f.	plea, prayer
exprimo, -ere, -pressi, -pressum	I exact, squeeze out
perinde ... quam...	as much as
cohibeo, -ere, -ui, -itum	I restrict
malitia, -ae, f.	wickedness, malice
pecco, -are, -avi, -atum	I commit an offence, do wrong
demereor, -eri, -itus sum	I oblige
immo	in fact
severitas, -atis, f.	strictness
obstinatus, -a, -um	stubborn
gratia, -ae, f.	(*here*) favour
inde	in consequence
magistratus, -us, m.	magistracy, period of office
ferme	(*here*) usually
inclino, -are, -avi, -atum	I go down hill
in modum (+ gen.)	like, in the manner of
suffragium, -ii, n.	vote
conquiro, -ere, -quisivi, -quisitum	I seek after
arceo, -ere, -cui, -ctum	I keep at bay
aequabilis, -e	consistent
constans, -antis	steady
repetundae (sc. *pecuniae*)	money or other things that are to be restored
from *repeto*	'I demand back'
infrango, -ere, -fregi, -fractum	I crush
avaritia, -ae, f.	greed
gratiarum actio, -onis, f.	vote of thanks
ambitio, -onis, f.	currying of favour

[22]

1 Magno adsensu celebrata sententia. non tamen senatus consultum perfici potuit, abnuentibus consulibus ea de re relatum. mox auctore principe sanxere ne quis ad concilium sociorum referret agendas apud senatum pro praetoribus prove consulibus grates, neu quis ea legatione fungeretur. 2 isdem consulibus gymnasium ictu fulminis conflagravit effigiesque in eo Neronis ad informe aes liquefacta. et motu terrae celebre Campaniae oppidum Pompei magna ex parte proruit; defunctaque virgo Vestalis Laelia, in cuius locum Cornelia ex familia Cossorum capta est.

22.1:

- What construction is *abnuentibus consulibus*?
- With reference to the Introduction, Section 6 (on Thrasea Paetus), consider why the consuls are disinclined to let Thrasea's proposal be put to the vote.
- What was the *concilium sociorum*?
- Why is *referret* in the subjunctive?

22.2:

- *isdem consulibus*: suggest an idiomatic translation for this phrase.
- *gymnasium*: what is this, and what connotations does such a building have? (You may wish to include consideration of the etymology of *gymnasium* in your answer.)
- Try reading out loud *effigiesque in eo Neronis ad informe aes liquefacta*. What do you think Tacitus' tone of voice would be like?
- Who were the Cornelii Cossi?

Stylistic Appreciation: How does Tacitus add colour to his account of the end of the year in this little chapter?

Discussion Point: What do you make of the 'ominous' destruction of Nero's Gymnasium and his effigy within? Why does Tacitus include this detail? Does he take this to be a sign of divine judgment? Do you think there is a place for 'prodigies' such as this in the writing of history? What are the forces that modern historians appeal to in order to impose meaningful patterns upon (amorphous) historical time?

adsensus, -us, m.	agreement
celebro, -are, -avi, -atum	(*here*) I praise
senatus consultum, -i, n.	decree of the senate
abnuo, -ere, -nui, -nutum	I deny
auctore principe	(*abl. absol.*) 'on the emperor's authority'
sancio, -ire, sanxi, sanctum	I enact a law (*sanxere* = *sanxerunt*)
(*sociorum*) *concilium, -ii,* n.	(provincial) council
pro praetor, -oris, m.	propraetor (*rank of provincial governor*)
pro consul, -ulis, m.	proconsul (*rank of provincial governor*)
legatio, -onis, f.	delegation
fungor, -i, functus sum (+ abl.)	I carry out
gymnasium	gymnasium
fulmen, -inis, n.	lightning
ictus, -us, m.	strike
conflagro, -are, -avi, -atum	I burst into flames
effigies, -ei, f.	statue, effigy
informis, -e	shapeless
aes, aeris, n.	bronze
liquefacio, -ere, -feci, -factum	I melt
motus terrae, motus terrae, m.	earthquake
celeber, -bris, -bre	populous
Campania, -ae, f.	Campania (*region of Italy*)
Pompei, -orum, m.pl.	Pompeii
magna ex parte	to a great extent
proruo, -ere, -rui, -rutum	I collapse, am demolished
defungor, -i, -functus sum	I die
virgo Vestalis, virginis Vestalis, f.	Vestal Virgin
Cossi, -orum, m.pl.	the Cossi (*a Roman family*)
capio, -ere, cepi, captum	(*here*) I appoint

[23]

1 Memmio Regulo et Verginio Rufo consulibus natam sibi ex Poppaea filiam Nero ultra mortale gaudium accepit appellavitque Augustam dato et Poppaeae eodem cognomento. locus puerperio colonia Antium fuit, ubi ipse generatus erat. **2** iam senatus uterum Poppaeae commendaverat dis votaque publice susceperat, quae multiplicata exolutaque. et additae supplicationes templumque fecunditatis et certamen ad exemplar Actiacae religionis decretum, utque Fortunarum effigies aureae in solio Capitolini Iovis locarentur, ludicrum circense, ut Iuliae genti apud Bovillas, ita Claudiae Domitiaeque apud Antium ederetur. **3** quae fluxa fuere, quartum intra mensem defuncta infante. rursusque exortae adulationes censentium honorem divae et pulvinar aedemque et sacerdotem. atque ipse ut laetitiae, ita maeroris immodicus egit. **4** adnotatum est, omni senatu Antium sub recentem partum effuso, Thraseam prohibitum immoto animo praenuntiam imminentis caedis contumeliam excepisse. secutam dehinc vocem Caesaris ferunt qua reconciliatum se Thraseae apud Senecam iactaverit ac Senecam Caesari gratulatum: unde gloria egregiis viris et pericula gliscebant.

23.1:

- Who were Memmius Regulus and Verginius Rufus? Discuss the significance of the phrase *Memmio Regulo et Verginio Rufo consulibus* for the genre in which Tacitus is writing.
- *dato et Poppaeae eodem cognomento*: what construction is this?

23.2:

- Parse *dis*.
- Explain what *certamen ad exemplar Actiacae religionis* refers to.

23.3:

- Explain the syntax of *quae* and of *quartum intra mensem defuncta infante*.
- Parse *censentium*.

23.4:

- State and explain the case of *Thraseam*.
- *apud Senecam iactaverit*: why do you think Nero would have wanted to tell Seneca in particular of his mercy towards Thrasea?
- Comment on Tacitus' choice of the verb *gliscebant* here.

Stylistic Appreciation: How in this chapter does Tacitus offer us a disturbing snapshot of the behaviour of the *princeps* and the senators in the reign of Nero?

Discussion Point: '*O homines ad servitutem paratos!*' ('Damn these fellows so ready to be slaves!'): so the emperor Tiberius reproached the senators of his time. Does this chapter suggest a similarly slavish senate? What factors in Rome's history and constitution led the senators to behave as they do in this chapter? Why is Tacitus so scornful of their conduct? Can you think of modern contexts – in your school, in society at large – where you might be able to observe similar forms of behaviour? What are the causes? What the consequences?

ultra (+ acc.)	beyond
appello, -are, -avi, -atum	I call
cognomentum, -i, n.	name
puerperium, -ii, n.	childbirth
Antium, -ii, n.	Antium (*modern Anzio, Nero's birthplace*)
genero, -are, -avi, -atum	I give birth to, produce
uterus, -i, m.	womb
commendo, -are, -avi, -atum	I entrust to the protection of
votum, -i, n.	vow
publice	(*here*) as a community
exsolvo, -ere, -solui, -solutum	I discharge (a vow)
supplicatio, -onis, f.	day of thanksgiving
fecunditas, -atis, f.	fertility
ad exemplar + gen.	based on the model of
Actiaca religio, -onis, f.	Festival of Actium
decerno, -ere, -crevi, -cretum	I decree
solium, -ii, n.	throne
Capitolinus Iuppiter, Iovis, m.	Capitoline Jupiter (*the greatest cult of Jupiter*)
ludicrum, -i, n.	show, games
circensis, -e	of the circus
ut ... ita...	as... so...
Bovillae, -arum, f.pl.	Bovillae (*a town near Rome*)
edo, -ere, edidi, editum	I put on (games)
fluxus, -a, -um	transitory, short-lived
defungor, -i, -functus sum	I die
adulatio, -onis, f.	flattery
censeo, -ere, -ui, censum	I propose
pulvinar, -aris, n.	ceremonial couch (*for the gods*)
maeror, -oris, m.	grief
immodicus, -a, -um	excessive
adnoto, -are, -avi, -atum	I observe (*here, impersonal passive*)
sub (+ acc.)	(*here*) just after
partus, -us, m.	birth
prohibeo, -ere, -ui, -itum	I forbid
praenuntius, -a, -um (+ gen.)	forshadowing
imminens, -entis	impending, imminent
contumelia, -ae, f.	affront, insult
dehinc	then
fero, ferre, tuli, latum	(*here*) I say
reconcilio, -are, -avi, -atum (+ dat.)	I reconcile (to)
iacto, -are, -avi, -atum	I boast
egregius, -a, -um	illustrious
glisco, -ere	I grow greater, swell

[33]

1 C. Laecanio M. Licinio consulibus acriore in dies cupidine adigebatur Nero promiscas scaenas frequentandi: nam adhuc per domum aut hortos cecinerat Iuvenalibus ludis, quos ut parum celebres et tantae voci angustos spernebat. **2** non tamen Romae incipere ausus Neapolim quasi Graecam urbem delegit: inde initium fore ut transgressus in Achaiam insignesque et antiquitus sacras coronas adeptus maiore fama studia civium eliceret. **3** ergo contractum oppidanorum vulgus, et quos e proximis coloniis et municipiis eius rei fama acciverat, quique Caesarem per honorem aut varios usus sectantur, etiam militum manipuli, theatrum Neapolitanorum complent.

33.1:
- What type of ablative is *cupidine*?
- Parse *cecinerat*.

33.2:
- *Neapolim*: briefly explain Nero's reasoning in selecting this city for his first public performance.
- Explain the syntax of *inde initium fore*.

33.3:
- What does the vocabulary of *oppidanorum vulgus* imply about these men?
- What type of verb is *sectantur*?

Stylistic Appreciation: How does Tacitus' syntax and language paint an intriguing picture of the emperor and his followers in this chapter?

Discussion Point: The 2006 BBC series *Ancient Rome: Rise and Fall of an Empire* claimed that aristocratic Romans' outrage at an emperor performing on stage would be comparable to what would be felt today if the Queen became a pole-dancer. What merit is there in this comparison? What Roman prejudices emerge in this chapter? Would Tacitus' distaste for Nero's theatrical tendencies have been universally shared?

in dies	day by day
cupido, -inis, f.	desire
adigo, -ere, -egi, -actum	I drive on
promiscus, -a, -um	public
scaena, -ae, f.	stage
frequento, -are, -avi, -atum	I appear frequently
Iuvenales ludi, -ium -orum, m.pl.	the Juvenile Games
ut	(*here*) as
parum	insufficiently
celeber, -bris, -bre	well-attended
angustus, -a, -um	limited
Neapolis (Gk acc. *-im*), f.	Neapolis (*Naples*)
quasi	as it were
deligo, -ere, -legi, -lectum	I choose
Achaia, -ae, f.	Achaea (*Roman province of mainland Greece*)
insignis, -e	famous
antiquitus	from of old, long-...
corona, -ae, f.	garland
studium, -ii, n.	enthusiasm
elicio, -ere, -licui, -licitum	I win, elicit
contraho, -ere, -traxi, -tractum	I assemble
oppidanus, -i, m.	townsman
municipium, -ii, n.	town
accio, -ire, accivi, accitum	I summon
usus, -us, m.	(*here*) duty, function
sector, -ari, -atus sum	I follow in the train of
manipulus, -i, m.	a maniple, a company (*military unit*)
Neapolitani, -orum, m.pl.	Neapolitans, citizens of Neapolis
compleo, -ere, -plevi, -pletum	I fill

[34]

1 Illic, plerique ut arbitrabantur, triste, ut ipse, providum potius et secundis numinibus evenit: nam egresso qui adfuerat populo vacuum et sine ullius noxa theatrum conlapsum est. ergo per compositos cantus grates dis atque ipsam recentis casus fortunam celebrans petiturusque maris Hadriae traiectus apud Beneventum interim consedit, ubi gladiatorium munus a Vatinio celebre edebatur. 2 Vatinius inter foedissima eius aulae ostenta fuit, sutrinae tabernae alumnus, corpore detorto, facetiis scurrilibus; primo in contumelias adsumptus, dehinc optimi cuiusque criminatione eo usque valuit ut gratia pecunia vi nocendi etiam malos praemineret.

34.1:
- State and explain the case of *secundis numinibus*.
- Parse *casus*.
- What is striking about the phrase *maris Hadriae*?
- What does 'Beneventum' mean and how does Tacitus play with the name?

34.2:
- What type of ablative is *corpore*?
- What type of clause is *ut* introducing here?
- What type of ablatives are *gratia pecunia vi nocendi*? What makes this phrase particularly effective?

Stylistic Appreciation: With reference to Tacitus' choice and position of words and other stylistic features, discuss how this chapter contributes to an impression of the perversity of Nero and his court.

Discussion Point: Why does Vatinius appal Tacitus so much? What about imperial Rome made figures such as Vatinius possible? Are there any comparable figures in later history or in the present day? What do you make of the link between physical and moral deformity: is physiognomy entirely dead in modern popular thought?

arbitror, -ari, -atus sum	I think
providus, -a, -um	providential, a sign of good omen
secundus, -a, -um	favourable
numen, -inis, n.	(*here*) will of the gods
noxa, -ae, f.	harm
theatrum, -i, n.	theatre
conlabor, -i, -lapsus sum	I collapse
per (+ acc.)	(*here*) in, by
compositus, -a, -um	written, made up, composed
cantus, -us, m.	song
grates, ium f. pl.	thanks rendered, thanksgiving
casus, -us, m.	accident
celebro, -are, -avi, -atum	I celebrate
petiturus (fut. partic. of *peto*)	'as he was on his way to'
traiectus, -us, m.	crossing
consido, -ere, -sedi, -sessum	I rest, sit down
munus, -eris, n.	(*here*) a (public) show
celeber, -bris, -bre	crowded, well-attended
edo, -ere, edidi, editum	I put on (a show)
foedus, -a, -um	foul
aula, -ae, f.	court
ostentum, -i, n.	marvel, wonder
sutrina taberna, -ae, f.	shoemaker's shop
alumnus, -a, -um (+ gen.)	brought up in
detortus, -a, -um	deformed
facetiae, -arum, f.pl.	sense of humour, wit
scurrilis, -e	scurrilous, offensive
in contumelias	'as the butt of insults'
adsumo, -ere, -sumpsi, -sumptum	I take on
dehinc	subsequently
criminatio, -onis, f.	accusation
valeo, -ere, -ui	I am powerful
gratia, -ae, f.	influence
mali, -orum, m.pl.	'crooks' (*refers to Nero's courtiers*)
praemineo, -ere	I outdo, surpass, am pre-eminent

[35]

1 Eius munus frequentanti Neroni ne inter voluptates quidem a sceleribus cessabatur. isdem quippe illis diebus Torquatus Silanus mori adigitur, quia super Iuniae familiae claritudinem divum Augustum abavum ferebat. **2** iussi accusatores obicere prodigum largitionibus, neque aliam spem quam in rebus novis esse: quin inter libertos habere quos ab epistulis et libellis et rationibus appellet, nomina summae curae et meditamenta. **3** tum intimus quisque libertorum vincti abreptique; et cum damnatio instaret, brachiorum venas Torquatus interscidit; secutaque Neronis oratio ex more, quamvis sontem et defensioni merito diffisum victurum tamen fuisse si clementiam iudicis exspectasset.

35.1:
- Parse *frequentanti*.
- State and explain the case of *isdem ... illis diebus* and discuss the effect of having two attributes (*isdem* and *illis*).
- Briefly outline who Torquatus Silanus is. What reasons does Nero have for wanting him to be killed?

35.2:
- Explain why Torquatus' employment of the titles *ab epistulis, a libellis* and *a rationibus* was dangerous.
- What type of genitive is *summae curae*?

35.3:
- State and explain the case of *defensioni*.
- Parse *victurum*.
- Who is referred to by *iudicis*? How would you describe Tacitus' tone here?

Stylistic Appreciation: How does Tacitus make this short passage a terrifying glimpse of Neronian Rome?

Discussion Point: To what extent, if any, do you think Torquatus is to blame for what happened to him? What does this episode reveal about the nature of monarchy in Rome under Nero? Or about monarchy in general? Do any similar episodes spring to mind from ancient or modern history?

munus, -eris, n.	(*here*) a (public) show
frequento, -are, -avi, -atum	I attend
voluptas, -atis, f.	pleasure
cesso, -are, -avi, -atum	I cease, rest
quippe	for in fact
adigo, -ere, -egi, -actum	I force
super (+ acc.)	in addition to
Iunia familia, -ae, f.	the Junian family (*Torquatus' family*)
claritudo, -inis, f.	distinction, fame
divus, -a, -um	divine
abavus, -i, m.	great-great-grandfather
fero, ferre, tuli, latum	(*here*) I claim
obicio, -ere, -ieci, -iectum	I bring a charge
prodigus, -a, -um (sc. *esse*)	extravagant
largitio, -onis, f.	hand-out, largesse
res novae, rerum novarum, f.pl.	revolution
quin	moreover that he... (*ind. stat. continues*)
ab epistulis	'for letters' – a label designating 'Private Secretary'
(a) libellis	'for petitions' – label designating 'Petitions Secretary'
(a) rationibus	'for book-keeping' – label designating 'Accountant'
appello, -are, -avi, -atum	I call
cura, -ae, f.	(*here*) administration
meditamentum, -i, n.	training exercise; first step on the path to [*summa cura*]
intimus, -a, -um	most intimate
vincio, -ire, vinxi, vinctum	I tie up, put in chains
abripio, -ere, -ripui, -reptum	I tear away
damnatio, -onis, f.	condemnation
insto, -are, -stiti, -statum	I am at hand
brachium, -ii, n.	arm
vena, -ae, f.	vein
interscindo, -ere, -scidi, -scissum	I sever
ex more	as usual
quamvis	although
sons, sontis	guilty (*referring to Torquatus*)
defensio, -onis, f.	defence
merito	with good reason
diffisus, -a, -um (+ dat.)	without confidence in
vivo, -ere, vixi, victum	I live (*fut. partic.* = *victurus*)
clementia, -ae, f.	mercy

[36]

1 Nec multo post omissa in praesens Achaia (causae in incerto fuere) urbem revisit, provincias Orientis, maxime Aegyptum, secretis imaginationibus agitans. dehinc edicto testificatus non longam sui absentiam et cuncta in re publica perinde immota ac prospera fore, super ea profectione adiit Capitolium. **2** illic veneratus deos, cum Vestae quoque templum inisset, repente cunctos per artus tremens, seu numine exterrente, seu facinorum recordatione numquam timore vacuus, deseruit inceptum, cunctas sibi curas amore patriae leviores dictitans. **3** vidisse maestos civium vultus, audire secretas querimonias, quod tantum itineris aditurus esset, cuius ne modicos quidem egressus tolerarent, sueti adversum fortuita aspectu principis refoveri. ergo ut in privatis necessitudinibus proxima pignora praevalerent, ita populum Romanum vim plurimam habere parendumque retinenti. **4** haec atque talia plebi volentia fuere, voluptatum cupidine et, quae praecipua cura est, rei frumentariae angustias, si abesset, metuenti. senatus et primores in incerto erant procul an coram atrocior haberetur: dehinc, quae natura magnis timoribus, deterius credebant quod evenerat.

36.1:

- What type of ablative is *multo*?
- What is the *Capitolium* and what is its significance?

36.2:

- *illic ... inceptum*: analyse how the syntax of this sentence helps to articulate its sense.
- What type of ablative is *amore*?

36.3:

- What are the tenses of the infinitives *vidisse ... audire*? What do you think the change of tense conveys? What construction here necessitates the use of infinitives?
- State and explain the case of *itineris*.
- What type of gerundive is *parendum*?

36.4:

- State and explain the mood of *haberetur*.

Stylistic Appreciation: How does Tacitus create in this chapter a powerfully damning account of the hypocrisy and corruption of both ruler and ruled in the time of Nero?

Discussion Point: In this chapter Tacitus seems to delve deep into Nero's psychology, reporting his secret hopes and his greatest fears: is this within a historian's remit? What aspects of the relationship between the emperor and the people does Tacitus want us to dwell on? Do you accept Tacitus' scathing judgment on the selfish priorities of the *plebs*?

omitto, -ere, -misi, -missum	I leave aside
in incerto	uncertain, a matter of debate
Oriens, -entis, m.	the East
imaginatio, -onis, f.	imagination
agito, -are, -avi, -atum	I mull over
dehinc	then
edictum, -i, n.	public proclamation
testificor, -ari, -atus sum	I declare
perinde ... ac...	as much... as...
super (+ abl.)	about
profectio, -onis, f.	departure
Capitolium, -ii, n.	the Capitoline Hill
veneror, -ari, -atus sum	I worship
artus, -us, m.	limb
tremo, -ere, -ui	I tremble
numen, -inis, n.	divine power, divinity
recordatio, -onis, f.	remembrance
desero, -ere, -ui, -sertum	I abandon
inceptum, -i, n.	purpose, undertaking
levis, -e	(*here*) unimportant
dictito, -are, -avi, -atum	I say repeatedly
querimonia, -ae, f.	complaint
modicus, -a, -um	(*here*) brief
egressus, -us, m.	excursion, trip
tolero, -are, -avi, -atum	I bear, endure
suetus, -a, -um	accustomed
fortuita, -orum, n.pl.	misfortunes
aspectus, -us, m.	sight
refoveo, -ere, -fovi, -fotum	I revive
ut ... ita...	just as... so...
necessitudo, -inis, f.	relationship
pignus, -oris, n.	tie, bond
praevaleo, -ere, -ui	I have superior force, prevail
volens, -entis	(*here*) welcome
voluptas, -atis, f.	pleasure
cupido, -inis, f.	desire
praecipuus, -a, -um	greatest, especial
res frumentaria, rei frumentariae, f.	corn supply
angustiae, -arum, f.pl.	shortage
metuo, -ere, -ui, -utum	I fear
primores, -um, m.pl.	leading men
coram (adv.)	among them, close at hand
habeo, -ere, -ui, -itum	(*here*) I consider
quae natura (sc. *est*)	as is the usual way
deterius	(*here*) the worse alternative

[37]

1 Ipse quo fidem adquireret nihil usquam perinde laetum sibi, publicis locis struere convivia totaque urbe quasi domo uti. et celeberrimae luxu famaque epulae fuere quas a Tigellino paratas ut exemplum referam, ne saepius eadem prodigentia narranda sit. **2** igitur in stagno Agrippae fabricatus est ratem cui superpositum convivium navium aliarum tractu moveretur. naves auro et ebore distinctae, remigesque exoleti per aetates et scientiam libidinum componebantur. volucres et feras diversis e terris et animalia maris Oceano abusque petiverat. **3** crepidinibus stagni lupanaria adstabant inlustribus feminis completa et contra scorta visebantur nudis corporibus. iam gestus motusque obsceni; et postquam tenebrae incedebant, quantum iuxta nemoris et circumiecta tecta consonare cantu et luminibus clarescere. **4** ipse per licita atque inlicita foedatus nihil flagitii reliquerat quo corruptior ageret, nisi paucos post dies uni ex illo contaminatorum grege (nomen Pythagorae fuit) in modum solemnium coniugiorum denupsisset. inditum imperatori flammeum, missi auspices, dos et genialis torus et faces nuptiales, cuncta denique spectata quae etiam in femina nox operit.

37.1:
- What polarity in Roman thought is Tacitus dwelling on in the first sentence?
- Explain the use of the infinitives *struere* and *uti*.
- Who is Tigellinus?

37.2:
- Explain the mood of *moveretur*.
- How does the phrase *Oceano abusque* conjure an atmosphere of exoticism?

37.3:
- What is effective in the syntax of *iam gestus motusque obsceni*?
- What type of genitive is *nemoris*?

37.4:
- Parse *denupsisset*. What is significant about Tacitus' use of this verb?
- Briefly explain the references to: *flammeum; auspices; genialis torus*. What do you think is the effect of these densely-packed terms from the ritual lexicon of Roman marriage?

Stylistic Appreciation: How does Tacitus generate an overpowering atmosphere of debauchery and decadence in his account of Tigellinus' banquet?

Discussion Point: Which tenets of traditional Roman morality are broken in this banquet? Is the sexual misconduct of leaders a perennial source of scandal? Does Tacitus' evident outrage at this banquet come from the same angle as ours at similar stories today? (What, for instance, are the similarities, what the differences between Nero's orgy and modern 'bunga bunga' parties?)

adquiro, -ere, -quisivi, -quisitum	I win
perinde	as
struo, -ere, struxi, structum	I set up
convivium, -ii, n.	banquet
celeber, -bris, -bre (+ abl.)	(*here*) celebrated for
luxus, -us, m.	luxury
epulae, -arum, f.pl.	banquet
prodigentia, -ae, f.	extravagance, 'prodigality'
stagnum, -i, n.	lake
fabricor, -ari, -atus sum	I construct
ratis, -is, f.	raft, ship
tractus, -us, m.	towing
ebur, eboris, n.	ivory
distinctus, -a, -um	embellished
remex, -igis, m.	rower
exoletus, -a, -um	degenerate, perverted [ppp of *exolesco, -ere*]
volucris, -is, m.	bird
fera, -ae, f.	wild beast
abusque (+ abl.)	all the way from
crepido, -inis, f.	bank, quayside
lupanar, -aris, n.	brothel
inlustris, -e	noble
completus, -a, -um (+ abl.)	filled with
scortum, -i, n.	(low-class) prostitute, whore
visor, -i, visus sum	(*here*) I am on view
gestus, -us, m.	gesture
obscenus, -a, -um	filthy
iuxta	nearby
nemus, -oris, n.	grove
circumiectus, -a, -um	surrounding
consono, -are, -ui	I resound
claresco, -ere, -ui	I shine
(in)licitus, -a, -um	(un)lawful
foedo, -are, -avi, -atum	I defile, pollute
flagitium, -ii, n.	outrage, abomination
corruptus, -a, -um	depraved
contaminatus, -a, -um	perverted (*contaminati,* m.pl. = perverts)
grex, gregis, m.	herd
in modum (+ gen.)	in the manner of
coniugium, -ii, n.	marriage
denubo, -ere, -psi, -ptum (+ dat.)	I marry (*of a woman marrying a man*)
indo, -ere, -didi, -ditum	I put on
flammeum, -i, n.	bridal veil
auspex, -icis, m.	soothsayer
dos, dotis, f.	dowry
genialis torus, -i, m.	marriage bed
(nuptialis) fax, facis, f.	(wedding) torch
operio, -ire, operui, opertum	I hide

[38]

1 Sequitur clades, forte an dolo principis incertum (nam utrumque auctores prodidere), sed omnibus quae huic urbi per violentiam ignium acciderunt gravior atque atrocior. **2** initium in ea parte circi ortum quae Palatino Caelioque montibus contigua est, ubi per tabernas, quibus id mercimonium inerat quo flamma alitur, simul coeptus ignis et statim validus ac vento citus longitudinem circi corripuit. neque enim domus munimentis saeptae vel templa muris cincta aut quid aliud morae interiacebat. **3** impetu pervagatum incendium plana primum, deinde in edita adsurgens et rursus inferiora populando, antiit remedia velocitate mali et obnoxia urbe artis itineribus hucque et illuc flexis atque enormibus vicis, qualis vetus Roma fuit. **4** ad hoc lamenta paventium feminarum, fessa aetate aut rudis pueritiae, quique sibi quique aliis consulebant, dum trahunt invalidos aut opperiuntur, pars mora, pars festinans, cuncta impediebant. **5** et saepe dum in tergum respectant lateribus aut fronte circumveniebantur, vel si in proxima evaserant, illis quoque igni correptis, etiam quae longinqua crediderant in eodem casu reperiebant. **6** postremo, quid vitarent quid peterent ambigui, complere vias, sterni per agros; quidam amissis omnibus fortunis, diurni quoque victus, alii caritate suorum, quos eripere nequiverant, quamvis patente effugio interiere. **7** nec quisquam defendere audebat, crebris multorum minis restinguere prohibentium, et quia alii palam faces iaciebant atque esse sibi auctorem vociferabantur, sive ut raptus licentius exercerent seu iussu.

38.1:
- Parse *prodidere*.
- What type of ablative is *omnibus*?

38.2:
- Comment on Tacitus' selection of the word *mercimonium*.
- State and explain the case of *morae*.

38.3:
- How is Tacitus' use of verbs in this sentence particularly effective?

38.4:
- State and explain the case of *rudis pueritiae*.

38.5:
- Parse *circumveniebantur*.

38.6:
- Explain the mood of *vitarent*.

38.7:
- What type of dative is *sibi*?

Stylistic Appreciation: How does Tacitus' language in this chapter make the outbreak of the Great Fire both dramatic and moving?

Discussion Point: Did Nero start the Fire? If not, is Tacitus right to raise the possibility he did? Does he want us to believe that Nero was behind it? Can you think of contemporary examples of 'insinuation' (maybe from journalism)?

prodo, -ere, -didi, -ditum	(*here*) I record
circus, -i, m.	the Circus Maximus (*Rome's race track*)
contiguus, -a, -um	adjoining to, next to
mercimonium, -ii, n.	wares
alo, -ere, alui, alitum	I feed, nourish
citus, -a, -um	swift
longitudo, -inis, f.	length
corripio, -ere, -ripui, -reptum	I seize, tear into
munimentum, -i, n.	solid defences
saeptus, -a, -um	fenced in
cinctus, -a, -um	surrounded
pervagor, -ari, -atus sum	I spread over, traverse
plana, -orum, n.pl.	the level ground
edita, -orum, n.pl.	higher areas
inferiora, -um, n.pl.	lower parts
populor, -ari, -atus sum	I ravage
anteeo, -ire, -ivi/ -ii, -itum	I outstrip
remedium, -ii, n.	(*here*) counter-measures
velocitas, -atis, f.	speed
obnoxius, -a, -um	vulnerable
artus, -a, -um	narrow
enormis, -e	irregular
vicus, -i, m.	street
lamentum, -i, n.	lamentation
paveo, -ere	I am frightened
rudis, -e	inexperienced, tender
opperior, -iri, oppertus sum	I wait for
evado, -ere, -vasi, -vasum	I escape
reperio, -ire, repperi, -rtum	I find
longinquus, -a, -um	remote
casus, -us, m.	(*here*) situation
ambiguus, -a, -um	uncertain
compleo, -ere, -plevi, -pletum	I fill
sternor, -i, stratus sum	I fling myself down
diurus, -a, -um	daily
victus, -us, m.	food
caritas, -atis, f.	love
nequeo, -ere, -ivi, -itum	I am unable
quamvis	although
pateo, -ere, -ui	I lie open
effugium, -ii, n.	escape
intereo, -ire, -ii, -itum	I die
mina, -ae, f.	threat
restinguo, -ere, -stinxi, -stinctum	I extinguish
fax, facis, f.	torch
auctor, -oris, m.	(*here*) authority
vociferor, -ari, -atus sum	I yell
raptus, -us, m.	looting
licenter	freely
exerceo, -ere, -ui, -itum	I carry out

[39]

1 Eo in tempore Nero Antii agens non ante in urbem regressus est quam domui eius, qua Palatium et Maecenatis hortos continuaverat, ignis propinquaret. neque tamen sisti potuit quin et Palatium et domus et cuncta circum haurirentur. 2 sed solacium populo exturbato ac profugo campum Martis ac monumenta Agrippae, hortos quin etiam suos patefecit et subitaria aedificia extruxit quae multitudinem inopem acciperent; subvectaque utensilia ab Ostia et propinquis municipiis pretiumque frumenti minutum usque ad ternos nummos. 3 quae quamquam popularia in inritum cadebant, quia pervaserat rumor ipso tempore flagrantis urbis inisse eum domesticam scaenam et cecinisse Troianum excidium, praesentia mala vetustis cladibus adsimulantem.

39.1:
- What is the case of *Antii*?
- To what imperial residence does Tacitus refer here? What is the *Palatium*?
- Parse *haurirentur* and explain its mood.

39.2:
- How does *solacium* fit into this sentence grammatically?
- What is *Ostia*?

39.3:
- State and explain the case of *ipso tempore*.
- Parse *adsimulantem*. With which word is it agreeing in this sentence?

Stylistic Appreciation: How does this passage present a fascinating account of Nero's reaction to the Fire?

Discussion Point: What are we to make of Tacitus' sudden change of tack in his treatment of Nero? Is your picture of the emperor altered by this chapter? 'Fiddling while Rome burns' has become proverbial: is it fair that Nero should be best remembered in this context? What elements of Nero's response to the fire are recognizable from modern disaster relief? Nero's practical and popular relief measures failed to alter public perception of the emperor: why? Can you think of other historical or modern examples, in which practical relief measures and political campaigning became intertwined?

ago, -ere, egi, actum	(*here*) I stay, spend time
Palatium, -ii, n.	Palatine Hill
Maecenatis horti, -orum, m.pl.	Gardens of Maecenas
continuo, -are, -avi, -atum	I connect
propinquo, -are, -avi, -atum	I approach
sisto, -ere, stiti, statum	I stop
haurio, -ire, hausi, haustum	I consume
solacium, -ii, n.	consolation, relief
exturbatus, -a, -um	driven out
profugus, -a, -um	homeless
monumentum, -i, n.	public building
quin etiam	and even
patefacio, -ere, -feci, -factum	I throw open
subitarius, -a, -um	makeshift, emergency
inops, -opis	destitute
extruo, -ere, -xi, -ctum	I put up
subveho, -ere, -vexi, -vectum	I carry up
utensilia, -ium, n.pl.	provisions
Ostia, -ae, f.	Ostia (*Rome's port*)
propinquus, -a, -um	neighbouring
municipium, -ii, n.	town
minuo, -ere, -ui, -utum	I reduce
usque ad	right down to
terni, -ae, -a	three
nummus, -i, m.	sesterce (*Roman coin*)
in inritum	to no effect
pervado, -ere, -vasi, -vasum	I spread
flagro, -are, -avi, -atum	I blaze
domesticus, -a, -um	private, domestic
scaena, -ae, f.	stage
Troianus, -a, -um	of Troy
excidium, -ii, n.	destruction
vetustus, -a, -um	ancient
adsimulo, -are, -avi, -atum	I compare

[40]

1 Sexto demum die apud imas Esquilias finis incendio factus, prorutis per immensum aedificiis ut continuae violentiae campus et velut vacuum caelum occurreret. necdum positus metus aut redierat plebi spes: rursum grassatus ignis patulis magis urbis locis; eoque strages hominum minor, delubra deum et porticus amoenitati dicatae latius procidere. **2** plusque infamiae id incendium habuit quia praediis Tigellini Aemilianis proruperat videbaturque Nero condendae urbis novae et cognomento suo appellandae gloriam quaerere. quippe in regiones quattuordecim Roma dividitur, quarum quattuor integrae manebant, tres solo tenus deiectae: septem reliquis pauca tectorum vestigia supererant, lacera et semusta.

40.1:
- State and explain the case of *aedificiis*.
- Why is *violentiae* in the dative?
- Parse *hominum*.

40.2:
- What type of genitive is *infamiae*?
- State and explain the case of *solo*.
- Parse *supererant*.

Stylistic Appreciation: Analyse how Tacitus uses language to dramatize the losses in the second fire.

Discussion Point: How do you think Nero's demolition of buildings to make fire-breaks was received? Considering how Nero was to use the land cleared of houses after the Fire, is it understandable that conspiracy theories arose about his involvement? When have similar theories been popularised in recent times? Is Tacitus right to record this sort of rumour in his *Annals*?

demum	at last
imus, -a, -um	foot of
Esquiliae, -arum, f.pl.	Esquiline Hill
proruo, -ere, -rui, -rutum	I demolish
per immensum	'over a vast area'
continuus, -a, -um	relentless
violentia, -ae, f.	violence
velut	as it were
occurro, -ere, -curri, -cursum (+ dat.)	I block, resist
necdum	not yet
pono, -ere, posui, positum	(*here*) I lay aside
grassor, -ari, -atus sum	I run riot
patulus, -a, -um	spacious, open
strages, -is, f.	slaughter, destruction
delubrum, -i, n.	temple
porticus, -us, f.	colonnade
amoenitas, -atis, f.	enjoyment
dicatus, -a, -um (+ dat.)	dedicated to
procido, -ere, -cidi, -cisum	I fall, am destroyed
infamia, -ae, f.	scandal
praedium, -ii, n.	estate
Aemilianus, -a, -um	Aemilian
prorumpo, -ere, -rupi, -ruptum	I break out
condo, -ere, -didi, -ditum	I found (a city)
cognomentum, -i, n.	name
quippe	indeed
regio, -onis, f.	district
integer, -ra, -rum	undamaged
solum, -i, n.	ground
tenus (+ abl.)	as far as, down to
vestigium, -ii, n.	trace
lacer, -era, -erum	mangled
semustus, -a, -um	half-burnt

[41]

1 Domuum et insularum et templorum quae amissa sunt numerum inire haud promptum fuerit: sed vetustissima religione, quod Servius Tullius Lunae et magna ara fanumque quae praesenti Herculi Arcas Evander sacraverat, aedesque Statoris Iovis vota Romulo Numaeque regia et delubrum Vestae cum Penatibus populi Romani exusta; iam opes tot victoriis quaesitae et Graecarum artium decora, exim monumenta ingeniorum antiqua et incorrupta, ut quamvis in tanta resurgentis urbis pulchritudine multa seniores meminerint quae reparari nequibant. **2** fuere qui adnotarent XIIII Kal. Sextiles principium incendii huius ortum, quo et Senones captam urbem inflammaverint. alii eo usque cura progressi sunt ut totidem annos mensesque et dies inter utraque incendia numerent.

41.1:

- *numerum inire haud promptum fuerit*: what do you think this suggests about the number of buildings destroyed?
- What kind of ablative is *vetustissima religione*?
- Pick out and briefly comment on the significance of **two** of the sacred sites mentioned by Tacitus.

41.2:

- Explain the mood of *adnotarent*.
- What type of clause is introduced by *eo usque ... ut...*?

Stylistic Appreciation: How does Tacitus' use of language in this passage invest his account of the fire's destruction with drama and pathos?

Discussion Point: Why does Tacitus select the monuments and works of art he does for mention in this chapter? What about them contributes to the sense of irreparable loss he is evoking? To what extent is the attitude of the *seniores* here recognizable? And of those who observed the rather contrived coincidences? Why do you think Tacitus includes this sort of bizarre observation in his history?

insula, -ae, f.	block of flats
numerum ineo, -ire, -ii	I reach a number, count
promptus, -a, -um	easy
vetustus, -a, -um	old, ancient
religio, -onis, f.	holiness, sanctity
ara, -ae, f.	altar
fanum, -i, n.	shrine
Hercules, -is, m.	Hercules
Arcas, -adis	Arcadian (*from Arcadia, region of Greece*)
sacro, -are, -avi, -atum	I consecrate
Stator, -oris, m.	'the Stayer' (*a title of Jupiter*)
voveo, -ere, vovi, votum	I vow, devote
Numa, -ae, m.	Numa (*second king of Rome*)
regia, -ae, f.	palace
delubrum, -i, n.	shrine
Penates, -ium, m.pl.	household gods
exuro, -ere, -ussi, -ustum	I burn
decus, -oris, n.	glory, pride
exim	then
monumentum, -i, n.	monument
ingenium, -ii, n.	(*here*) man of genius
incorruptus, -a, -um	undamaged
quamvis	although
pulchritudo, -inis, f.	beauty
resurgo, -ere, -surrexi, -surrectum	I recover, rise again
seniores, -um, m.pl.	older men
memini, -isse	I remember
reparo, -are, -avi, -atum	I restore
nequeo, -ire, -ivi, -itum	I am unable
adnoto, -are, -avi, -atum	I notice
principium, -ii, n.	beginning
Senones, -um, m.pl.	the Senonian Gauls
inflammo, -are, -avi, -atum	I set fire to
cura, -ae, f.	study
totidem	the same number of
numero, -are, -avi, -atum	I count

[42]

1 Ceterum Nero usus est patriae ruinis extruxitque domum in qua haud proinde gemmae et aurum miraculo essent, solita pridem et luxu vulgata, quam arva et stagna et in modum solitudinum hinc silvae inde aperta spatia et prospectus, magistris et machinatoribus Severo et Celere, quibus ingenium et audacia erat etiam quae natura denegavisset per artem temptare et viribus principis inludere. **2** namque ab lacu Averno navigabilem fossam usque ad ostia Tiberina depressuros promiserant squalenti litore aut per montes adversos. neque enim aliud umidum gignendis aquis occurrit quam Pomptinae paludes: cetera abrupta aut arentia ac, si perrumpi possent, intolerandus labor nec satis causae. Nero tamen, ut erat incredibilium cupitor, effodere proxima Averno iuga conisus est; manentque vestigia inritae spei.

42.1:
- Analyse the design of *Nero usus est patriae ruinis extruxitque domum,* thinking particularly about the contrasts Tacitus is drawing.
- State and explain the case of *miraculo.* What does the subjunctive *essent* indicate here?
- What type of dative is *quibus?*

42.2:
- Parse *depressuros.*
- How does Tacitus' choice and position of words in *squalenti litore aut per montes adversos* convey the difficulty of this project?

Stylistic Appreciation: How does Tacitus underscore the extravagance and vanity of Nero's building programme after the fire?

Discussion Point: What are we to make of the contrast between *ars* and *natura* in this chapter? Have you encountered this polarity elsewhere in the classical world? Was it admirable to be an *incredibilium cupitor*? Is it admirable now? Nero was the last emperor of his dynasty (the Julio-Claudians); the emperors of the next (Flavian) dynasty built all over Nero's great *rus in urbe.* Why do you think they did this? How might the fact that the dynasty to which Nero belonged ended with his death have affected our understanding of him?

ceterum	but
ruina, -ae, f.	destruction
proinde ... quam...	so much... as...
gemma, -ae, f.	jewel
miraculum, -i, n.	source of wonder
solitus, -a, -um	familiar
pridem	for a long time
luxus, -us, m.	luxury
vulgo, -are, -avi, -atum	I popularise, make common
arvum, -i, n.	field
stagnum, -i, n.	lake
in modum (+ gen.)	in the manner of
solitudo, -inis, f.	wildnerness
hinc ... inde...	on this side... on that side...
prospectus, -us, m.	view
magister, -ri, m.	(*here*) architect
machinator, -oris, m.	engineer
audacia, -ae, f.	boldness
denego, -are, -avi, -atus	I refuse
tempto, -are, -avi, -atum	I try
vires, -ium, f.pl.	(*here*) wealth, resources
inludo, -ere, -lusi, -lusum (+ dat.)	I fool away, squander
Avernus lacus, -us, m.	lake Avernus (*in the Bay of Naples*)
navigabilis, -e	navigable
fossa, -ae, f.	(*here*) canal
ostium, -ii, n.	mouth (of a river)
Tiberinus, -a, -um	of the river Tiber
deprimo, -ere, -pressi, -pressum	I sink, dig out
squalens, -entis	barren
adversus, -a, -um	(*here*) intervening
umidus, -a, -um	moist
occurro, -ere, -curri, -cursum	I occur
Pomptinae paludes, -um, f.pl.	the Pomptine marshes
abruptus, -a, -um	sheer
arens, -entis	dry
intolerandus, -a, -um	unendurable
incredibilis, -e	impossible, incredible
cupitor, -oris, m.	lover of, enthusiast for
iugum, -i, n.	hill
conitor, -i, -nisus sum	I strive
vestigium, -ii, n.	trace
inritus, -a, -um	vain

[43]

1 Ceterum urbis quae domui supererant non, ut post Gallica incendia, nulla distinctione nec passim erecta, sed dimensis vicorum ordinibus et latis viarum spatiis cohibitaque aedificiorum altitudine ac patefactis areis additisque porticibus quae frontem insularum protegerent. 2 eas porticus Nero sua pecunia extructurum purgatasque areas dominis traditurum pollicitus est. addidit praemia pro cuiusque ordine et rei familiaris copiis finivitque tempus intra quod effectis domibus aut insulis apiscerentur. 3 ruderi accipiendo Ostienses paludes destinabat utique naves quae frumentum Tiberi subvectassent onustae rudere decurrerent; aedificiaque ipsa certa sui parte sine trabibus saxo Gabino Albanove solidarentur, quod is lapis ignibus impervius est; 4 iam aqua privatorum licentia intercepta quo largior et pluribus locis in publicum flueret, custodes; et subsidia reprimendis ignibus in propatulo quisque haberet; nec communione parietum, sed propriis quaeque muris ambirentur. 5 ea ex utilitate accepta decorem quoque novae urbi attulere. erant tamen qui crederent veterem illam formam salubritati magis conduxisse, quoniam angustiae itinerum et altitudo tectorum non perinde solis vapore perrumperentur: at nunc patulam latitudinem et nulla umbra defensam graviore aestu ardescere.

43.1:
- How does the design of *dimensis vicorum ordinibus et latis viarum spatiis cohibitaque aedificiorum altitudine* suggest the imposition of order?
- Explain the mood of *protegerent*.

43.2:
- What construction is *effectis domibus*?

43.3:
- Explain the syntax of *accipiendo*.

43.4:
- Why is *haberet* subjunctive?

43.5:
- Explain the mood of *perrumperentur*.
- Why is the infinitive *ardescere* used here?

Stylistic Appreciation: In what ways does Tacitus make this passage a thought-provoking and ambivalent account of Nero's attempts to improve the city?

Discussion Point: Is Tacitus' assessment of Nero's building works fair? How does Nero's programme of improvements compare to the approaches of other governments, in the modern day or through history, to catastrophes?

Gallicus, -a, -um	of the Gauls
distinctio, -onis, f.	demarcation
erigo, -ere, -rexi, -rectum	I build
dimetior, -iri, -mensus sum	I measure out
vicus, -i, m.	street
cohibeo, -ere, -ui, -itum	I restrict
altitudo, -inis, f.	height
patefacio, -ere, -feci, -factum	I leave open
porticus, -us, f.	colonnade
protego, -ere, -texi, -tectum	I protect
purgo, -are, -avi, -atum	I clear
pro (+ abl.)	(*here*) according to
rei familiaris copiae, -arum, f.pl.	personal wealth
finio, -ire, -ivi, -itum	I prescribe, define
apiscor, -i, aptus sum	I obtain
rudus, -eris, n.	rubble
Ostienses paludes, -um, f.pl.	the marshes of Ostia
destino, -are, -avi, -atum	I assign
Tiberis, -is, m.	river Tiber
subvecto, -are, -avi, -atum	I carry up
onustus, -a, -um	loaded with
trabes, -is, f.	wooden beam
solido, -are, -avi, -atum	I reinforce, support
lapis, -is, m.	stone
impervius, -a, -um	resistant to
licentia, -ae, f.	unrestrained behaviour
largior, -ius	(*here*) 'in greater abundance'
in publicum	for public use
subsidium, -ii, n.	means, equipment
reprimo, -ere, -pressi, -pressum	I stop, extinguish
propatulum, -i, n.	an accessible position
communio, -onis, f.	sharing
paries, -etis, m.	party-wall
proprius, -a, -um	one's own
ambio, -ire, -ivi, -itum	I encircle
utilitas, -atis, f.	usefulness
decor, -oris, m.	beauty
salubritas, -atis, f.	health
conduco, -ere, -duxi, -ductum	(*here*) I am conducive
angustiae, -arum, f.pl.	narrowness
perinde	so much, so readily
vapor, -oris, m.	heat
patulus, -a, -um	open
latitudo, -inis, f.	wide space
aestus, -us, m.	heat
ardesco, -ere, arsi	I burn, grow hot

[44]

1 Et haec quidem humanis consiliis providebantur. mox petita dis piacula aditique Sibyllae libri, ex quibus supplicatum Vulcano et Cereri Proserpinaeque ac propitiata Iuno per matronas, primum in Capitolio, deinde apud proximum mare, unde hausta aqua templum et simulacrum deae perspersum est; et sellisternia ac pervigilia celebravere feminae quibus mariti erant. 2 sed non ope humana, non largitionibus principis aut deum placamentis decedebat infamia quin iussum incendium crederetur. ergo abolendo rumori Nero subdidit reos et quaesitissimis poenis adfecit quos per flagitia invisos vulgus Christianos appellabat. 3 auctor nominis eius Christus Tiberio imperitante per procuratorem Pontium Pilatum supplicio adfectus erat; repressaque in praesens exitiabilis superstitio rursum erumpebat, non modo per Iudaeam, originem eius mali, sed per urbem etiam quo cuncta undique atrocia aut pudenda confluunt celebranturque. 4 igitur primum correpti qui fatebantur, deinde indicio eorum multitudo ingens haud proinde in crimine incendii quam odio humani generis convicti sunt. et pereuntibus addita ludibria, ut ferarum tergis contecti laniatu canum interirent, aut crucibus adfixi aut flammandi, atque ubi defecisset dies in usum nocturni luminis urerentur. 5 hortos suos ei spectaculo Nero obtulerat et circense ludicrum edebat, habitu aurigae permixtus plebi vel curriculo insistens. unde quamquam adversus sontes et novissima exempla meritos miseratio oriebatur, tamquam non utilitate publica sed in saevitiam unius absumerentur.

44.1:
- Briefly explain Tacitus' reference to the *Sibyllae libri*.
- Parse *celebravere*.

44.2:
- Explain the syntax of *rumori abolendo*.

44.3:
- Where is Judaea, and why is it described as *originem eius mali*?

44.4:
- Whom does *pereuntibus* describe? Explain the syntax of this word.

44.5:
- Parse *obtulerat*.
- How does the design of *non utilitate publica, sed in saevitiam unius absumerentur* underline Nero's cruelty?

Stylistic Appreciation: How is the hypocrisy and cruelty of the emperor brought out particularly vividly in this chapter?

Discussion Point: Tacitus seems to view Rome as a sink-hole for the empire: when and where have similar views been widely held? Are they current today? How plausible is Tacitus' claim that cruel treatment of a hated minority aroused popular sympathy? Are there more recent instances of this? Christian sources for Nero's executions of Christians make no mention of his allegations of arson: why do you think this is? Whom are we to believe?

piaculum, -i, n.	means of appeasing
Sibyllae libri, -orum, m.pl.	the Sibylline books (*ancient works of prophecy*)
supplico, -are, -avi, -atum	I pray to (*supplicatum [est] is an impersonal passive*)
propitio, -are, -avi, -atum	I appease
matrona, -ae, f.	married woman
haurio, -ire, hausi, haustum	I draw (water)
simulacrum, -i, n.	statue
perspargo, -ere, -spersi, -spersum	I sprinkle over
sellisternium, -ii, n.	sacred banquet
pervigilium, -ii, n.	vigil
largitio, -onis, f.	lavish gifts
placamentum, -i, n.	appeasement
decedo, -ere, -cessi, -cessum	I subside
aboleo, -ere, -evi, -etum	I wipe out, eliminate
subdo, -ere, -didi, -ditum	I frame
reus, -i, m.	defendant; culprit; (*here*) scapegoat
quaesitus, -a, -um	elaborate
adficio, -ere, -feci, -fectum	I inflict
flagitium, -ii, n.	outrage
invisus, -a, -um	hated
procurator, -oris, m.	governor (of a province)
supplicium, -ii, n.	death-penalty
exitiabilis, -e	deadly
pudendus, -a, -um	shameful
confluo, -ere, -fluxi	I flow together
celebro, -are, -avi, -atum	(*here*) I become popular
corripio, -ere, -ripui, -reptum	I arrest
fateor, -eri, fassus sum	I confess
indicium, -ii, n.	evidence
ludibrium, -ii, n.	humiliation
fera, -ae, f.	wild beast
tergum, -i, n.	(*here*) skin, hide
contectus, -a, -um	covered with (*ferarum tergis*)
laniatus, -us, m.	tearing
crux, crucis, f.	cross
adfixus, -a, -um	(*here*) nailed to
deficio, -ere, -feci, -fectum	I end, fail
uro, -ere, ussi, ustum	I burn
habitus, -us, m.	dress, clothing
auriga, -ae, m.	charioteer
permixtus, -a, -um	mingled with
curriculum, -i, n.	chariot
sons, sontis	guilty
novissimus, -a, -um	(*here*) most extreme
meritus, -a, -um	deserving
miseratio, -onis, f.	compassion
tamquam	as though
absumo, -ere, -sumpsi, -sumptum	I do away with

[45]

1 Interea conferendis pecuniis pervastata Italia, provinciae eversae sociique populi et quae civitatium liberae vocantur. inque eam praedam etiam dii cessere, spoliatis in urbe templis egestoque auro quod triumphis, quod votis omnis populi Romani aetas prospere aut in metu sacraverat. **2** enimvero per Asiam atque Achaiam non dona tantum sed simulacra numinum abripiebantur, missis in eas provincias Acrato ac Secundo Carrinate. ille libertus cuicumque flagitio promptus, hic Graeca doctrina ore tenus exercitus animum bonis artibus non induerat. **3** ferebatur Seneca quo invidiam sacrilegii a semet averteret longinqui ruris secessum oravisse et, postquam non concedebatur, ficta valetudine quasi aeger nervis cubiculum non egressus. tradidere quidam venenum ei per libertum ipsius, cui nomen Cleonicus, paratum iussu Neronis vitatumque a Seneca proditione liberti seu propria formidine, dum persimplici victu et agrestibus pomis ac, si sitis admoneret, profluente aqua vitam tolerat.

45.1:
- What were the *civitates liberae*, and what does Tacitus want to suggest by *vocantur* here?

45.2:
- State and explain the case of *missis*.
- What does Tacitus mean by *Graeca doctrina ore tenus exercitus*?
- What type of ablative is *bonis artibus*?

45.3:
- Parse *tradidere*. What is the meaning of *trado* in this context? What is its subject?
- With which noun are the participles *paratum* and *vitatum* agreeing?
- State and explain the tense of *tolerat*.

Stylistic Appreciation: What is there in this section to contribute to our impression of Nero, and how does Tacitus' use of language draw attention to his wickedness?

Discussion Point: In his search for funds, Nero turns the empire upside down and shakes it. When have countries or empires more recently behaved similarly? What impression of Nero as an emperor does this give? What sort of things would *Graeca doctrina* have entailed? Who in our times might most closely fit Tacitus' acid description of Carrinas the hypocrite? Is Seneca much better? Are we to view his withdrawal from public life as principled or craven?

confero, -ferre, -tuli, -latum	(*here*) I raise (funds)
pervasto, -are, -avi, -atum	I ravage
everto, -ere, -verti, -versum	I ruin
cedo, -ere, cessi, cessum	(*here*) I fall victim (*cess<u>ere</u> = cess<u>erunt</u>*)
spolio, -are, -avi, -atum	I plunder
egero, -ere, -gessi, -gestum	I carry off
votum, -i, n.	vow
prospere	in prosperity
sacro, -are, -avi, -atum	I consecrate
enimvero	and what is more
simulacrum, -i, n.	statue
numen, -inis, n.	deity
Acratus, -i, m.	Acratus (*agent of Nero*)
Secundus Carrinas, -atis, m.	Secundus Carrinas (*agent of Nero*)
ille ... hic...	the former... the latter...
flagitium, -ii, n.	outrage
promptus, -a, -um	ready
doctrina, -ae, f.	learning
os, oris, n.	(*here*) speech
tenus (+ abl.)	as far as
exerceo, -ere, -ui, -itum	I train in, practise
induo, -ere, -ui, -utum	I imbue
sacrilegium, -ii, n.	sacrilege
semet	= *se*
longinquus, -a, -um	remote
secessus, -us, m.	retirement
concedo, -ere, -cessi, -cessum	I allow
fingo, -ere, finxi, fictum	I feign, invent
valetudo, -inis, f.	(*here*) ill-health
aeger, -gra, -grum	sick
nervus, -i, m.	muscle
cubiculum, -i, n.	bedroom
trado, -ere, -didi, -ditum	(*here*) I record
venenum, -i, n.	poison
proditio, -onis, f.	betrayal
proprius, -a, -um	one's own
formido, -inis, f.	fear
persimplex, -icis	very simple
victus, -us, m.	food
agrestis, -e	of the countryside
poma, -ae, f.	fruit
sitis, -is, f.	thirst
admoneo, -ere, -ui, -itum	I urge
profluens, -entis	running
vitam tolero, -are, -avi, -atum	I support my life

4. Commentary

DOI: 10.11647/OBP.0035.03

The assigned portion of text begins *in medias res*. We parachute right into the middle of a meeting of the Roman senate that took place towards the end of the year 62 (15.20.1). Tacitus' account of it began in the previous paragraph (15.19) and continues until 15.22.1. The set text carries on for a bit, covering the end of AD 62 and the beginning of AD 63 (15.22.2 – 15.23), before vaulting over nine sections (15.24 – 15.32). We re-enter the narrative in 15.33 (the beginning of AD 64) and are then asked to read continuously until the end of 15.45. The text breaks off with the unsuccessful attempt by Nero to have his old tutor Seneca poisoned. There is a certain rationale behind this stopping and starting. Those in charge of setting the text excised with surgical precision those portions of the *Annals* that cover the military situation in the Near East, specifically Rome's ongoing conflict with Parthia (15.1–18; 24–32). The focus of the assigned portion is squarely on Italy and Rome – the city, the senate, and, not least, the imperial court, with the corresponding personnel, in particular the emperor Nero.[66]

Section 1: *Annals* 15.20–23

Thematically, the four chapters of *Annals* 15.20–23 can be divided as follows:
- i.   20.1–22.1: Report of a senate meeting that took place towards the end of AD 62 (continuing on from 15.19).
- ii. 22.2: Review of striking prodigies that occurred in the year AD 62.
- iii. 23.1–4: Start of Tacitus' account of AD 63, with extensive coverage of the birth and death of Nero's daughter Claudia Augusta.

---

66 This cut-and-paste approach, while understandable, results in a distortion of Tacitus' overall picture of the Neronian principate. In particular the geopolitical dimension of his text, the way in which he interweaves centre and periphery, Rome and the world, disappears from view. It is important to bear in mind here that Nero's reign ended when provincial governors decided to march on Rome.

(1) 20.1–22.1: THE MEETING OF THE SENATE

Chapters 1–18 of *Annals* 15 cover developments in Rome's war against Parthia. In 15.19 (i.e. the chapter before the set text starts), Tacitus' focus shifts back to domestic matters. Unethical senatorial careerism comes back onto the agenda. He records that members of Rome's ruling élite increasingly exploited a legal loophole to circumvent a stipulation of the *lex Papia Poppaea de maritandis ordinibus* ('Papian-Poppaean law on marrying categories'). The law, which was part of Augustus' legislative initiatives concerning morals and marriage, ensured preferential treatment of candidates for high-powered posts in the imperial administration who had one or more children.[67] As Cassius Dio put it (53.13.2): 'Next he [sc. Augustus] ordained that the governors of senatorial provinces should be annual magistrates, chosen by lot, except when a senator enjoyed a special privilege because of the large number of his children or because of his marriage.'[68] To receive the legal benefits without going through the trouble of raising children, childless careerists began to adopt young men shortly before the appointment or election procedure, only to release them again soon after securing the desired post. This practice of 'fictive adoption' (*ficta* or *simulata adoptio*), which, as Tacitus notes in his inimitable style, enabled the practitioners to become fathers without anxiety and childless again without experiencing grief (*sine sollicitudine parens, sine luctu orbus*), caused massive resentment among those who invested time and effort in the raising of children. They appealed to the senate, which issued a decree that no benefits of any kind be derived from such sham adoptions (15.19.4, the last sentence of the chapter):

> factum ex eo senatus consultum, ne simulata adoptio in ulla parte muneris publici iuvaret ac ne usurpandis quidem hereditatibus prodesset.

> [A senatorial decree was thereupon passed, ruling that a feigned adoption should not assist in any way in gaining a public appointment, nor even be of use in taking up an inheritance.]

---

67 The law was introduced by the bachelors (!) Marcus *Papius* Mutilus and Quintus *Poppaeus* Secundus, two of the consuls of AD 9 (hence *lex Papia Poppaea*). This piece of legislation was an adjustment of the more famous (and, among members of the ruling élite, highly unpopular) *lex Julia de maritandis ordinibus* ('Julian law on marrying categories') that Augustus passed in 18 BC. For further details (including our sources in translation) see Cooley (2003) 353–72.

68 For Cassius Dio, we cite the translation by Earnest Cary in the Loeb Classical Library (Cambridge, Mass. and London 1914–1927).

Then a sudden transition in narrative registers occurs. With the first word of the set text (*exim*), we join the senate meeting, in which this decree came to pass, and witness the next item on the agenda in 'real time' (as it were): the lawsuit against the Cretan power-broker Claudius Timarchus. From then on we we get a blow-by-blow account of the proceedings and are even treated to a direct speech from the Stoic Thrasea Paetus (20.3–21.4). This meeting of the senate, which suddenly comes to life, is the last event of AD 62 that Tacitus reports in detail. As such it harks back to how his account of the year began at 14.48: also with a lawsuit and a meeting of the senate in which the same figure starred as here – Thrasea Paetus. For a proper appreciation of 15.20–22, and in particular its protagonist, we therefore need to know of this earlier occasion – which we accordingly discuss at some length in our Introduction (see section 6).

Chapter 20

20.1 Exim Claudius Timarchus Cretensis reus agitur, ceteris criminibus ut solent praevalidi provincialium et opibus nimiis ad iniurias minorum elati: una vox eius usque ad contumeliam senatus penetraverat, quod dictitasset in sua potestate situm an pro consulibus qui Cretam obtinuissent grates agerentur.

The section consists of two sentences:

a. *exim ... elati;*
b. *una ... agerentur.*

They feature more or less parallel syntax: in each case, a main clause (*exim ... agitur; una ... penetraverat*) is followed by a sequence of subordinate clauses. In thematic terms, however, the design is obliquely asymmetrical. The first main clause sets up the entire scene, whereas the second main clause harks back not to the first main clause (its apparent syntactic counterpart) but to the subordinate constructions that follow it: *una vox* correlates antithetically with *ceteris criminibus*. The design downplays the generalizing *cetera crimina*: they are awkwardly tagged on in an ablative absolute and further elaborated in an elliptical *ut*-clause, in contrast to the one specific *vox*, which is the subject and in first position. Sandwiched as they are between two main clauses that lead from the introduction of the defendant to the one offence (the *una vox*) that brought him to the attention of the senate, they are syntactically glossed over.

exim Claudius Timarchus Cretensis reus agitur, ceteris criminibus ut solent praevalidi provincialium et opibus nimiis ad iniurias minorum elati: The main clause – *exim Claudius Timarchus Cretensis reus agitur* – is straightforward enough. But then the syntax starts to get difficult. Tacitus continues, awkwardly, with a nominal ablative absolute, i.e. an ablative absolute that is missing the participle (in this case the present participle of *esse*, which does not exist in Latin): 'the rest of the charges being...' The subsequent *ut*-clause, too, has its problems. Against standard word order, Tacitus places the verb at the beginning (*solent*). The fact that it is in the indicative helps to clarify the meaning of *ut* ('as'). But an infinitive that would complete the main verb *solent* is nowhere to be seen. The entire rest of the *ut*-clause is taken up by one long subject phrase: *praevalidi provincialium et opibus nimiis ad iniurias minorum elati*. The missing infinitive with the verb *soleo* is not in itself unusual (it frequently has to be supplied from context), but here it generates an exceptionally open-ended construction:

> 'the rest of the charges being such as provincial strongmen tend to...'

Well? What *is* the infinitive that has gone absent without leave? Two possible options are *accusari* ('tend to be accused of') or, with a slight semantic slippage from *crimina* in the sense of 'charges' to *crimina* in the sense of 'crimes', *committere* ('tend to perpetrate'). Since there is a break after the *ut*-clause (*una vox* starts the second main clause), we have to make up our own minds – or remain studiously and elegantly ambiguous in our translation, as does Woodman: 'Next, Claudius Timarchus, a Cretan, appeared as a defendant on the general charges customary for those paramount provincials whose elevation to excessive wealth results in injury to lesser people.'[69]

exim: The temporal marker ('thereupon', 'thereafter') is typical of Tacitus' habit to flag up the generic affiliations of his text, as he purports to record events in their order of occurrence and gives the impression (arguably correct) that he used archival data, such as official records of the senate's business (the *acta senatus*) in compiling his *Annals*. But his formal commitment to annalistic writing ought not to obscure that he proceeded selectively and arranged his material in such a way that further meaningful patterns emerge. The two lawsuits that frame his account of AD 62, each

---

69   Woodman (2004) 315.

starring Thrasea Paetus, are an excellent example of his practice. An interesting tension ensues between Tacitus' artful design and strategic selectivity on the one hand and, on the other, the apparently artless recording of events in chronological order implied by temporal markers such as *exim*.

Claudius Timarchus Cretensis: Claudius Timarchus is otherwise unknown, yet is clearly a powerful Cretan, whose name specifies a hybrid freedman combining hints of the doddery emperor with Greek 'Ruling-Élite' (as Tacitus' indignant remarks on jumped-up *nouveaux* provincial types caustically spell out: see below).[70] Crete (along with Cyrenaica) was a 'senatorial' province governed by an ex-praetor ('pro-consul') – as opposed to an 'imperial' province under the direct control of the *princeps*. In his *Geography*, Strabo (c. 63 BC – AD 23) includes an extensive discussion of this split, which was a key feature of the reorganization of the Roman empire under Augustus. The passage is worth citing in full since it yields valuable insights into the logic of the Augustan settlement that defined the career opportunities of the senatorial élite under the principate (17.3.25):[71]

> But the Provinces have been divided in different ways at different times, though at the present time they are as Augustus Caesar arranged them; for when his native land committed to him the foremost place of authority and he became established for life as lord of war and peace, he divided the whole empire into two parts, and assigned one portion to himself and the other to the Roman people; to himself, all parts that had need of a military guard (that is, the part that was barbarian and in the neighbourhood of tribes not yet subdued, or lands that were sterile and difficult to bring under cultivation, so that, being unprovided with everything else, but well provided with strongholds, they would try to throw off the bridle and refuse obedience), and to the Roman people all the rest, in so far as it was peaceable and easy to rule without arms; and he divided each of the two portions into several Provinces, of which some are called 'Provinces of Caesar' and the others 'Provinces of the People.' And to the 'Provinces of Caesar' Caesar sends *legati* and procurators, dividing the countries in different ways at different times and administering them as the occasion requires, whereas to the 'Provinces of the People' the people send praetors or proconsuls, and these Provinces also are brought under different divisions whenever expediency requires.

---

70 We owe this observation to John Henderson: 'Claudius' recalls Nero's predecessor the emperor Claudius (the hero of Robert Graves' *I, Claudius*), whereas 'Timarchus' combines the two Greek words *timê* ('honour', 'distinction') and *archê* ('power', 'rule').

71 We cite the translation by H. L. Jones in the Loeb Classical Library (Cambridge, Mass. and London, 1932), slightly adjusted.

Put differently, Augustus arranged things in such a way that the emperor retained exclusive control over the army, without denying other members of the ruling élite the opportunity to enrich themselves and enhance their careers by taking up positions in provincial government.[72] The administration of what Strabo calls the 'Provinces of the People' was ultimately the responsibility of the senate, and cases that could not be decided by the governor on the spot were referred back to Rome.

praevalidi provincialium et opibus nimiis ad iniurias minorum elati: The massive subject-phrase of the '*ut solent...*' clause. Tacitus has placed the key words at the beginning (*praevalidi*) and the end (*elati*). *praevalidi* is an adjective functioning as a noun ('the supremely powerful') and takes a partitive genitive (*provincialium*). *elati* is the perfect passive participle of *effero*, also functioning as a noun and governing the ablative phrase *opibus nimiis* together with prepositional phrase *ad iniuriam minorum*. The overall design is therefore chiastic. Tacitus uses this phrase to type-cast Timarchus. He is not interested in the accused as an individual, but as the representative of a specific social group: the provincial super-élite. Several stylistic touches reinforce the tremendous power and wealth that this élite has at its disposal, notably the strengthened adjective *prae-validus* (in nice alliteration with *provincialium*, deftly reproduced by Woodman in English with 'paramount provincials': see above), the emphasis on *excessive* (*nimiis*) wealth, and the choice of the vivid participle *elati*, which suggests elevation above common mortals. Tacitus contrasts the excessively powerful with their inferiors (*minorum*) and implies that such a differential in power and resources almost *inevitably* results in harm for those at the lower end of the pecking order: the preposition *ad* here

---

72 In his account of the arrangement put in place by Augustus, Cassius Dio reports and shreds the ideological veneer (53.12.1–3): 'In this way he [sc. Augustus] had his supremacy ratified by the senate and by the people as well. But as he wished even so to be thought a man of the people, while he accepted all the care and oversight of the public business, on the ground that it required some attention on his part, yet he declared he would not personally govern all the provinces, and that in the case of such provinces as he should govern he would not do so indefinitely; and he did, in fact, restore to the senate the weaker provinces, on the ground that they were peaceful and free from war, while he retained the more powerful, alleging that they were insecure and precarious and either had enemies on their borders or were able on their own account to begin a serious revolt. His professed motive in this was that the senate might fearlessly enjoy the finest portion of the empire, while he himself had the hardships and the dangers; but his real purpose was that by this arrangement the senators should be unarmed and unprepared for battle, while he alone had arms and maintained soldiers.'

conveys a sense of function, purpose, or result (*OLD* G). These are men 'raised by their excessive wealth *so as to* inflict harm on their inferiors.' The construction hints at Tacitus' pessimistic view of human nature.

For those of you who have read Cicero, *in Verrem* 2.1.53–69, at AS-level, provincial exploitation during the late republic will be a familiar topic. Tacitus mentions it at the very beginning of the *Annals*, where he surveys different social groups and their reasons for welcoming, or at least accepting, the new world order of the Augustan principate (1.2.2):

> neque provinciae illum rerum statum abnuebant, suspecto senatus populique imperio ob certamina potentium et avaritiam magistratuum, invalido legum auxilio, quae vi ambitu, postremo pecunia turbabantur.
> [Neither were the provinces ill-disposed towards that state of affairs, given that they had become disillusioned by the regime of the senate and the people on account of the warring among the powerful and the greed of the magistrates and because of the ineffective protection afforded by the laws: they tended to be rendered invalid by sheer force, political manipulation, and, ultimately, bribery.]

Our passage suggests that the principate did by no means bring an end to provincial exploitation, even though the type of suffering inflicted on subject peoples changed: under imperial rule, the provinces were at least no longer ransacked by civil-war parties (cf. *certamina potentium*) fighting it out on their territory, with at times terrible costs to the indigenous population. Greed of magistrates, however, seems to have remained a constant.[73]

una vox eius usque ad contumeliam senatus penetraverat, quod dictitasset in sua potestate situm [sc. *esse*] an pro consulibus qui Cretam obtinuissent grates agerentur: In contrast to what precedes it, the syntax of this sentence is reasonably straightforward, if intricate:

- we have a main clause (verb: *penetraverat*)
- this leads up to the subordinate *quod*-clause (verb: *dictitasset*; for the subjunctive, see below)
- *dictitasset* in turn introduces an indirect statement, with *situm* (sc. *esse*) as infinitive and an implied *id* as subject accusative, which takes the *an*-clause as predicate ('... that it resided in his power whether...')
- within the *an*-sentence, finally, we have a relative clause (*qui Cretam obtinuissent*), with *pro consulibus* as antecedent.

---

73 See further Brunt (1961), with discussion of our passage at 215–17.

Yet despite the intricate syntax, the meaning of this clause is crystal clear: an insolent utterance earned the uppity Cretan provincial a court-appearance in Rome. The contrast between the hazy syntax that characterizes the stretch *ceteris criminibus ... minorum elati* and the precise syntax in the sentence that follows is thematically appropriate. Tacitus distinguishes two types of accusations by means of the antithesis *ceteris criminibus* and *una vox*. The *cetera crimina*, so he suggests, are charges that tend to be levied against provincial strongmen as a matter of course (*solent*), with the strong *implication* being (which does not, however, amount to an *assertion*) that the charges are genuine. But Tacitus never specifies what Timarchus' abuse and exploitation of his fellow-provincials consisted in. On the other hand, he goes into great detail about the one utterance (yes, a mere *utterance*, however arrogant and frequently repeated) that rubbed the Roman overlords the wrong way. The switch from opaque to precise syntax gives Tacitus' Latin an insidious spin: the casual indifference of the obscure and elliptical sentence construction that characterizes his presentation of the *cetera crimina* would seem to suggest that the Romans do not really care all that much about Timarchus' acts of transgression against his fellow-provincials, whereas the detailed elaboration of the one (seemingly inconsequential) boast that affected Roman majesty reflects the hyper-attentive indignation that ensues as soon as Roman sentiments are at stake. Taken thus, Tacitus' syntax would seem to mock the priorities of the senate when it comes to the administration of justice in the provinces and to expose its over-blown sense of self-importance – without of course in any way whitewashing Timarchus, who emerges as another specimen in his pessimistic 'anthropology of power': in Tacitus' book, all sheep are black.

una vox eius usque ad contumeliam senatus penetraverat: The sentence, which follows in stark asyndeton, contains a fourfold contrast to what precedes: (i) *una vox* picks up *ceteris criminibus*; and *usque ad contumeliam senatus* harks back to *ad iniuriam minorum*, correlating and contrasting (ii) *iniuriam* and *contumeliam* as well as (iii) the objective genitives *minorum* and *senatus*. In addition, while both *elati* and *penetraverat* contain the sense of crossing a boundary or norm, (iv) *solent* suggests that the *cetera crimina* are par for the course, whereas *penetraverat* underscores the apparent singularity of this one particular transgression. Tacitus makes the perceived gravity of this 'crime' very clear – it is the one that made Timarchus' case different from the usual: both *usque ad* ('right up to', 'as far as') and *penetraverat* suggest that this additional offence outweighs the others in seriousness. But the correlation of *contumeliam senatus* with *iniuriam minorum* hints at irony: one is made to wonder what sort of political system it is, in which a verbal slight of superiors counts as a more serious transgression than the systematic exploitation of the powerless. (It is worth bearing in mind that Tacitus composed the *Annals* after a long public career that included the administration of the plum province.)

dictitasset: (= *dictitavisset*) Normal Latin verbs can be re-formed with -*to* or -*so* (first conjugation) to produce so-called 'frequentative' forms. This indicates that the action keeps happening: so *rogito* = I keep asking, ask persistently (from '*rogo*'); *curso* = I run about constantly (from '*curro*'). Here, *dictito* re-doubles the frequentative form '*dicto*' (formed from '*dico*') to bring out that Timarchus kept bragging about his power incessantly. The subjunctive mood indicates that it is not a *fact* that Timarchus said these things but an *accusation* (with an implied verb that governs the indirect statement): 'because (people claimed) he had kept saying that...' Miller calls it 'subjunctive of the charge, virtual oblique.'[74] This subtlety of Latin is one of the ways in which Tacitus can report scurrilous allegations in his history without actually endorsing them himself.

in sua potestate situm an pro consulibus qui Cretam obtinuissent grates agerentur: Here we have the insult that grated with the senate (via the proconsular governor, the senate's representative in the province): Timarchus claimed that it was *his* decision whether votes of thanks were given to the proconsuls in charge of the province. The exposed position of *in sua potestate* underscores the hubris of Timarchus. Meanwhile, age-old myth maintained that 'All *Cretans* are liars' – and made merry with the paradox that arises *when a Cretan tells you so*...

pro consulibus ... grates agerentur: *pro* and *consulibus* (in the dative) are to be taken together ('proconsuls' – originally 'stand-ins for consuls'). *grates* is in the nominative plural; the word is a poeticism: '*grates* was originally a religious term for thanks to a god but was first used = *gratias* by poets and then (from Curtius) by writers of elevated prose. In [the *Annals*] Tacitus greatly prefers it to *gratias*, which he reserves for speeches.'[75] At the time, provincial assemblies could decree a vote of thanks for their Roman governors, which

---

74 Miller (1973) 69.
75 Martin and Woodman (1989) 140.

a delegate would then convey to Rome and announce in the senate. The practice has republican roots. At *in Verrem* 2.2.13, for example, Cicero notes that from all of Sicily only Messana sent a legate to Rome to praise Verres for his provincial administration (and this legate, Heius, combined praise with demands to have the personal property that Verres had stolen from him returned). Given that ex-governors had to give an account of their term in office, such votes of thanks could come in handy – apart from offering a neat opportunity for aristocratic self-promotion. Votes, of course, can be bought or manipulated, and this is the form of corruption at issue here.

20.2 quam occasionem Paetus Thrasea ad bonum publicum vertens, postquam de reo censuerat provincia Creta depellendum, haec addidit: *quam* is a connecting relative (= *eam*). The subordinate *postquam*-clause, seemingly introduced as a mere afterthought, again allows Tacitus to underscore Roman priorities by way of syntax: just as with the ablative absolute *ceteris criminibus* and the incomplete *ut-solent* clause in the previous sentence, the construction conveys the sense that those matters of most urgent and direct concern *to the provincials* do not hold anyone's attention *at Rome*. By reporting the verdict on the defendant (note that Timarchus is not mentioned by name again – he is just *'reus'*) in a postponed subordinate clause, Tacitus gives the impression that Paetus dispatched briskly and dismissively with the case at hand. One could argue that the pluperfect with *postquam* here 'implies not only temporal precedence, but a logical relationship';[76] and that is true insofar as the wider reflections to follow presuppose the satisfactory closure of the specific case at issue. But Paetus (and Tacitus) very much focus on the general principles that ought to define the *Roman* approach to imperial rule rather than the particular crimes of the provincial Timarchus or the plight of the Cretans. There is, then, arguably no logical relationship in place. Rather, the punishment imposed on the culprit – the main concern from the point of view of the provincials – is quickly glossed over on the way to Paetus' main concern, the behavioural standards of Rome's ruling élite.

Paetus Thrasea: Tacitus here reverses his names, from the usual Thrasea Paetus to *Paetus Thrasea*. We may wonder why. Are we simply dealing with a further instance of *variatio*, which is such a hallmark of his style, keeping his prose distinctive, unpredictable and interesting? Or is Tacitus perhaps making an oblique point that under the principate matters are not as they ought to

---

76   Miller (1973) 70 and 64.

be (or traditionally were)? We may at any rate savour the nomenclature (with the help of observations supplied by John Henderson): what are we are dealing with in the case of Thrasea Paetus are two *cognomina*. To appreciate this point calls for a brief excursion on Roman naming conventions. The *cognomen* was the third element in a Roman name, coming after the praenomen ('given name') and the *nomen gentile* ('family name'). It was often a nickname, but could, like the *nomen gentile*, become hereditary. Here are some (famous) examples:

praenomen	*nomen gentile*	*cognomen*	**English meaning of *cognomen***
Marcus	Tullius	Cicero	Mr. Chickpea
Publius	Ovidius	Naso	Mr. Conk
Quintus	Horatius	Flaccus	Mr. Flabby or Flap-eared
Gaius	Julius	Caesar	Mr. Hairy

And here is John Henderson on the role of the cognomen in Roman (invective) rhetoric: 'Now equating a fellow-citizen of some distinction with his *cognomen* was the most cliché *topos* in all Roman civic discourse (*sermo*), and their wonderfully rustic *mos* of cultivating peasant gibes at features of the body had even *defined* Roman liberty as levelling obloquy. Hung with glee, and worn with pride, round the necks of highest and lowest in society, this habitual "standing epithet" was there ready to be trotted out, at any instant, in whatever context. The "informal" pet name picking out a self, there to hug or to hurt its bearer, picked on a blunt and crude archaic image-repertoire of deformity and dysfunction to stamp them, stomp on them, stamp them into the ground.'[77]

As it happens, both Paetus and Thrasea are *cognomina*, the former Latin, the latter Graecizing, each highly appropriate to the character in question: *paetus* means 'squinty', Θρασύς (*thrasus*) means 'reckless.' They compound to make our philosophizing senator Mr. Squinty-Bold: a Roman politician with a Greek philosophical mindset, who just so happens to 'spot' (askance) and 'boldly' seize an opportunity to pull off... a 'reverse' (cf. *vertens*). Put differently, Tacitus' inversion of his

---

77 Henderson (2004) 77. Another good example is Cicero's punning on Verres, which is also the Latin term for 'boar' – hence 'Mr. Porker'.

character's two nicknames reflects what Paetus is doing here. It is also the case that there was but one 'Thrasea', but several figures called Paetus. Caesennius *Paetus*, for example, has been busy messing up as a proconsular commander on the Eastern Front earlier in *Annals* 15.

ad bonum publicum vertens: Tacitus here anticipates Thrasea's sly re-definition of the issue under negotiation: Thrasea concentrates not on the specific case at hand, the diminished Roman *dignitas*, or the rights of provincials: his concern is rather with the overall ethos and behavioural standards of Rome's senatorial élite.

de reo censuerat provincia Creta depellendum: *censuerat* introduces an indirect statement. Its subject accusative has to be supplied from *de reo*, i.e. *eum* or *Timarchum* (the elision reinforces the sense that Thrasea does not really care all that much about the details of this case); the verb is the gerundive *depellendum* (sc. *esse*). Arguably the most famous instance of this construction is the notorious habit of Cato the Elder (234 – 149 BC) to close his speeches with the statement *ceterum censeo Carthaginem esse delendam* ('and by the way, I think that Carthage ought to be razed to the ground'). This may not be coincidental: Paetus' speech contains stylistic reminiscences of Cato the Elder's oratory (see below), and Tacitus may here be gently hinting at what is in store – as well as highlighting the affinity in character between Cato the Elder and Thrasea Paetus.

haec addidit: What follows is the longest direct speech in *Annals* 15. We do not know whether it is based on (in the sense of re-invents) one that Paetus actually delivered. (Officialdom rarely records unsuccessful proposals that are – as this one here – set aside as impertinent and out-of-order; Tacitus does – if it suits his aims of scandalized satire and his portrayal of Thrasea Paetus as an anachronistic throw-back to republican times.) The use of (often freely invented) direct speech is at any rate one of the areas in which ancient historiography differs from modern historiography. Virtually all Greek and Roman historiographers put speeches into the mouths of their characters. Tacitus uses this device comparatively rarely, but when he does he tries to give the speaker a distinctive style that differs from that of the surrounding narrative. The structure of the speech is as follows:

20.3:

a. Appeal to experience (*usu...*)

   b. Illustration (*sic*...)

   c. Gnomic generalization (*nam*...)

20.4:

   d. Conclusions to be drawn/ type of decision to be made (*ergo*...)

21.1–4:

   e. Elaboration of why this decision is necessary and beneficial (olim quidem...)

Thrasea's speech is shot through with formulations that point back to Cato the Elder and Sallust (86 – c. 35 BC) – two 'moralizing' authors from the middle and late republic, i.e. exactly the period in Roman history that Thrasea evokes as normative.

20.3: 'usu probatum est, patres conscripti, leges egregias, exempla honesta apud bonos ex delictis aliorum gigni. sic oratorum licentia Cinciam rogationem, candidatorum ambitus Iulias leges, magistratuum avaritia Calpurnia scita pepererunt; nam culpa quam poena tempore prior, emendari quam peccare posterius est.

usu probatum est: Thrasea opens by claiming that his argument is grounded in historical fact: 'proved by experience' is a strong claim to make and, if true, would instantly stamp his discourse on Roman moral legislation with special authority.

patres conscripti: *patres conscripti* is the formal term of address for the senators, dating back to the beginning of the republic. It is a shortened version of *patres et conscripti*, i.e. the original (patrician) members (*patres*) and those (plebeian) members *enlisted* (in Latin: *conscribo, -ere, -psi, -ptum*) at a later stage. See e.g. Livy 2.1.10 (we are in 509 BC, i.e. the year after the expulsion of the kings) – a passage that is worth citing in full since it brings out the powerful republican ideology built into the expression:

> Deinde, quo plus virium in senatu frequentia etiam ordinis faceret, caedibus regis deminutum patrum numerum primoribus equestris gradus lectis ad trecentorum summam explevit; traditumque inde fertur ut in senatum vocarentur qui patres quique conscripti essent: conscriptos, videlicet novum senatum, appellabant lectos. Id mirum quantum profuit ad concordiam civitatis iungendosque patribus plebis animos.

> [Then, to augment the strength of the senate by an increase of the order, he (sc. Brutus) filled up to the sum-total of 300 the number of the fathers, which had been depleted by the murders committed by the king, by enlisting

leading men of the equestrian rank. From that time it is said to have been
handed down that there be summoned into the senate those who were the
'Fathers' and those who were the 'Conscripted': they called the 'Conscripted'
(i.e. the new members of the senate) the Enrolled. It is wonderful how useful
this measure was for the harmony of the senate and for uniting the plebs
with the senators (*patres*).]

leges egregias, exempla honesta apud bonos ex delictis aliorum gigni:
An indirect statement introduced by *usu probatum est*, with *leges egregias,*
exempla honesta (in asyndetic sequence) as subject accusative and *gigni*
as infinitive. The adjectives *egregius* ('outstanding', from *ex + grex*) and,
especially, *honestus* (etymologically related to *honor, -oris* m., 'high
esteem', 'public office') recall the type of the noble Roman of old to which
Thrasea tries to conform – as does the adjective *bonus*, here used as a
noun ('the good'). But Thrasea's retrospective is also brutally realistic
insofar as he sacrifices a good deal of historical nostalgia for a pessimistic
anthropology. Even benchmarks of excellence achieved in the past, he
submits, did not come about from some moral fibre inherent in the
ancient Romans, but rather in reaction to criminal conduct. His *exempla*
are not outstanding deeds of shining glory but rather legal measures and
punitive sanctions. (See *OLD* s.v. *exemplum* 3 for the sense of 'a warning
example, deterrent; an exemplary punishment.') Put differently, the
norms that Thrasea evokes point to a social dynamic at variance with
an unambiguous glorification of the past. Even in republican and early
imperial times, sound legal measures arose 'among the good' (*apud bonos*)
only (?) as punitive *responses* to the crimes and transgressions of others
(*ex delictis aliorum*). While Thrasea thus contrasts the good, right-thinking,
proper Romans (*boni*) with unspecified 'others' (*alii*), the good themselves
come across as strangely passive insofar as they prove their moral fibre
only in reaction to negative stimuli. By invoking 'the good' Thrasea puts
moral pressure on his addressees, the senators, implying that they do not
merit this desirable label unless they vote in favour of his motion.

leges egregias, exempla honesta: Note the staccato-like asyndeton, the
strict parallel construction (noun + adjective; noun + adjective), and
comparative lack of adornment (apart from the whiff of alliteration in
egregias ~ exempla). This is very un-Tacitean style but perhaps adds a
flavour of Stoic 'rhetoric' or 'Catonic simplicity' to Thrasea's speech.
(The Stoics were all about logic, not rhetoric. Likewise, Cato the Elder

disapproved of flowery rhetoric as something alien to Roman common sense: his advice to public speakers was *rem tene, verba sequentur* – 'stick to the topic, and the words will come automatically.')

oratorum licentia Cinciam rogationem, candidatorum ambitus Iulias leges, magistratuum avaritia Calpurnia scita pepererunt: Thrasea continues asyndetically, listing three examples to illustrate the principle that misdeeds or moral failings tend to bring forth corrective legislative measures. The style has the simplicity of a catalogue, an impression reinforced by the remorselessly parallel design of the tricolon. Three nouns in the genitive plural (*oratorum, candidatorum, magistratuum*) specify the offending group. They depend on three nouns in the nominative singular, which indicate the nature of the offence (*licentia, ambitus, avaritia*). The three accusative objects follow the same pattern: in each case we first get the attribute that identifies the name of the measure taken (*Cinciam, Iulias, Calpurnia*) and then the legislative term that the attribute modifies (*rogationem, leges, scita*, though here at least Thrasea aims for variety: see below). A tabled display brings out the systematic approach to rhetorical illustration that Thrasea adopts:

Offending group	Nature of the offence	Name of measure to address it	Legislative term of the measure taken
oratorum	*licentia*	*Cinciam*	*rogationem*
candidatorum	*ambitus*	*Iulias*	*leges*
magistratuum	*avaritia*	*Calpurnia*	*scita*

Again, Tacitus uses style as means of ethopoiea ('projection of character'): Thrasea is utterly disinterested in dressing up his discourse with rhetorical flourishes. (As you may remember from reading Cicero at AS-level, Cicero, for one, likes to introduce some variety into his tricola, for instance by putting the last colon in chiastic order to the preceding two or using a *tricolon crescens*, where the cola increase in length.) Thrasea does not list the laws in chronological order:

lex Cincia de donis et muneribus: passed 204 BC

leges Iuliae de ambitu: passed 18 and 8 BC,

lex Calpurnia de rebus repetundis: passed 149 BC

Rather, he has designed his tricolon climactically with respect to the offending group: we move from public speakers (*oratores*), to candidates for public office (*candidati*), to office holders (*magistratus*). Thrasea chooses his examples carefully. All three pieces of legislation turn out to be relevant to the issue at hand.

Cinciam rogationem: The *lex Cincia de donis et muneribus* ('Cincian law on gifts and fees') was a plebiscite of 204 BC that, among other stipulations, prohibited gifts or payments of any kind to advocates. Tacitus already had occasion to mention the law at *Annals* 11.5–7 and 13.42.1 – indicating that financial compensation for acting as orator in court remained a hot-button issue under the principate.

Iulias leges: The *leges Iuliae de ambitu* ('Julian laws on bribery') were passed by Augustus in 18 BC and 8 BC. Cassius Dio 54.16.1: 'Among the laws that Augustus enacted was one which provided that those who had bribed anyone in order to gain office should be debarred from office for five years. He laid heavier assessments upon the unmarried men and upon the women without husbands, and on the other hand offered prizes for marriage and the begetting of children.' See also Suetonius, *Augustus* 34.1: *Leges retractavit et quasdam ex integro sanxit, ut sumptuariam et de adulteriis et de pudicitia, de ambitu, de maritandis ordinibus* ('He revised existing laws and enacted some new ones, for example, on extravagance, on adultery and chastity, on bribery, and on the encouragement of marriage among the various classes of citizens'). Put differently, by invoking this particular piece of Augustan legislation, Thrasea harks back to a previous item on the agenda of this particular senate-meeting, i.e. the tricksing of childless senators to reap the benefits Augustus accorded to procreating members of the ruling élite.

magistratuum avaritia: The phrase recalls Sallust, *Bellum Iugurthinum* 43.5, especially since Thrasea's speech will shortly rework another formulation from the same passage (see below 21.3: *invictus adversum gratiam animus*):[78]

> Itaque ex sententia omnibus rebus paratis conpositisque in Numidiam proficiscitur, magna spe civium cum propter artis bonas tum maxime quod adversum divitias invictum animum gerebat et avaritia magistratuum ante id tempus in Numidia nostrae opes contusae hostiumque auctae erant.

---

78 Translations of Sallust here and elsewhere are taken from the Loeb Classical Library edition by J. C. Rolfe (Cambridge, Mass. and London, 1921).

[Therefore, after everything was prepared and arranged to his satisfaction, Metellus left for Numidia, bearing with him the high hopes of the citizens, which were inspired not only by his good qualities in general, but especially because he possessed a mind superior to riches; for it had been the avarice of magistrates that before this time had blighted our prospects in Numidia and advanced those of the enemy.]

Calpurnia scita: The *lex Calpurnia de repetundis* ('Calpurnian law on the recovery of public funds') of 149 BC, proposed by the tribune of the people Lucius *Calpurnius* Piso, established Rome's first permanent court, the *quaestio de repetundis*, the same court in which Verres stood trial. One of its main functions was to try governors for extortion committed during their term of office.

rogationem ... leges ... scita: The procedure for passing each of the laws mentioned will have been similar, but Tacitus/ Thrasea opts for lexical variation. *rogatio* refers to a proposed measure that is put before a Roman assembly for approval – our 'bill.' Once approved, a *rogatio*/ bill becomes a *lex* ('law'). A *scitum*, which is the perfect participle of *scisco* ('to vote for', 'to approve'), is a resolution of a popular assembly. The word thus places the emphasis on the process of decision-making, and it is usually found with a genitive of the decision-making body, especially the people: *plebis scitum* ('plebiscite'), *populi scitum* ('the decree of the people'). For this reason, it does not work quite as well as *rogatio* or *lex* with an adjective attribute of the person responsible for drafting the bill or law because technically speaking the *scitum* that turned the *rogatio* of Piso into the *lex Calpurnia* was not that of Piso, but that of the people. The slight incongruity is more than made up for by the rhetorical effect of the lexical variety: it seems to imply that the examples could be further multiplied.

nam culpa quam poena prior [sc. *est*]**, emendari quam peccare posterius est:** The two *quam* go with the two comparatives *prior* and *posterius* and coordinate the four subjects: *culpa* and *poena*, *emendari* and *peccare*. Thrasea closes his opening gambit with a gnomic saying that is as intricate in rhetorical design as it is banal in content. He makes the same point twice, first with a pair of nouns, then with a pair of infinitives (functioning as nouns), juxtaposed (once again) asyndetically: crime precedes punishment, to be reformed comes after committing a transgression. But the order is for once chiastic: *culpa* correlates with *peccare*, *poena* with *emendari*, though there is a whiff of parallel design in the alliterative sequence *poena prior ~*

peccare posterius. The introductory *nam* has causal force but is perhaps best left untranslated (with a footnote to the examiners that this is a deliberate omission). The repetitious formulation of the argument, the variation of constructions and the expression of the thought from two opposite angles serve to emphasise Thrasea's point that the senators should make use of Timarchus' crime to create a good new law. The sentence stands in allusive dialogue with earlier Latin historiography, recalling passages in both Sallust and Livy: 'significant too is its [sc. Thrasea's speech] markedly Sallustian language and the fact that in its defence of the established order of things it echoes the conservatism of Cato the Censor [as reported by Livy] when he spoke against the repeal of the sumptuary Oppian law.'[79] Here are the two most pertinent passages. First, Sallust, *Bellum Iugurthinum* 85.12:

> Atque ego scio, Quirites, qui postquam consules facti sunt et acta maiorum et Graecorum militaria praecepta legere coeperint: praeposteri homines, *nam gerere quam fieri tempore posterius, re atque usu prius est.*

> [I personally know of men, citizens, who after being elected consuls began for the first time to read the history of our forefathers and the military treatises of the Greeks, preposterous creatures! *for though in order of time administration follows election, yet in actual practice it comes first.*]

The passage from Livy to consider concerns an episode from 195 BC. Two tribunes of the people proposed the abrogation of the Oppian law that had been passed during the war against Hannibal in 215 BC: it limited public indulgence in luxury items by women. Repeal of the law found much support. But the proposal met with adamant opposition from one of the consuls, Cato the Elder. The speech as given by Livy is too long to be quoted in its entirety. But the following extract towards the end should suffice to highlight affinities between his position and that adopted by Thrasea in Tacitus; it also conveys a good flavour of the period in Roman history and its most iconic representative that Thrasea is keen to evoke in support of his argument (34.4):[80]

> 'Saepe me querentem de feminarum, saepe de virorum nec de privatorum modo sed etiam magistratuum sumptibus audistis, diversisque duobus vitiis, avaritia et luxuria, civitatem laborare, quae pestes omnia magna imperia everterunt. haec ego, quo melior laetiorque in dies fortuna rei publicae est, quo magis imperium crescit – et iam in Graeciam Asiamque transcendimus

---

79   Martin (1969) 139.
80   The translation from Livy is taken from the Loeb Classical Library edition by E. T. Sage (Cambridge, Mass. and London, 1953).

omnibus libidinum inlecebris repletas et regias etiam adtrectamus gazas –, eo plus horreo, ne illae magis res nos ceperint quam nos illas. infesta, mihi credite, signa ab Syracusis inlata sunt huic urbi. iam nimis multos audio Corinthi et Athenarum ornamenta laudantes mirantesque et antefixa fictilia deorum Romanorum ridentes. ego hos malo propitios deos et ita spero futuros, si in suis manere sedibus patiemur. patrum nostrorum memoria per legatum Cineam Pyrrhus non virorum modo sed etiam mulierum animos donis temptavit. nondum lex Oppia ad coercendam luxuriam muliebrem lata erat; tamen nulla accepit. quam causam fuisse censetis? eadem fuit quae maioribus nostris nihil de hac re lege sanciundi: nulla erat luxuria quae coerceretur. *sicut ante morbos necesse est cognitos esse quam remedia eorum, sic cupiditates prius natae sunt quam leges quae iis modum facerent.* quid legem Liciniam excitavit de quingentis iugeribus nisi ingens cupido agros continuandi? quid *legem Cinciam* de donis et muneribus nisi quia vectigalis iam et stipendiaria plebs esse senatui coeperat? itaque minime mirum est nec Oppiam nec aliam ullam tum legem desideratam esse quae modum sumptibus mulierum faceret, cum aurum et purpuram data et oblata ultro non accipiebant. ...'

['You have often heard me complaining of the extravagance of the women and often of the men, both private citizens and magistrates even, and lamenting that the state is suffering from those two opposing evils, avarice and luxury, which have been the destruction of every great empire. The better and happier becomes the fortune of our commonwealth day by day and the greater the empire grows – and already we have crossed into Greece and Asia, places filled with all the allurements of vice, and we are handling the treasures of kings – the more I fear that these things will capture us rather than we them. Tokens of danger, believe me, were those statues which were brought to this city from Syracuse. Altogether too many people do I hear praising the baubles of Corinth and Athens and laughing at the mouldings worked in clay of our Roman gods. I refer that these gods be propitious to us, and I trust that they will be if we allow them to remain in their own dwellings. In the memory of our forefathers Pyrrhus, through his agent Cineas, tried to corrupt with gifts the minds of our men and women as well. Not yet had the Oppian law been passed to curb female extravagance, yet not one woman took his gifts. What do you think was the reason? The same thing which caused our ancestors to pass no law on the subject: there was no extravagance to be restrained. *As it is necessary that diseases be known before their cures, so passions are born before the laws which keep them within bounds.* What provoked the Licinian law about the five hundred iugera except the uncontrolled desire of joining field to field? What brought about *the Cincian law* except that the plebeians had already begun to be vassals and tributaries to the senate? And so it is not strange that no Oppian or any other law was needed to limit female extravagance at the time when they spurned gifts of gold and purple voluntarily offered to them. ...']

Already Cato the Elder, then, posited a causal link between Rome's triumphal military success abroad and a decline in morality (or at least self-restraint) at home. And like Thrasea, he correlates the passing of sumptuary legislation with the emergence of desires harmful to the fabric of Roman society. Unlike Thrasea, he actively invokes a past period of perfection during which such legislation was not yet required. But even for Cato this period is ancient history; and once corruption has set in, there is no way back. This is the fallen state of the Roman world that Thrasea inhabits as well.

20.4: ergo adversus novam provincialium superbiam dignum fide constantiaque Romana capiamus consilium, quo tutelae sociorum nihil derogetur, nobis opinio decedat, qualis quisque habeatur, alibi quam in civium iudicio esse.

After setting out and illustrating his principles, Thrasea proceeds to outline a course of action. He would like a decision that (*a*) checks further haughty behaviour on the part of provincials, i.e. is directed *adversus novam provincialium superbiam*; but also (*b*) meets Roman standards of excellence in terms of *fides* and *constantia* (*dignum fide constantiaque Romana capiamus consilium*). Both terms find further elaboration in the *quo*-clause: *fide* is picked up by *quo tutelae sociorum nihil derogetur*; and *constantia* by [*quo*] *nobis opinio decedat, qualis quisque habeatur, alibi quam in civium iudicio esse*. The *-que* after *constantia*, which links *fide* and *constantia*, is the first (!) connective in Thrasea's speech, but he instantly falls back into asyndetic mode. The two parts of the *quo*-clause (...*derogetur,* ... *decedat*) are unlinked, continuing the terse, unremitting, to-the-point accounting and enumeration that is a hallmark of the speech from the outset.

adversus novam provincialium superbiam: The adverb *adversus* helps to generate a sense of threat, which is magnified further by *novam* (basically 'new', but here with an extra edge – 'unprecedented'). In general, 'newness' carried a negative charge for a Roman audience, implying something never previously encountered, new and dangerous. (The Latin for 'revolutionary chaos' is *res novae*.) The noun *superbia*, too, is highly damning. It is not something the Romans tolerated in the territories under their control. The most famous articulation of the principle 'Squash the Proud' is the 'imperial mission' statement towards the end of *Aeneid* 6, where Anchises, in anticipation of the founding of Rome and her rise to world-empire, exclaims (6.851–53):

'tu regere imperio populos, Romane, memento

(hae tibi erunt artes), pacique imponere morem,

parcere subiectis et debellare superbos.'

[You, Roman, be mindful of ruling the people with your power of command (be these your arts), to impose custom upon peace, to spare the vanquished, and to squash the proud.]

Thrasea draws a stark, idealised antithesis between the provincials (*provincialium*) and the Romans (*Romana*), the former exhibiting arrogance (*superbiam*), the latter more noble qualities (*fide constantiaque*).

dignum fide constantiaque Romana ... consilium: *dignum ... consilium* forms an impressive hyperbaton. The attribute (in predicative position) and the noun it modifies encase two key Roman values. *fides* is a key concept in how the Romans thought about social relations, and dictionary entries ('confidence', 'loyalty', 'trustworthiness', 'credibility') convey only a limited sense of the full semantic range and force of the qualities at issue: *fides* underwrites socio-economic exchanges, defines political interactions, and justifies Roman rule. In relationships that were both reciprocal (with party rendering some, but not necessarily the same, kind of service to the other) and asymmetrical (with one party being much more powerful than the other), a commitment to *fides* on both sides operated as a (partial) counterweight to steep inequalities in power.[81] *constantia* – often paired with *gravitas* and the opposite of fickleness ('steadfastness') – is one of the republican virtues that Cicero likes to bring into play when talking about the moral fibre of his clients or the Roman ancestors.[82] But it was not an entirely unproblematic quality, especially in a political system such as republican and imperial Rome that depended much on compromise and consensus. An unwavering ('obstinate') attitude of adversaries could paralyse the political process. At *pro Sestio* 77, for instance, Cicero identifies obstinate persistence (*pertinacia aut constantia*) on the part of a tribune as a frequent source of riots. And as we have seen in our discussion of Thrasea Paetus' behaviour in the context of Atilius' treason trial (see Introduction, section 6), haughty disregard for the social scripts of imperial politics, while perhaps soliciting approval as an admirable display

---

81   Hölkeskamp (2004)
82   See e.g. *pro Quinto Roscio* 7, *pro Cluentio* 197, *de Domo Sua* 39, *pro Balbo* 13 with Schofield (2009) 201–4.

of *constantia*, might also be regarded as a self-serving pursuit of *gloria*, with dysfunctional consequences for the terms of interaction between senate and *princeps*.

capiamus: a hortative subjunctive: Thrasea rallies his colleagues to support his views.

quo tutelae sociorum nihil derogetur, nobis opinio decedat...: The relative pronoun *quo* (in the ablative of means or instrument, referring back to *consilium*) introduces a clause that elaborates on *fides* and *constantia* in parallel design:

	Dative	**Subject**	**Verb**
fides	*tutelae sociorum*	*nihil*	*derogetur*
constantia	*nobis*	*opinio*	*decedat*

Both *derogari* and *decedere* contain the idea of removal or subtraction, yet in antithetical correlation: nothing ought to be removed from Roman *fides* (with the emphatic *nihil* stressing the uncompromising disposition of Thrasea); but if the Romans do not get rid of the idea that the actions or opinions of provincials have influence in Rome, their *constantia* (here in the sense of 'firmness of purpose') will be diminished. Both parts of the *quo*-clause thus reinforce the Roman sense of superiority vis-à-vis the provincial subjects. *Fides* manifests itself in the proper guardianship of those entrusted to one's care; *constantia* in an attitude of indifference towards attempts of provincials to gain any sort of purchase on political decision-making in Rome.

qualis quisque habeatur, alibi quam in civium iudicio esse: An indirect statement dependent on *opinio decedat*. The phrasing *alibi quam* ('anywhere else but') makes the point powerfully that no other opinion than that of Roman citizens should matter and combines with the earlier *nihil* to reinforce the impression that Thrasea's way of thinking is unconditional and categorical: he is not one to budge from principles, not even an inch. *qualis* refers to the type, quality, or character of a person and stands in predicative position to *quisque*: 'of which quality or worth each individual is to be regarded.' Hence: '... let us adopt a policy..., whereby (*quo*)... we depart from the opinion that what each man is held to be like rests somewhere other than in the judgment of his fellow citizens.'[83]

in civium iudicio: Thrasea draws a determined line between citizens and non-citizens. The emphasis on citizenship and on Rome as a civic community has a republican ring to it. It sidelines, by passing over in silence, other, more salient distinctions – as the one between the emperor and everyone else. (Especially for members of the ruling élite, the *iudicium principis* was of course a key factor.) Conversely, the notion that the worth of a person lies in the judgement of some individual or social group goes against the Stoic principle of the self-sufficiency of excellence, which does not require external validation of any kind. Thrasea here adjusts his philosophical affiliations to the realities of Roman politics.

Chapter 21

21.1: *Olim quidem* **non modo praetor aut consul sed privati etiam mittebantur qui provincias viserent et quid de cuiusque obsequio videretur referrent; trepidabantque gentes de aestimatione singulorum:** *at nunc* **colimus externos et adulamur, et quo modo ad nutum alicuius grates, ita promptius accusatio decernitur.**

Thrasea proceeds by drawing a sharp contrast between 'back then' (*olim*) and 'nowadays' (*nunc*). Word order underscores the strength of feeling: the key adverbs *olim* and *nunc* are placed in front position and find reinforcement through two strategic particles: *quidem*, which is usually placed directly after the word it emphasizes and here endows *olim* with special resonance ('in the good old days, as you well know'); and the strongly adversative *at*. The order is chiastic: temporal adverb (*olim*) + particle (*quidem*) :: particle (*at*) + temporal adverb (*nunc*). Thrasea correlates and contrasts the past and the present by means of lexical and thematic inversions. For the past, he invokes the high magistrates of the republic (*praetor, consul*) as well as any non-office-holders on top (*privati*); for the present, he opts for an undifferentiated 'we' (*colimus, adulamur*), as if to underscore the contemporary irrelevance of key political categories from republican times (see further below on *privati*). The collective self-indictment is reinforced by the contrast between the collective 'we' and the preceding *de aestimatione*

---

83   Woodman (2004) 315.

singulorum: in the past, entire people (*gentes*) stood in fear of the assessment of *single individuals*; now *all* Romans are beholden to the whim and will of some random provincial. In the course of the sentence, Thrasea sketches out a complete reversal of republican realities in imperial times: we are moving from one random Roman lording it over every provincial to one random provincial lording it over every Roman. At the centre of the design Thrasea places the antithesis *de cuiusque obsequio* – *ad nutum alicuius*. *obsequium* indicates '(slavish) obedience', *nutus* ('nod', but here in the technical sense of 'a person's nod as the symbol of absolute power') refers to someone's virtually unlimited power to get things done by a mere jerk of the head. By means of two strategic omissions Thrasea manages to suggest that complete nonentities are now in charge at Rome: after *alicuius* we must mentally supply *provincialis* ('by some provincial or other'); and the ablative of agency with *decernitur* (*a provincialibus*) is also only implied. In effect, Thrasea argues that the Romans have allowed their provincial subjects to become their overlords – a complete inversion of what things used (and ought) to be.

non modo praetor aut consul sed privati etiam mittebantur: Thrasea claims here that in the olden days not just high-ranking officials but even *privati* (citizens without office or *imperium*) were dispatched to run affairs abroad. He is here using *privatus* in the technical 'republican' sense, i.e. 'non-office holder.' In the early empire, *privatus* became (also) an antonym of *princeps* – i.e. it could be used to refer to any Roman (including high magistrates) as opposed to the emperor. Commentators see in Thrasea's gesture to republican times a reference to the so-called *legatio libera*. The term referred to the senatorial privilege of travelling at public expense (like a legate) to look after their personal interests without the requirement of taking on civic duties. Provincials were expected to entertain and support such travellers like a Roman official on public business and bitterly complained about this additional burden. Cicero, for one, tried (unsuccessfully) to outlaw this practice.[84] There were, then, good reasons why provincials feared these 'legates' – not because they represented Roman law and order (as Thrasea intimates), but because they constituted a particularly insidious form of provincial exploitation. Note also that Thrasea misrepresents the practice: these 'legates' were not 'sent' by the senate – they received a special privilege to go. The distortions and the hyperbole – both clearly

---

84   Kolb (2000) 36–7.

conducive to Thrasea's argument – raise interesting questions about his character (and Tacitus' use of characterization). Are we to imagine Thrasea deliberately deviating from the truth to further his case? Or would he and his audience (perhaps even Tacitus?) share a somewhat inaccurate and certainly nostalgic conception of republican times?

qui provincias viserent et quid de cuiusque obsequio videretur referrent: The verbs of the relative clause – *viserent* and *referrent* – are in the subjunctive, indicating purpose: these people, Thrasea claims (incorrectly: see previous note), were sent *in order to* inspect and report. What did they report on? Thrasea supplies the answer in the indirect question (hence the subjunctive) *quid … videretur. video* in the passive with neuter pronoun as subject means 'to seem good, right, proper', so in essence, these Roman visitors issued reports on 'what seemed proper about the obedience of each individual.' There is an insidious, subjective touch to *videretur*: *videri*, in the sense 'to seem', presupposes the eye of a beholder to whom something *appears* to be the case without it necessarily *being* the case, and the verb therefore routinely takes a dative of a person whose perspective is at issue. Thrasea could have added *eis* but leaves it out, generating a wrong impression of objectivity.

cuiusque: The word makes clear that Thrasea imagines the inspection and reporting to have been far-reaching, extending to every single provincial – a hyperbole bordering on the absurd. It evokes association of Hesiod's droves of immortals who walk the earth in disguise and report on the conduct of humans (*Works & Days* 252–55) or the prologue of Plautus' *Rudens*, where the minor divinity Arcturus develops a 'Big Jupiter is watching you' theology – or, indeed, modern totalitarian regimes and their systems of mass-surveillance.

trepidabantque gentes de aestimatione singulorum: The -*que*, so rare in Thrasea's speech, links *mittebantur* (cause) and *trepidabant* (effect) particularly tightly. The overall design is chiastic – subject (*praetor, consul, privati*) verb (*mittebantur*) :: verb (*trepidabant*) subject (*gentes*) – which results in the emphatic placement of *trepidabant* at the beginning of the second main clause and underscores the dynamic of 'cause and effect.' The contrast between *gentes* (entire nations) and *singulorum* (individuals) brings out the power individual magistrates were able to exercise in the old days. *aestimatio* here seems to refer to a general 'assessment' or 'appraisal', but it is also a technical term in law, where it refers specifically to the assessment of damages and their pecuniary value, the insidious implication being that any *aestimatio* by any Roman will cost Rome's subject people – dearly.

colimus externos et adulamur: Thrasea pleonastically uses two verbs with almost identical meanings ('we court and flatter') to lay on thick the weakness and cravenness of modern officials, which reflects badly on the entire ruling élite (Thrasea implicates himself and everyone else present by switching into the first person plural). There is a note of contempt here, especially in the word *externos* ('foreigners').

quo modo ad nutum alicuius grates, ita promptius accusatio decernitur: A highly condensed mode of expression. Written out in full, the sentence would run: *quo modo ad nutum alicuius [provincialis] grates [a provincialibus decernuntur], ita promptius accusatio [a provincialibus] decernitur.* Although Timarchus' 'crime' was to claim control over votes of thanks, Thrasea frightens the senators by pointing out that perversely empowered provincials are even quicker (*promptius*) to press charges against Roman officials than to decree votes of thanks – only to frustrate expectations in the following sentence.

21.2: decernaturque et maneat provincialibus potentiam suam tali modo ostentandi: sed laus falsa et precibus expressa perinde cohibeatur quam malitia, quam crudelitas.

We have reached the point where Thrasea presents his key paradox. His speech now makes a surprising turn. Up till now his focus has been on whipping up outrage at provincial conceit and the unwholesome inversion of imperial hierarchies. Now Thrasea suggests that he minds neither the provincials bringing charges nor boasting about their power – the real problem lies elsewhere: the corruption in Rome. In what seems at first sight a counterintuitive move, he argues that the provincials ought to retain the right to press charges; but they should be prohibited from issuing (which inevitably means 'selling') votes of thanks. The principle has wider applications: there is an implicit analogy here between the insincere or extorted *laus* that provincials lavish on Roman governors and the insincere or extorted *laus* that Roman senators lavish on the *princeps*. As Rudich puts it, perhaps over-assertively: 'Thrasea Paetus' message was only thinly masked by rhetorical generalities and must accordingly have been perceived by his audience as an attack on their own practice of *adulatio*.'[85]

decernaturque: Thrasea is again elliptical: to complete the first phrase, one needs to supply *accusatio* from the previous sentence. The mood is subjunctive. The present subjunctive can be used in the third person to give orders ('jussive subjunctive'), here translating as 'let it [sc. an accusation] be decreed.'

et maneat provincialibus potentiam suam tali modo ostentandi: The syntax here is rather unusual: the genitive of the gerund (*ostentandi*), which takes *potentiam suam* as accusative object, lacks a noun on which it depends and one might have expected an infinitive instead. This is, however, not the only place in the *Annals* where this construction occurs: Tacitus also uses it at 15.5 (*vitandi*) and 13.26 (*retinendi*). As Miller points out, 'it is extremely unlikely that in all three instances the same odd construction has been caused by the same accident of textual transmission. It is more probably an example of Tacitean experimentation with language' – in this case the blurring between the use of the gerund and the infinitive.[86] The *potentia* refers specifically to the last thing Thrasea had mentioned, i.e. the power of provincials to charge Roman officials with maladministration. He argues that the provincials should still be able to bring cases against corrupt governors; what must be stopped (as he goes on to argue) are the false or corrupt votes of thanks. The verb *ostento* (another frequentative) carries the idea of parading or showing off and suggests that Thrasea considers the powers he would like the provincials to retain rather inconsequential. There is a mocking tone to his concession: the '*potentia*' of the provincials does not amount to much. (For Tacitus on real power vs pomp and show, see 15.31: ... *inania tramittuntur*.)

sed laus falsa et precibus expressa perinde cohibeatur quam malitia, quam crudelitas: Thrasea falls back into asyndetic mode – here reinforced by the anaphora of *quam*: <u>*quam*</u> *malitia,* <u>*quam*</u> *crudelitas* – to proclaim his counterintuitive conviction that contrived praise is as much in need of policing as (*perinde ... quam* = as much as) *malitia* ('wickedness') and *crudelitas* ('cruelty'). The elegant simplicity of *quam malitia, quam crudelitas*

---

85 Rudich (1993) 77.
86 Miller (1973) 52.

(which come with the force of punches to the face) contrasts with the slightly contorted expression *laus falsa et precibus expressa*, in the course of which *laus*, a positive notion, comes gradually undone. The first attribute (*falsa*) seems to refer to provincials 'selling' their votes of thanksgiving, whereas the second attribute (*precibus expressa* – from *exprimere* 'to squeeze out') refers to Roman governors extorting votes of thanksgiving from their provincial subjects. Either form of 'praise' is morally corrupt and potentially the result of cruel behaviour. The assimilation of *laus* to *malitia* and *crudelitas* conjures a world of rampant immorality in which key ethical and semantic distinctions have broken down.

21.3: plura saepe peccantur, dum demeremur quam dum offendimus: This aphoristic phrase sums up Thrasea's attitude to provincial government. Paradoxically, he claims that trying to win favour frequently amounts to a greater crime than causing offence. The sequence *peccantur – demeremur – offendimus* is climactic: we begin with an impersonal passive, move on to the 1st person plural of a deponent (*demeremur*), and end up with *offendimus*, which is active in form and meaning. The alliteration of *p* and *d* and the neat antithesis in *dum demeremur quam dum offendimus*, stressed by the anaphora of *dum*, also help to make this remark shine.

quaedam immo virtutes odio sunt: The word *immo* (here unusually placed second) puts a novel, corrective spin on the preceding sentence. It explains why causing offence – an apparent negative – ought not to be considered a cause for concern. Even certain *positive* qualities (*virtutes*) trigger hatred.

severitas obstinata, invictus adversus gratiam animus: The phrase stands in apposition to *virtutes*, indicating two examples of just such excellent if unpopular qualities. The overall design is a majestic chiasmus – noun (*severitas*) + attribute (*obstinata*) :: attribute (*invictus*) + noun (*animus*) – that comes with three special twists: (i) Thrasea again puts on display his aversion to connectives: the two *virtutes* are listed one after the other, asyndetically. (ii) The overall arrangement is climactic both in quantitative and thematic terms: the second half is significantly longer because *invictus*, the attribute of *animus*, is in predicative position and governs the additional phrase *adversus gratiam*; and there is an increase in intensity from *obstinata* ('resolute') to *invictus*, which signifies an even higher degree of determination and resolve than *obstinatus*: the subtle military metaphor makes the evocation of a strong, incorruptible Roman mind especially arresting. (Note that as gloss on Greek *amachos* ('unconquerable') *invictus* means 'invinc-*ible*', so it only appears to match the past participle *obstinata*.) Thrasea invokes a mindset so firm of purpose that no attempt to curry favour has any effect. (iii) He twists standard Latin word order out of shape: usually, adjectives in attributive position indicating degree (such as *obstinata*) come before the noun they modify, whereas adjectives in predicative position (as is the case with *invictus* here) come after the noun they modify. Overall, the expression evokes the moral discourse of republican Rome and, more specifically, Sallustian idiom: see *Bellum Iugurthinum* 43.5 (*...quod adversum divitias invictum animum gerebat*), cited in full above at 20.3.

21.4 inde initia magistratuum nostrorum meliora ferme et finis inclinat, dum in modum candidatorum suffragia conquirimus: quae si arceantur, aequabilius atque constantius provinciae regentur. nam ut metu repetundarum infracta avaritia est, ita vetita gratiarum actione ambitio cohibebitur.'

inde initia magistratuum nostrorum meliora ferme et finis inclinat: The word *inde* ('in consequence') continues Thrasea's claim that certain excellent qualities (*virtutes*) such as a strict resolve and a mind steeled against attempts at ingratiation are liable to incur hatred. The line of reasoning here seems to be as follows: the majority (cf. *ferme*) of Roman magistrates approach their term in office with sound ethics but a feeble disposition; they start out governing with *obstinata severitas* and rejecting anyone trying to curry favour (hence *initia ... meliora*) – only to encounter resistance or hatred; unable to endure being the source and target of negative emotions, they let themselves be corrupted towards the end. The ellipsis of a verb in the first half (literally, 'the beginnings of our magistracies [sc. are] generally better') seems to enact the sense of the early promise quickly slipping away; it also reinforces the antithesis between *initia* and *finis*. For someone as reluctant to waste time on connectives as Thrasea, his use of *et*, which oddly correlates a verb omitted (*sunt*) with the one main verb in the sentence (*inclinat*), stands out. The sentence bubbles with sound effects, especially the alliteration and homoioteleuton of *i*, *m* and *f* (see the underlining) all drawing the listeners' attention to the speaker's diagnosis of Rome's political ills. Note also the long, seven-word build up with those resounding polysyllables, and then the simple, self-enacting, anticlimactic *finis inclinat*.

dum in modum candidatorum suffragia conquirimus: A *suffragium* is a vote cast in an assembly (for a candidate, resolution, or such like), and the phrase *suffragia conquirere* refers to the canvassing of votes – a common occurrence before elections. In the context of provincial administration, however, Thrasea presents the practice as demeaning and distinctly undesirable: governors ought not to behave like candidates for political office chasing the popular vote. By using the first person plural (*conquirimus*) Thrasea suggests that it is not just the reputation of the individual miscreant that is at issue here but that of the entire senate (with one implication being: we, sc. you, have all done it!): governors represent Rome's ruling élite as a whole, and the behaviour of one reflects on everyone else.

quae si arceantur, aequabilius atque constantius provinciae regentur: *quae* is a connecting relative (= *ea*) and refers back to the practice of courting favour with provincials to receive a vote of thanks. Thrasea here switches from moral indictment to asserting the tangible benefits of his proposed measure: if governors refrain from canvassing or buying votes, the provinces will be run better and more consistently. Note the use of moods: we get a potential subjunctive in the protasis (*arceantur*), and a future indicative in the apodosis (*regentur*: the provinces *will* be run...). *If* the appropriate measures are taken, so Thrasea seems to suggest, *then* the desired outcome is not in doubt: it will not just kick in *potentially*, but with certainty. (In other words, it should be a no-brainer.)

aequabilius atque constantius: The phrase is strongly reminiscent of a passage in Sallust. See *Bellum Catilinae* 2.3–4:

> Quodsi regum atque imperatorum animi virtus in pace ita ut in bello valeret, *aequabilius atque constantius* sese res humanae haberent, neque aliud alio ferri neque mutari ac misceri omnia cerneres. Nam imperium facile eis artibus retinetur quibus initio partum est.

> [Now if the mental excellence with which kings and rulers are endowed were as potent in peace as in war, human affairs would run an evener and steadier course, and you would not see power passing from hand to hand and everything in turmoil and confusion; for empire is easily retained by the qualities by which it was first won.]

The two passages share a number of parallels: in each case, the matter at issue is the mental disposition of those in power in a time of peace.

The construction – a conditional sequence – is the same (though note that Sallust uses a present counterfactual). And both authors trace a similar trajectory from positive beginnings to eventual decline. Syme suggests that the Sallustian idiom lends support to Thrasea Paetus' mission to 'recall ancient dignity in an oration defending the honour of the senatorial order.'[87] To reinforce the Sallustian ring of the phrase, Thrasea for once even suspends his dislike of connectives and uses a rare *atque*.

metu repetundarum infracta avaritia est: Thrasea abbreviates: *metu repetundarum* stands for *metu pecuniarum repetundarum* or *metu quaestionis repetundarum*. *pecuniae repetundae* was a technical legal term meaning 'the recovery of extorted money', but *pecuniae* is often omitted. The *quaestio de repetundis* (the Roman extortion court) was the first permanent criminal court or tribunal in Rome, established in 149 BC by the *lex Calpurnia* (mentioned above) to try cases of extortion by provincial governors. Thrasea's (blatantly disingenuous) claim that these courts had defeated officials' greed is stressed by the vivid verb *infracta ... est* and by the position of *avaritia* inside the components of the verb – a design that seems to enact the crushing of the greed.

vetita gratiarum actione ambitio cohibebitur: In fine style, Thrasea finishes with a succinct summary of his proposal: ban votes of thanks (the ablative absolute *vetita ... actione* replaces a conditional clause) and corruption will end (the future here follows the same confident logic as *regentur* above).

Chapter 22

22.1: Magno adsensu celebrata sententia. non tamen senatus consultum perfici potuit abnuentibus consulibus ea de re relatum. mox auctore principe sanxere, ne quis ad concilium sociorum referret agendas apud senatum pro praetoribus proue consulibus grates, neu quis ea legatione fungeretur.

magno adsensu celebrata [sc. *est*] **sententia:** The ellipsis of *est* gives the impression of a pithy parallelism, with two phrases in which an attribute (*magno, celebrata*) is followed by a noun (*adsensu, sententia*). The use of

---

the passive both here and in the following sentence keeps Thrasea in the limelight. The other senators remain an anonymous collective. And the meaningful/meaningless round of applause rings out hollow here to celebrate a stand-out tableau – nailing Tacitus' equivalent of the 'Cretan liar' paradox to imperial Rome.

non tamen senatus consultum perfici potuit abnuentibus consulibus ea de re relatum [sc. *esse*]: The subject of the sentence is *consultum*, modified by *senatus* in the genitive. A 'resolution of the senate' was not technically speaking a law, but it had the force of law, especially in foreign and provincial affairs. Here it did not come to pass since the consuls, who presided over the proceedings, intervened. The ablative absolute *abnuentibus consulibus* has causal force, with *abnuentibus* introducing an indirect statement, with the infinitive again in the passive: *relatum*, sc. *esse*. The consuls P. Marius and L. Afinius object to an actual resolution on formal grounds: the matter before the senate was whether Timarchus was guilty or not, and Thrasea had used the occasion to scrutinize key principles of provincial government. This part of his argument was *extra causam*, and while it received the enthusiastic support of the majority of senators, the consuls were wary to add new items, especially those of far-reaching consequences, to the official agenda *ad hoc* since they had not yet been able to check whether they had the support of the emperor. And this particular proposal came from Thrasea, who had already upset the emperor on previous occasions with his independence. More specifically, the passage here harks back to the incident with which Tacitus begins his account of the year 62: the *maiestas*-trial of the praetor Antistius at 14.48–49 (cited and discussed in the Introduction, Section 6). Just as the two speeches by Thrasea mirror each other, so does the reaction of the presiding consuls. Their negative intervention here recalls their reaction at 14.49: *at consules, perficere decretum senatus non ausi, de consensu scripsere Caesari* ('The consuls, however, not venturing to complete the senatorial decree in form, wrote to the emperor and stated the opinion of the meeting'). The scenario affords us telling insights into the workings of the imperial system, and the interrelation of power and character. Thrasea speaks his mind, without regard for the consequences. The moral majority retains its protective anonymity but can be fired up. The consuls, who are ultimately responsible, don't want to stick their necks out. Thrasea does not care what the *princeps* thinks or how he may react;

for almost everyone else the mind and disposition of the emperor is the yardstick for their own thoughts and actions. The historian knows that traditional forms of good governance always hand officials tools to block unwelcome reform; in the Caesars' Rome, at any rate, Tacitus shows, the public pageant of government was pure rigmarole.

mox auctore principe...: In this case there is no hint that Nero felt slighted by Thrasea's proposal; instead, he himself put forward such a motion soon afterwards. The temporal adverb *mox* presumably refers to a point in time in the same year (AD 62). Rudich even argues that Thrasea's proposal played into Nero's hands and interprets the reluctance of the consuls to have the motion passed differently: 'It is no accident that the consuls were reluctant to promulgate Thrasea Paetus' motion to abolish provincial thanksgivings..., while Nero, on the other hand, approved it. Though it was intended to oppose imperial *adulatio*, the emperor was exploiting Thrasea Paetus' move for the opposite purpose, that is, of depriving the Senate of another fraction of its political prestige.'[88] We have suggested a somewhat different explanation for the consuls' hesitation. And Rudich's reading leaves open the question as to why Thrasea's proposal received the enthusiastic support of the senate. What do *you* think is going on? And does your Tacitus want us to fathom, to wonder, or to flounder?

sanxere: (= *sanxerunt*, i.e. the senators). In AD 11, Augustus had passed a law that stipulated an interval of 60 days between the end of a governor's tenure and the proposal of a vote of thanks. See Cassius Dio 56.25.6: 'He also issued a proclamation to the subject nations forbidding them to bestow any honours upon a person assigned to govern them either during his term of office or within sixty days after his departure; this was because some governors by arranging beforehand for testimonials and eulogies from their subjects were causing much mischief.' Now Nero's proposal aimed to ban the practice altogether. It is not entirely clear whether his measure was effective, ineffectual to begin with, or fell into abeyance after a while.

ne quis ... referret agendas apud senatum ... grates, neu quis ea legatione fungeretur: After votes of thanks were made in the council, a delegation was sent to Rome to report it to the senate. The law aimed to end both aspects of this practice (i.e. the voting of thanks and the dispatch of a

---

88   Rudich (1993) 77.

delegation). The sentence has an air of formality and may well be modelled on the language of the decree itself. *referret* introduces an indirect statement with *agendas* [sc. *esse*] as verb and *grates* as subject accusative.

ne quis ... neu quis: *quis* = *aliquis*. ('After *si, nisi, num* and *ne,* | *ali-* goes away.')[89]

concilium sociorum: This institution, which had Hellenistic and republican precedents, came into its own under Augustus, as an important site of communication between the centre of imperial power in Rome and the provinces: 'in each province, the altar to Rome and Augustus provided an official cult centre, and its service provided an occasion for assembly. The *concilium* met, usually, once a year, and after the rites discussed any business that concerned the province. Any formal expressions of thanks would be voted here, and conveyed by a delegation to the Senate.'[90]

pro praetoribus prove consulibus: *prove* = *pro* + the enclitic *ve*. *pro praetoribus* refers to the *legati Augusti pro praetore* who governed the imperial provinces ('propraetorian governors of the emperor'); *pro consulibus* refers to the governors of senatorial provinces, who since the time of Augustus all carried the title of proconsuls: see e.g. Suetonius, *Augustus* 47. The normal formulation would have been the inverse, i.e. *proconsul legatusve*.[91] The passage is a good example of what Syme has diagnosed as one of the perversities of Tacitean style: 'The terminology of the Roman administration was awkward or monotonous. Tacitus varies or evades it. ... he will go to any lengths or contortions rather than denominate the governor of an imperial province by the exact title.'[92] Tacitus means to press, to expose, all official language for its emptiness, inanity, fantasy.

(II) 22.2: REVIEW OF STRIKING PRODIGIES THAT OCCURRED IN AD 62

22.2 Isdem consulibus gymnasium ictu fulminis conflagravit effigiesque in eo Neronis ad informe aes liquefacta. et motu terrae celebre Campaniae

---

89   We owe this jingle to George Lord.
90   Miller (1973) 71. The last monographic treatment of the *concilia* is Deininger (1965).
91   Koestermann (1968) 203.
92   Syme (1958) I 343–44.

oppidum Pompei magna ex parte proruit; defunctaque virgo Vestalis Laelia, in cuius locum Cornelia ex familia Cossorum capta est.

We are still in AD 62, but Tacitus now looks back and reviews the *omina* and *prodigia* – strange natural occurrences that indicated the displeasure of the gods – that had happened over the course of this year. This is a regular feature of his narrative and serves a variety of purposes. (i) To begin with, it is a key generic marker of annalistic historiography, in terms of both content and form. The Romans themselves traced the beginnings of the practice of writing year-by-year chronicles to the custom of the *pontifex maximus* recording on a board (*tabula*) kept on display outside his place of residence (a) the names of the high magistrates and (b) key events of public significance, not least those of a religious nature such as prodigies, on a yearly basis. The recording started from scratch each year, but the priesthood of the pontiffs also archived the information thus collected. Some – but by no means all – historiographers of the Roman republic adopted an approach and style to the writing of history that mimicked the information displayed on the board of the high priest, presumably in part to endow their narratives with the official and/ or religious authority of a national chronicle.[93] (ii) A key element of annalistic historiography is the repeated reference to consuls – as such, it is an inherently republican form of thinking about history and recalls a period in which the consuls were the highest magistrate in the Roman commonwealth (and the city-state scale of Rome could be governed by yearly flights of officials); annalistic historiography thus stands in latent tension to the existence of a *princeps* (as well as a worldwide empire). (iii) In addition to the names of magistrates, annals tended to note down anything that concerned the interaction between Rome's civic community and the gods. Prodigies are divine signs, and their recording situates the narrative within a supernatural context.

[*Extra Information: Tacitus and religion*

'Tacitus and religion' is a complex topic that defies exhaustive discussion in the present context. What follows are some pointers for how Tacitus integrates the sphere of the divine into his narrative universe. Griffin, for instance, identifies four supernatural forces to which Tacitus appeals in his narrative to render events intelligible: (i) divine intervention; (ii) fate, in the Stoic sense of an unalterable chain of natural causes; (iii) destiny, as determined by the time

---

93   Gotter and Luraghi (2003) 35.

of our birth, i.e. by the stars; (iv) 'fortune' or 'chance.'[94] Not all of these factors are mutually reconcilable from a theological point of view.[95] More generally speaking, Tacitus' narrative universe offers a fractured metaphysics: he brings into play mutually incompatible conceptions of the gods, invokes their power and presence in various ways, but only to turn a narrative corner and lament their inefficaciousness. Here is a look at some representative passages that are particularly pertinent for an appreciation of 15.23. To begin with, it is important to stress that Tacitus recognizes the gods as a force in history that strikes emperors and senators alike. See, for instance, *Annals* 14.22.4:

> Isdem diebus nimia luxus cupido infamiam et periculum Neroni tulit, quia fontem aquae Marciae ad urbem deductae nando incesserat; videbaturque potus sacros et caerimoniam loci corpore loto polluisse. secutaque anceps valetudo iram deum adfirmavit.

> [About the same date, Nero's excessive desire for extravagance brought him disrepute and danger: he had entered in the spring of the stream that Quintus Marcius conveyed to Rome to swim; and by bathing his body he seemed to have polluted the sacred waters and the holiness of the site. The grave illness that followed confirmed the wrath of the gods.]

The gods, then, go beyond sending signs of warning. They cause havoc, and not only for the *princeps*. In the wake of the conspiracy of Piso, the wrath of the gods somehow encompasses all of Roman society. *Annals* 16.13.1–2 is particularly striking because it conflates divine anger with the savagery of the *princeps*:

> Tot facinoribus foedum annum etiam di tempestatibus et morbis insignivere. vastata Campania turbine ventorum, qui villas arbusta fruges passim disiecit pertulitque violentiam ad vicina urbi; in qua omne mortalium genus vis pestilentiae depopulabatur, nulla caeli intemperie quae occurreret oculis. sed domus corporibus exanimis, itinera funeribus complebantur; non sexus, non aetas periculo vacua; servitia perinde et ingenua plebes raptim extingui, inter coniugum et liberorum lamenta, qui dum adsident, dum deflent, saepe eodem rogo cremabantur. equitum

---

94   Griffin (2009) 168–69.

95   For instance: in a Stoic universe, in which everything unfolds according to a predetermined chain of natural causes, gods lose their independent agency and 'chance' has no place. (It is therefore important to note that the passage where he seems to allude to Stoic fate is very obscure: see Martin (2001) 148–49, cited by Griffin (2009) 168 n. 2, who also points out that Tacitus does not always use *fatum* in the technical Stoic sense of the term.)

senatorumque interitus, quamvis promisci, minus flebiles erant, tamquam communi mortalitate saevitiam principis praevenirent.

[Upon this year, disgraced by so many shameful deeds, the gods also imposed their mark through violent storms and epidemics. Campania was laid waste by a whirlwind, which wrecked the farms, the fruit trees, and the crops far and wide and carried its violence to the vicinity of the capital, where the force of a deadly disease decimated the human population at all levels of society, even though there was no visible sign of unwholesome weather conditions. But the houses were filled with lifeless bodies, the streets with funerals. Neither sex nor age gave immunity from danger; slaves and the free-born population alike died like flies, amid the laments of their wives and children, who, while tending (to the ill) and mourning (the deceased), (became infected, died, and) often were burnt on the same pyre. The deaths of knights and senators, while likewise indiscriminate, gave less rise to lamentation, since it appeared as if they were cheating the savagery of the emperor by undergoing the common lot.]

And soon afterwards, Tacitus steps back from his account of the bloodshed caused by Nero to reflect on his narrative and the impact it may have on the reader – before invoking the larger supernatural horizon in which imperial history and its recording in Tacitus' text has unfolded (*Annals* 16.16.2):

ira illa numinum in res Romanas fuit, quam non, ut in cladibus exercituum aut captivitate urbium, semel edito transire licet.

[It was that wrath of divine forces against the Roman state, which one cannot, as in the case of beaten armies or captured towns, mention once and for all and then move on.]

What these passages illustrate is the uncertainty principle. In some cases, divine retribution for an act of transgression is virtually instantaneous: witness the illness that befell Nero shortly after his inadvisable swim. In other cases, the gap in time between portent and the advent of doom is disconcertingly long: one could have supposed that the melting down of Nero's statue heralded his imminent demise – but at the point in time his end was still four years in the coming. Too big a gap generates disbelief in the efficacy of prodigies – and the gods. Tacitus himself draws attention to this problem at *Annals* 14.12.1–2, in the wake of the alleged conspiracy of Agrippina against Nero that ended in her death (the passage also includes an early appearance of Thrasea Paetus):

Miro tamen certamine procerum decernuntur supplicationes apud omnia
pulvinaria, utque quinquatrus, quibus apertae insidiae essent, ludis annuis
celebrarentur, aureum Minervae simulacrum in curia et iuxta principis
imago statuerentur, dies natalis Agrippinae inter nefastos esset. Thrasea
Paetus silentio vel brevi adsensu priores adulationes transmittere solitus
exiit tum senatu, ac sibi causam periculi fecit, ceteris libertatis initium
non praebuit. prodigia quoque crebra et inrita intercessere: anguem enixa
mulier, et alia in concubitu mariti fulmine exanimata; iam sol repente
obscuratus et tactae de caelo quattuordecim urbis regiones. quae adeo sine
cura deum eveniebant, ut multos postea annos Nero imperium et scelera
continuaverit.

[However, with a remarkable spirit of emulation among the leading men
thanksgivings were decreed at all shrines, further that the festival of
Minerva, at which the assassination attempt was discovered, be celebrated
by annual games, that a golden statue of Minerva and next to it an effigy
of the emperor be put up in the curia, and that Agrippina's birthday be
included among the inauspicious dates. This time, Thrasea Paetus, who
was wont to let earlier instances of flattery pass either in silence or with
a curt assent, walked out of the senate, creating a source of danger for
himself, without opening up a gateway to freedom for the others. Portents,
too, appeared, frequent and futile: a woman gave birth to a snake, another
was killed by a thunderbolt during intercourse with her husband; the sun,
again, was suddenly eclipsed and the fourteen regions of the capital were
struck by lightning. These events happened so utterly without any concern
of the gods that Nero continued his reign and his crimes for many years
to come.]

Tacitus here mercilessly exposes the hypocrisy of the religious adulation
that the emperor attracted: in spite of the fact that the son murdered his
mother, emperor and senators engage in communal thanksgiving to
the gods that the mother did not manage to murder her son. Given this
perversion of the truth and the way that the divinities are implicated in the
crime (as the agents who supposedly helped to uncover Agrippina's plot),
the numerous signs of divine displeasure do not come as a surprise. Yet
Tacitus goes on to dismiss the *prodigia* as ineffectual because the warning
they supposedly constituted resulted neither in a change of behaviour
and ritual amendment to avert the apparently imminent danger nor in
supernatural punishment of the real criminal, the emperor. The fact that
Nero kept on living a life of crime for years to come suggests to Tacitus that
the apparent portents lacked divine purpose. Moreover, as the passage from
Annals 16 that we just cited illustrates, before Nero gets his comeuppance

he visits Roman society like a wrathful divinity himself. Ultimately, divine efficacy in Roman history has become inscrutable and unpredictable. The world that Tacitus records eludes easy understanding. Some aspects of it are both re-prehensible and incom-prehensible. Communication at all levels is seriously distorted. No one's listening to sage correctives in the senate-house (from our Saint Thrasea), and no one's listening to alarm-bells set off by that other throwback voice looking out for Rome – heaven-sent scary stuff.]

isdem consulibus: The name of the consuls is one – but no longer the power-indicator – dating system available in imperial Rome.

gymnasium ictu fulminis conflagravit effigiesque in eo Neronis ad informe aes liquefacta: For the *Neronia*, a quinquennial festival along the model of the Greek Olympic Games first celebrated in AD 60 (Tacitus covers it at *Annals* 14.20–21, which we cite and discuss below), Nero had built the first public *gymnasium* in Rome. Tacitus mentions its dedication at the very end of his account of AD 61 (14.47): *gymnasium eo anno dedicatum a Nerone praebitumque oleum equiti ac senatui Graeca facilitate* ('In the course of the year, Nero consecrated a gymnasium, oil being supplied to the equestrian and senatorial orders – a Greek form of liberality').[96] The slippage from AD 60 to AD 61 merits some comments. Griffin uses *Ann.* 14.47 as evidence that 'in 61 he [sc. Nero] dedicated his new public baths in Rome, a complex that included a gymnasium. He marked the occasion by a free distribution of oil to senators and equites, who were clearly meant to be attracted to athletics by the free offer' – but acknowledges in an endnote that our other sources have the gymnasium, and in the case of Suetonius, also the baths, dedicated and in use during the Neronia in AD 60.[97] To fix the clash, she suggests that 'it is possible that Tacitus' date refers to the dedication of the whole complex, the gymnasium alone being finished by the Neronia.'[98] But this is hardly compelling given that Tacitus, unlike Suetonius, does not even mention the

---

96 Griffin (1984) 44 with page 247 n. 44.

97 See Cassius Dio 61.21.2 and Suetonius, *Nero* 12.3: *Instituit et quinquennale certamen primus omnium Romae more Graeco triplex, musicum gymnicum equestre, quod appellavit Neronia; dedicatisque thermis atque gymnasio senatui quoque et equiti oleum praebuit* ('He was likewise the first to establish at Rome a quinquennial contest in three parts, after the Greek fashion, that is in music, athletics, and riding, which he called the *Neronia*; at the same time he dedicated his baths and gymnasium, supplying every member of the senatorial and equestrian orders with oil').

98 Griffin (1984) 247 n. 44.

baths at 14.47: he only speaks of the dedication of the gymnasium. Perhaps something else entirely is going on: could Tacitus have slyly shifted the date of the dedication of the gymnasium back a year so that he could correlate the endings of his accounts of AD 61 (14.47) and AD 62 (15.22)? Has the desire for a suggestive artistic design here overruled the principle of chronological accuracy?

The term *gymnasium* itself, at any rate, is a loanword from the Greek (γυμνάσιον/ *gymnasion*, a place where one stripped to train 'naked', or γυμνός/ *gymnos* in Greek). As the name suggests, it was a quintessentially Greek institution – a place for athletic exercise (in particular wrestling), communal bathing, and other leisure pursuits (such as philosophy). Our sources suggest that Nero himself fancied a career as a wrestler – linked to his sponsorship of gymnasia: 'his interest in pursuing a somewhat less dangerous career [than fighting as a gladiator] in wrestling is well attested. He certainly built gymnasia at Rome, Baiae, and Naples; wrestlers competed at his Neronia; he enjoyed watching them in Naples; and he actually employed court wrestlers, *luctatores auli*. Contemporary rumor had it that he intended himself to compete in the next Olympic Games among the athletes, for he wrestled constantly and watched gymnastic contests throughout Greece...'[99]

Tacitus mentions the occurrence without commentary, but there was little need for one. In part, the structure of his narrative provides an eloquent interpretation: it is hardly coincidental that he should have concluded his account of AD 61 with the dedication of the gymnasium by Nero and his account of AD 62 with instances of divine wrath directed against the building and the statue of the emperor contained therein. The artful design that ensues stands out even more clearly if we recall that the mention of Nero's dedication of the gymnasium comes right after the obituary for Memmius Regulus (consul of 31) and that the paragraph that follows the meltdown of the statue begins with the consulship of his son (also named Memmius Regulus). Tacitus thus chiastically interrelates the end of 61, the end of 62, and the beginning of 63:

> End of 61: obituary of Memmius Regulus *pater* (14.47: cited below); dedication of Nero's gymnasium (14.47).

> End of 62: conflagration of Nero's gymnasium (15.22); beginning of 63: reference to the consulship of Memmius Regulus *filius* (15.23).

---

99   Champion (2003) 80.

Tacitus thus twins the abomination and disaster of the imperial court – Nero is the last scion of the Julio-Claudian dynasty – with an image of continuity in the form of republican lineage.

effigiesque in eo Neronis ad informe aes liquefacta: Statues of emperors (and other members of the imperial family or household) were ubiquitous in imperial Rome. They ensured the visual presence of the *princeps* in a wide variety of settings, raised the represented figure above the status of ordinary mortals, and more generally constituted an important medium for projecting an image of the reigning *princeps* to different social groups within the empire: 'Representations of Roman emperors and empresses crafted in marble or bronze functioned as surrogates for real imperial bodies, artistic evocations of the imperial presence that were replicated and disseminated everywhere in the Empire. Just as the corporeal being of the emperor, as supreme ruler of the Mediterranean, was endowed with his divine essence or genius, and came to be elevated conceptually above the bodies of his subjects, so too imperial images were conceived differently from those of private individuals. Unlike most of their subjects, the emperor or empress could exist as effigies in multiple bodies that took the form of portrait statues populating every kind of Roman environment such as *fora, basilicae,* temples, baths, military camps and houses.'[100] The quotation comes from an article with the title 'Execution in Effigy: Severed Heads and Decapitated Statues in Imperial Rome', which focuses on the destruction of statuary after the death of an emperor. New *principes*, especially if they belonged to a different dynasty, tended systematically to do away with the artistic representations of their predecessors. The melting-down of Nero's likeness constitutes a divine anticipation of the iconoclasm that lay in store for his images upon his death. Divine displeasure at the Hellenizing shenanigans of the emperor could not have been articulated more clearly. There is no better way to portend Nero's sticky end than the complete destruction of the statue. One captures a sense of satisfaction in the extreme formulation *ad informe aes* – Tacitus clearly enjoys the image of golden-boy Nero's statue being melted down into a shapeless lump as a result of the conflagration. The lightning bolt is the hallmark of Jupiter: so this message comes from the top.

---

100   Varner (2005) 67. On imperial statuary see further Vout (2007) and Gladhill (2012).

et motu terrae celebre Campaniae oppidum Pompei magna ex parte proruit: *Pompe(i)i, ~orum* is a second declension masculine plural noun, here standing in apposition to *celebre Campaniae oppidum*, the subject of the sentence. This earthquake, which Seneca, in his *Natural Histories* 6.1.2, dates to AD 63, predated the famous eruption of Vesuvius in 79 during the reign of Titus, which *totally* destroyed Pompeii and the neighbouring city of Herculaneum. Hence there is a proleptic point in *magna ex parte*: Tacitus and his readers would of course have read this passage with the later catastrophe in mind, turning the earthquake mentioned here into an ominous prefiguration of greater evil to come, though not specifically related to the reign of Nero (but easily relatable to the imminent fall of the first dynasty of Caesars). Seismic activity has natural causes but frequently features the same temporal logic as prodigies, insofar as a minor tremor or eruption – at times many years in advance – is then followed by a cataclysmic outbreak. Likewise, prodigies constituted a preliminary indication of divine displeasure that issued a warning of an imminent disaster (but also afforded a precious window of opportunity to make amends, appease the gods, and thus avert it). The Romans understood extreme natural events as divinely motivated signs, but were unaware of – or refused to believe in – the ineluctability of natural disasters such as earthquakes or volcanic eruptions; they preferred to invest in the conviction that proper communication with the gods constituted *some* safeguard against crises and chaos. But is that so different from contemporary religious creeds?

magna ex parte proruit: The scale of the destruction was already immense and hints at the violence of the quake.

defunctaque virgo Vestalis Laelia: The Vestal Virgins (six at any one time, who, upon entering the college, took a vow of chastity and stayed in position for thirty years or until they died) were priestesses of Vesta, the Roman goddess of the hearth. Devoted in the main to the cultivation of the sacred fire, which was not supposed to go out since it symbolized the eternity of the Roman state, they were associated with the well-being of the Roman commonwealth and its continuity in time. Any change in personnel owing to a premature death or other event affecting the smooth functioning of the college therefore amounted to an affair of state. Laelia was perhaps the daughter of D. Laelius Balbus.[101]

---

101 Laelia is Nr. 2161 in Jörg Rüpke's compendium of all religious officials from ancient Rome of whom we have any record. See Rüpke (2008).

in cuius locum Cornelia ex familia Cossorum capta est: Candidates for the priesthood, girls between 6 and 12 years of age, were offered by their families for the honour. When they were selected by the chief priest (*Pontifex Maximus*), he said, '*te, Amata, capio*' (I take you, beloved one): this is the reason for the verb here.[102] The Cornelia in question might have been the daughter of Cornelius Cossus, one of the consuls of AD 60.[103] Tacitus' readers would know her gruesome destiny. In AD 91, when she had become *Vestalis maxima*, the emperor Domitian had her accused of *incestum* ('sexual impurity and hence profanation of the religious rites'). She was found guilty and, despite pleading her innocence, executed by being buried alive. See Suetonius, *Domitian* 8.4 and the harrowing account by Pliny, *Letters* 4.11.6–13.

The Cornelii Cossi went *all* the way back to the 5th century BC, i.e. the early years of republican Rome. A member of this branch of the *gens Cornelia*, Aulus Cornelius Cossus, was the second one of just three Roman generals ever who won the so-called *spolia opima* ('rich spoils') – the armour stripped from an opposing general after he had been killed in single combat (in Cossus' case the king of the Etruscan town Veii, Lars Tolumnius: see Livy 4.17–20 for the details). Reflect, *before* reading on, that the sacred institution of the Vestal priesthood (with its impeccable republican pedigree and personnel) provided for the replenishment of its stock of girls in case of loss: you won't find monarchy coping half so smoothly with the perils menacing its self-perpetuation. *Now* read on:

(III) 23.1–4: Start of Tacitus' account of AD 63: the birth and death of Nero's daughter by Sabina Poppaea, Claudia Augusta

Chapter 23

Tacitus' account of the year AD 63 comprises *Annals* 15.23–32. The set text only includes the initial paragraph (23) and then vaults forward to the start of AD 64 at 15.33. The stretch left out primarily covers – in spectacularly telling contrast – military developments in the Near East. In the meantime, we have a royal birth! A daughter! A dead duck.

---

102 See Wildfang (2006), Ch. 3: 'Vestal initiation – the rite of *captio*'.
103 Koestermann (1968) 62.

23.1 Memmio Regulo et Verginio Rufo consulibus natam sibi ex Poppaea filiam Nero ultra mortale gaudium accepit appellavitque Augustam dato et Poppaeae eodem cognomento. locus puerperio colonia Antium fuit, ubi ipse generatus erat.

Memmio Regulo et Verginio Rufo consulibus: This is the standard annalistic formula for opening a year, especially in the latter portions of the *Annals*: 'Tacitus introduces a new year with various formulae in *Annals* 1–6, but in the later books his desire for *variatio* seems to cease: in fact, all extant year-beginnings, except for two [that for AD 58 at 13.34 and that for AD 65 at 15.48], are introduced by a standard ablative absolute of the type *x y consulibus*.'[104]

Memmio Regulo: C. Memmius Regulus, the son of P. Memmius Regulus, one of the consuls of 31, who died in 61. Tacitus records the death at 14.47, as his penultimate entry for that year, adding an overall appreciation of the character:

> Eo anno mortem obiit Memmius Regulus, auctoritate constantia fama, in quantum praeumbrante imperatoris fastigio datur, clarus, adeo ut Nero aeger valetudine, et adulantibus circum, qui finem imperio adesse dicebant, si quid fato pateretur, responderit habere subsidium rem publicam. rogantibus dehinc, in quo potissimum, addiderat in Memmio Regulo. vixit tamen post haec Regulus, quiete defensus et quia nova generis claritudine neque invidiosis opibus erat.

> [The year saw the end of Memmius Regulus, whose authority, firmness, and character had earned him the maximum of glory possible in the shadows cast by imperial greatness. So true was this that Nero, indisposed and surrounded by sycophants predicting the dissolution of the empire, should he go the way of fate, answered that the nation had a resource. To the further inquiry, where that resource was specially to be found, he added: 'In Memmius Regulus.' Yet Regulus survived: he was shielded by his quietude of life; he sprang from a recently ennobled family; and his modest fortune aroused no envy.]

Verginio Rufo: L. Verginius Rufus, a name that points far into the future. He crushed the revolt of Gaius Julius Vindex against Nero in AD 67/68. Twice he declined to be hailed emperor. Pliny records the inscription that

---

104 Bartera (2011) 161. Whether this standardization 'reflects the political irrelevance of the consuls, who become, so to speak, "sclerotic" dating devices' (*ibid.*), is another matter.

Rufus chose for his tombstone (6.10.4; 9.19.1): *hic situs est Rufus, pulso qui Vindice quondam | imperium adseruit non sibi, sed patriae* ('Here lies Rufus, who once defeated Vindex and protected the imperial power not for himself, but for his country'). He died in 97, during his third consulship, at the ripe old age of 83. Pliny devotes an entire letter to the event, in which he tells us that it was Tacitus himself who delivered the funeral oration as the suffect consul, who took Rufus' place (2.1.1–6).

The laconic recording of the two consuls for 63 according to annalistic convention point Tacitus' readers, in the case of Memmius Regulus, back to the recent past (as commemorated by Tacitus in his *Annals*) and, in the case of Verginius Rufus, forward into the distant future. The text thus evokes both dynastic succession and annalistic sequence as two complementary grids for imposing patterns on historical time:

Reigns	'Dynasty'	Emperors	Annalistic sequence	Consuls
14–37		Tiberius	[...] 31 [...]	Memmius Regulus *pater*
37–41	Julio-Claudian	Caligula	[...]	
41–54		Claudius	[...]	
54–68		Nero	[...] 63 [...]	Memmius Regulus *filius*, Verginius Rufus
68–69		Galba, Otho, Vitellius	[...]	
69–79		Vespasian	[...]	
79–81	Flavian	Titus	[...]	
81–96		Domitian	[...]	
96–98	Nerva-Antonine	Nerva	[...] 97 [...]	Verginius Rufus, Cornelius Tacitus
98–117		Trajan	[...]	

'Imperial history' has its natural centre of gravity in the reigning *princeps*.
But by opting for an annalistic approach, Tacitus ensures that a pattern
of 'republican history' remains in place. The very simplicity of associating
each year with the name of the consuls in office (whether initially elected or
suffect) generates a sense of order and continuity in time more fundamental
than the changing dynasties that rule at Rome. Just thinking about the
names of the consuls – and in what other years they or their fathers held
the consulship (a natural thing to do, from a Roman reader's point of view)
– creates chronological vectors. In this case, the web of associations called
into being by the laconic dating device *Memmio Regulo et Verginio Rufo
consulibus* spans all three 'dynasties', from the Julio-Claudian through the
Flavian and beyond, to Tacitus' present. There is, then, an ideology built
into the annalistic approach to Roman history: emperors come and go; but
each year, consuls *still* enter into their office and maintain (a semblance
of) republican continuity. This way of thinking about time existed outside
Tacitus' narrative as well, of course. But through strategic arrangement of
his material, our author activates the pattern as a meaningful foil for his
imperial history: here it is his obituary of Memmius Regulus *pater* at 14.47,
at the end of his account of 61, which obliquely sets up his son's entry
into the consulship in 63, especially when paired with the references to
Nero's gymnasium (see above). Without this obituary, readers would have
had much greater difficulties in associating the son with his father (and
his consulship in 31) or in thinking ahead to the death of Verginius Rufus
during his third consulship (and the figure who would take his place and
deliver the funeral oration). And far less melodrama to savour.

natam sibi ex Poppaea filiam Nero ... accepit: The advanced position
of *natam*, right after the annalistic formula, reinforces the sense of a new
beginning also for the imperial household – which Tacitus crushes a few
lines later (see below, 23.3: *quartum intra mensem defuncta infante*). The
undramatic record of who held the consulship stands in stark contrast to
the triumphs and tragedies of the imperial household. The switch from
the names of the two highest magistrates of the Roman state, subordinate
in power only to the *princeps* himself, to the birth of a baby girl destined
to pass away after a few months creates a tension between the republican
frame or matrix of Tacitus' narrative and its principal subject matter. The
names of the imperial couple Poppaea and Nero in the first sentence about
AD 63 instantly counterbalance those of Memmius Regulus and Verginius

Rufus and refocus attention from republican office to the doings of the imperial family.

Poppaea: Nero was Poppaea Sabina's third husband, and she his second wife – after Octavia. She enters the *Annals* at 13.45 (in his account of the year AD 58) as the wife of the knight Rufrius Crispinus. The paragraph opens programmatically with the sentence *non minus insignis eo anno impudicitia magnorum rei publicae malorum initium fecit* ('a no less striking instance of immorality proved in the year the beginning of grave public calamities') and continues as follows:

> There was in the capital a certain Poppaea Sabina, daughter of Titus Ollius, though she had taken the name of her maternal grandfather, Poppaeus Sabinus, of distinguished memory, who, with the honours of his consulate and triumphal insignia, outshone her father: for Ollius had fallen a victim to his friendship with Sejanus before holding the major offices. She was a woman possessed of all advantages but good character (*huic mulieri cuncta alia fuere praeter honestum animum*). For her mother, after eclipsing the beauties of her day, had endowed her alike with her fame and her looks: her wealth was adequate for her standing by birth. Her conversation was engaging, her wit not without point (*sermo comis nec absurdum ingenium*); she paraded modesty, and practised wantonness (*modestiam praeferre et lascivia uti*). In public she rarely appeared, and then with her face half-veiled, so as not quite to satiate the beholder, – or, possibly, because that look suited her. She was never sparing of her reputation, and drew no distinctions between husbands and adulterers (*famae numquam pepercit, maritos et adulteros non distinguens*): vulnerable neither to her own nor to alien passion, where material advantage offered, that's where she transferred her desires (*neque adfectui suo aut alieno obnoxia, unde utilitas ostenderetur, illuc libidinem transferebat*). Thus whilst living in the wedded state with Rufrius Crispinus, a Roman knight by whom she had had a son, she was seduced by Otho [sc. the future emperor], with his youth, his voluptousness, and his reputed position as the most favoured of Nero's friends: nor was it long before adultery was mated to matrimony (*nec mora quin adulterio matrimonium iungeretur*).

Otho praised the beauty and charms of his wife in the presence of Nero – either, so Tacitus submits in the following paragraph (13.46), because he was so smitten with love that he could not help himself (*amore incautus*) or because he deliberately wished to inflame the emperor's desire with a view to a threesome that would have reinforced his own influence at court by the additional bond of joint ownership in one woman (*si eadem femina poterentur [sc. he and Nero], id quoque vinculum potentiam ei adiceret*). The plan misfired: once brought into the presence of the emperor, Poppaea succeeded in getting Nero infatuated with her, but, after the first adulterous night, played hard to get by insisting that she could not give up her marriage to Otho. To get rid of his rival, Nero broke his ties of friendship with Otho, debarred him from court, and ultimately appointed him as governor of Lusitania (present-day Portugal); there he remained for ten years until the outbreak of civil war in 68. After recording the appointment, Tacitus abruptly discontinues his account of what happened between Nero and Poppaea. One person who is an absent presence during this narrative stretch is Nero's first wife Octavia, the daughter of his predecessor Claudius. Tacitus has Poppaea mention Acte (Nero's concubine), but not Octavia. But once she displaced the emperor's concubine, she also managed to have Octavia banished and, ultimately, killed – a gruesome sequence of events to which Tacitus devotes significant narrative space to end *Annals* 14 with a bang. Upon the trumped-up charge of having committed adultery with the prefect of the praetorian guard and then procured an abortion, Octavia was executed by Nero's henchmen at the age of 20: after putting her in binds and opening her veins, they cut off her head and paraded it through the streets of Rome. Much to the delight of Poppaea.

Poppaea herself was accidentally kicked to death by Nero in AD 65, when she was again pregnant, with the emperor acting just like other tyrants in the Greco-Roman tradition, such as Periander of Corinth.[105] Tacitus narrates the incident and its aftermath at 16.6, underscoring again how much the emperor loved his wife and would have liked to have children:

> Post finem ludicri Poppaea mortem obiit, fortuita mariti iracundia, a quo gravida ictu calcis adflicta est. neque enim venenum crediderim, quamvis quidam scriptores tradant, odio magis quam ex fide: quippe liberorum cupiens et amori uxoris obnoxius erat. corpus non igni abolitum, ut Romanus mos, sed regum externorum consuetudine differtum odoribus conditur tumuloque Iuliorum infertur. ductae tamen publicae exsequiae laudavitque ipse apud rostra formam eius et quod divinae infantis parens fuisset aliaque fortunae munera pro virtutibus.

> [After the close of the festival, Poppaea met her end through a chance outburst of anger on the part of her husband, who felled her with a kick

---

105   See Diogenes Laertius, *Life of Periander*: 'However, after some time, in a fit of anger, he killed his wife by throwing a footstool at her, or by a kick, when she was pregnant, having been egged on by the slanderous tales of concubines, whom he afterwards burnt alive.' We cite the translation by R. D. Hicks in the Loeb Classical Library (Cambridge, Mass. and London, 1925) – with thanks to John Henderson for the reference.

during pregnancy. That poison played its part I am unable to believe, though
the assertion is made by some writers less from conviction than from hatred;
for Nero was desirous of children, and love for his wife was a ruling passion.
The body was not cremated in the Roman style, but, in conformity with the
practice of foreign courts, was embalmed by stuffing with spices, then laid
to rest in the mausoleum of the Julian clan. Still, a public funeral was held;
and the emperor at the Rostra eulogized her beauty, the fact that she had
been the mother of an infant daughter now divine, and other favours of
fortune which did duty for virtues.]

ultra mortale gaudium: While Nero's delight at becoming a father
is a (mock-) sympathetic touch, Tacitus portrays him as emotionally
incontinent, unable to restrain himself in either joy (as here) or grief (see
below 23.3: *atque ipse ut laetitiae ita maeroris immodicus egit*). The phrase *ultra*
mortale is also a not particularly subtle reminder of the ever-crazier tyrant's
delusions of divinity (apart from setting up the upcoming apotheosis of his
moribund daughter).

appellavitque Augustam dato et Poppaeae eodem cognomento: The
daughter's *nomen gentile* was Claudia, to which Nero decided to add the
honorific title Augusta. Within the *Annals*, the passage is part of a sequence,
stretching back to the very beginning of the work: at *Annals* 1.8, Tacitus
records that Augustus, in his will, posthumously conferred this title on his
wife Livia: ... *cuius testamentum inlatum per virgines Vestae Tiberium et Liviam*
heredes habuit. Livia in familiam Iuliam nomenque Augustum adsumebatur
('His will, brought in by the Vestal Virgins, specified Tiberius and Livia
as heirs, Livia to be adopted into the Julian family and the Augustan
name'). At *Annals* 12.26, he mentions that Claudius bestowed the honour
on his wife Agrippina, in the context of his adoption of her son Nero:
rogataque lex, qua in familiam Claudiam et nomen Neronis transiret. augetur
et Agrippina cognomento Augustae ('and the law was carried providing for
his adoption into the Claudian family and the name of Nero. Agrippina
herself was dignified by the title of Augusta'). Here the honorands are a
newborn baby – and a concubine-turned-wife. The absurd devaluation
of what in earlier times was a precious honour thus matches the degree
of Nero's emotional excess. Tacitus expresses his disapproval obliquely
with a break in syntax after *Augustam*. Instead of simply stating that Nero
conferred the honour to his infant daughter and her mother, he provides
the information that Poppaea, 'too' (or 'even': see the *et*) received the
title *Augusta* in a lengthy ablative absolute (*dato ... cognomento*). 'Poppaea'

sounded (gob-smackingly?) incongruous when yoked to the austere yeoman ethnic 'Sabinus'; tacking on holy 'Augusta' completed the effect.

colonia Antium: Antium (modern Anzio) was a coastal town in Latium south of Rome (see *Map of Italy*). Nero founded a colony of veterans there (hence *colonia* – though *this* species of self-perpetuation carried an oddly Greek name, 'Antion', 'Opposite'/ 'Against'; perhaps not coincidentally, back in 37 CE when *he* was born, as L. Domitius Ahenobarbus, his uncle Caligula was just succeeding Tiberius as emperor, before soon losing it with everybody). Many Roman nobles had sea-side villas in the region, but it became a particularly significant location for the imperial family. It was where Augustus received a delegation from the Roman people that acclaimed him *pater patriae*.[106] The emperor Gaius (Caligula) was born there (and so according to Suetonius, *Caligula* 8.5, at one point even considered making it the new capital!) – as was Nero, who also took it upon himself to raze the villa of Augustus to the ground so he could rebuild it on a grander scale. He was in Antium when news of the fire of Rome reached him (*Annals* 15.39, discussed below).

23.2 iam senatus uterum Poppaeae commendaverat dis votaque publice susceperat, quae multiplicata exsolutaque. et additae supplicationes templumque fecunditatis et certamen ad exemplar Actiacae religionis decretum, utque Fortunarum effigies aureae in solio Capitolini Iovis locarentur, ludicrum circense, ut Iuliae genti apud Bovillas, ita Claudiae Domitiaeque apud Antium ederetur.

Here we reach our first example of what Stephen Oakley has aptly called 'corporate servility' in the set text:[107] The senate tries to match the anxious expectation of the emperor before and his joy after the birth of his daughter by intensifying communication with the gods on behalf of the imperial family. This was an excellent way to show loyalty and devotion to the *princeps*;[108] on occasion, however, it backfired. In his biography of Caligula, Suetonius mentions instances in which the emperor demanded that those

---

106 Suetonius, *Augustus* 58.
107 Oakley (2009a) 188, with reference to 14.64.3. As he points out, the examples are innumerable – and need to be appreciated as such: 'The instances of servile behaviour that Tacitus chronicles are legion, and all readers will have their favourites; any selection that is not copious is false to the tone of his writing.'
108 See *Annals* 2.69.2 and elsewhere.

who had made vows for his health when he was sick kept them after his return to health (27):

> Votum exegit ab eo, qui pro salute sua gladiatoriam operam promiserat, spectavitque ferro dimicantem nec dimisit nisi victorem et post multas preces. alterum, qui se periturum ea de causa voverat, cunctantem pueris tradidit, verbenatum infulatumque votum reposcentes per vicos agerent, quoad praecipitaretur ex aggere.

> [A man who had made a vow to fight in the arena, if the emperor recovered, he compelled to keep his word, watched him as he fought sword in hand, and would not let him go until he was victorious, and then only after many entreaties. Another who had offered his life for the same reason, but delayed to kill himself, he turned over to his slaves, with orders to drive him decked with sacred boughs and fillets through the streets, calling for the fulfilment of his vow, and finally hurl him from the embankment.]

Nevertheless, the practice remained a standard element in the peculiar social dynamic that unfolded between the emperor and other members of Rome's ruling élite in imperial times. We (and Tacitus) tend to see the proposed honours as manifestations of corporate servility. It is therefore useful to recall that there is another cultural logic in play. Thus Ittai Gradel argues that this was a technique for the senators to get some purchase on the behaviour of the *princeps*: 'Honours were a way to define the status or social position of the person or god honoured, but it was also a way to tie him down. The bestowal of honours to someone socially superior, whether man or god, obliged him to return them with benefactions. Or, we might say, to rule well. It could indeed be honourable to reject excessive honours, and for example, the elder Scipio had excelled in this *gloria recusandi*. On the other hand, refusing honours also entailed rejecting the moral obligations that went with them, even to the point of recognizing no bonds whatsoever. So it would be socially irresponsible to reject all such proposals.'[109]

iam senatus uterum Poppaeae commendaverat dis votaque publice susceperat, quae multiplicata exsolutaque [sc. *sunt*]: As with his account of Nero's reaction, Tacitus manages to convey his distaste in how he represents the senate. The front position of the adverb *iam* helps to generate the impression of escalation: already during Poppaea's pregnancy, the senate had decided to turn the wellbeing of her unborn child into an affair of state.

---

109   Gradel (2002) 59.

The priesthood of the Arval Brothers, which consisted of senators, vowed sacrifices in case of a successful delivery. After the birth, the manifestations of joy, so Tacitus implies, knew no bounds: collectively, the senate joined in with the emperor's excessive reaction to the birth by multiplying and fulfilling their – proliferating – vows. The Arval Brothers too fulfilled their vows, as recorded in their *Acta* under 21 January 63: *in Capitolio uota soluta quae susceperant pro partu et incolumitate Poppaeae.*[110] When the couple returned from Antium with their newborn, the Arval Brotherhood celebrated their arrival with sacrifices to *Spes*, *Felicitas* (or *Fecunditas*), and *Salus Publica*. (Tacitus' *publice* possibly alludes to the occasion, though he refrains from providing details.)

et additae supplicationes templumque fecunditatis et certamen ad exemplar Actiacae religionis decretum, utque Fortunarum effigies aureae in solio Capitolini Iovis locarentur, ludicrum circense, ut Iuliae genti apud Bovillas, ita Claudiae Domitiaeque apud Antium ederetur: Tacitus now gives more specific details of what the vows consisted in, in his usual elliptical style:

– *et additae* [sc. *sunt*] *supplicationes*

– *templumque fecunditatis et certamen ad exemplar Actiacae religionis decretum* [sc. *est*]

Tacitus now switches construction, using *decretum* [*est*] as an elegant pivot: the verb governs both the nouns *templum* and *certamen* (as subjects) and the following *ut*-clause (analysed in more detail below):

– *utque Fortunarum effigies aureae in solio Capitolini Iovis locarentur, ludicrum circense, ut Iuliae genti apud Bovillas, ita Claudiae Domitiaeque apud Antium ederetur*

In other words, we have (i) public thanksgivings (*supplicationes*); (ii) a temple to Fertility (*templum*); (iii) highly prestigious public games (*certamen*); (iv) the dedication of two golden statues to the two Fortunes (*effigies*); and (v) circus races (*ludicrum circense*). Polysyndeton (the alternating *et ... -que ... et ... -que*) underscores the impression of excess – just as Tacitus' persistent use of the passive voice from *multiplicata exsolutaque* onwards (*additae, decretum, locarentur, ederetur*) suggests a loss of purposeful agency on the part of the senate.

---

110   See Smallwood (1967) 24; Scheid (1998) 76.

supplicationes: 'In times of crisis, the senate sometimes decreed public days of prayer, on which the whole citizenry, men, women, and children, went from temple to temple throughout the city praying for divine aid (*supplicationes*). In turn, a favorable outcome of such prayers led to public days of thanksgiving, on which the citizen body gave thanks for their deliverance.'[111]

et certamen ad exemplar Actiacae religionis: After his victory over Mark Antony at Actium (on the coast of Western Greece) in 31 BC, Octavian founded the city of Nicopolis ('Victory City') nearby. Every five years, it was to hold Greek games in memory of the victory, modelled on the Games at Olympia: see Suetonius, *Augustus* 18. A Roman colony may have been set up in the vicinity. But, as R. A. Gurval points out, 'Nicopolis was, above all, a Greek city with Greek institutions. Its local government, coinage, and public inscriptions were Greek.'[112] In establishing Greek forms of entertainment in Italy and Rome, the senate, then, seems to have tried to pander to the philhellenic passions of the emperor – much to the ire of Tacitus, who despised the Greeks. We have already had occasion to discuss Nero's ill-fated gymnasium (see above on 15.22.2). The topic will resurface forcefully later on in the set text. Here it is important to note that the senators clearly knew how to please their *princeps*. But in Tacitus' narrative, the contrast between the foundational victory of Octavian at Actium, which brought to an end a century of intermittent civil bloodshed, and the successful birth of Nero's doomed baby daughter remains: it strikingly underscores the utter lack of proportion in the farcical measures proposed.

Fortunarum effigies: Two sister goddesses of Fortune were worshipped in Antium, and their images are taken to the Capitol in Rome in a lunatic's idea of honouring Antium, the birthplace of Nero's *un-fortunate* daughter.

Capitolini Iovis: Jupiter Optimus Maximus Capitolinus was Rome's supreme divinity; he had his main temple in Rome on the Capitoline Hill.

---

111   Hickson Hahn (2007) 238. She goes on to note the problem in terminology that ensues: 'The term "supplication" (*supplicatio*) illustrates this problem [i.e. how to determine whether a visual representation of prayer constituted a petition, oath, or thanksgiving] well. The Romans used the same word to identify public days of prayer and offering for propitiation, expiation, and thanksgiving.'
112   Gurval (1995) 69.

ludicrum circense ut Iuliae genti apud Bovillas ita Claudiae Domitiaeque apud Antium ederetur: *ludicrum circense ... ederetur* is the second part of the *ut*-clause, in asyndetic continuation of *Fortunarum effigies ... locarentur*. At issue are races in the circus, which already were established at Bovillae in honour of the *gens Julia* (see *Map of Italy*). (The town of Bovillae, about ten miles from Rome, was a colony of Alba Longa, which in turn was founded by Aeneas' son Iulus.) Now Antium was to receive games as well, in honour of the *gens Claudia* and the *gens Domitia* (the dative singular *genti* is to be supplied with both *Claudiae* and *Domitiae*). Nero shared ancestors with all three *gentes*. His mother Agrippina was the daughter of Agrippina maior (who in turn was the daughter of Augustus' daughter *Julia* and his general Agrippa) and Germanicus (the son of Nero *Claudius* Drusus); Nero's father was Cn. *Domitius*. But the extraordinary honour he now accorded to Antium – in implicit rivalry with Bovillae – suggests a deliberate attempt to step outside the shadow of Augustus. John Humphrey's analysis of the stone circus at Bovillae is suggestive here:[113]

> Fully-built stone circuses will be seen to be very rare outside Rome at such an early date. Undoubtedly it was the special connection of the Julian *gens* with Bovillae that prompted the construction of this circus, for the reputed origin of Julus was at nearby Alba Longa whence the ancient cults had been transferred to Bovillae prior to the Augustan period. Under Tiberius at the end of AD 16 a shrine to the Julian *gens* and a statue of the divine Augustus were dedicated at Bovillae. Augustus may have established a college of youths (*collegia iuvenum*) at Bovillae, while in AD 14 Tiberius established the *sodales Augustales* which administered the cult of the *gens Iulia*. Both organizations may have been involved with the games at Bovillae. Circus games are specifically alluded to in AD 35 ... and in AD 63 (circus games given in honour of the Julian cult) [with reference to our passage]; by implication these circus games had also been held in previous years. Thus the circus was probably used chiefly for games held under the close auspices of the emperor or the cult of the emperor, and it may have been located in close proximity to the shrine (*sacrarium*) of the Julian *gens*. ... It is hard to resist the conclusion that the monumental entertainment buildings of Bovillae, like some of its other public buildings, were a special project of Augustus and Tiberius.

The passage also should put into perspective the sacral investment on the part of both Nero and the senate. Nero's predecessors and in particular Augustus had set high benchmarks in terms of honours received and self-promotion, and if he wanted to stand out against them – a virtual

---

113   Humphrey (1986) 565–66.

requirement of someone who took on the role of *'princeps'*: the elevated position of 'the first or most outstanding member of society' required permanent justification, not least vis-à-vis those who had held that role before. Nero could clearly not hold his own in terms of military achievement, so he decided to excel in a field of social practice on which no *princeps* had hitherto left a conspicuous mark: cultural activities cultivated in Greece. Meanwhile, as John Henderson reminds us, what he forgot was the meaning of the dual Fortunes' rule over Antium – 'Fortune' and (her *opposite* number) 'Mis-Fortune' (Or as Horace puts it at *Odes* 1.35.1–4: *O diva, gratum quae regis Antium,* | *praesens vel imo tollere de gradu* | *mortale corpus vel superbos* | *vertere funeribus triumphos*; 'Divine Fortune, who rules over pleasing Antium, ready to raise a mortal body from the lowest rung or change proud triumphs into funeral processions'). He might have reflected both on what befell the *gens Iulia* when Bovillan Augustus' daughter Julia was born (he divorced her mother Scribonia and took the baby 'on the same day': Dio 48.34.4) and that these games were most likely one feature of Tiberius' celebration of Augustus' death and deification (or *'deathification'*). And as for the Claudian clan, it was more lunacy to insist *simultaneously* on *both* Nero's adoptive *and* birth lineage; and it was less than fortunate a reminder to recall the end of the last Claudian princess Octavia, whose gruesome death Tacitus had just recounted at the end of the previous book.

23.3 quae fluxa fuere, quartum intra mensem defuncta infante. rursusque exortae adulationes censentium honorem divae et pulvinar aedemque et sacerdotem. atque ipse ut laetitiae, ita maeroris immodicus egit.

quae fluxa fuere quartum intra mensem defuncta infante: *quae* is a connecting relative (= *ea*). *fuere* = *fuerunt*. All the efforts were as written on water. Tacitus announces this anticlimax with laconic brevity and a mocking *f*-alliteration. *quartum intra mensem defuncta infante* is a good example of another hallmark of Tacitean style, that is, the surprising distribution of information across main and subordinate clauses. Here the 'vital' element is packed into a (causal) ablative absolute, with the participle (*defuncta*) and noun (*infante*) further delayed for special effect. The language is very matter-of-fact and unelaborated, again contrasting the simple reality of the death with the extravagant honours previously listed. In terms of syntax (and placement in the sentence) the phrase mirrors *dato et Poppaeae eodem cognomento* at 23.1 and the two ablative absolutes thus bracket the birth and the death of Nero's daughter, adding to the overall sense of futility and finality.

rursusque exortae [sc. *sunt*] **adulationes censentium honorem divae et pulvinar aedemque et sacerdotem:** The *rursusque* ('and again') at the beginning of the sentence gives a sense of despair to Tacitus' words: for him, the new outpouring of sycophantic adulation is depressingly predictable. The verb *exorior* hints at novelty, and the proposed honours were indeed unprecedented: (i) deification (*honorem divae*); (ii) a sacred couch (*pulvinar*); (iii) a temple (*aedem*); and (iv) a priest (*sacerdotem*). All four items are accusative objects of *censentium* (the genitive plural present active participle of *censeo*, dependent on *adulationes*: 'of those, who...'). Tacitus again employs polysyndeton to stress the profusion of honours showered on the dead baby by the supine senators and (as with the ablative absolute) to set up a correlation (this time on the level of style) between the events at her birth and upon her death. (See above 23.2 '*et additae...*')

honorem divae: The senators proposed to deify the baby-girl. Accordingly, Tacitus calls Poppaea 'mother of the divine infant' (*divinae infantis parens*) at *Annals* 16.6.2. The move may seem preposterous (and Tacitus' dry laconic account presents it as such). But we are supposed to recall what other emperors had dreamed up in this respect. Here is Cassius Dio's account of how Caligula reacted to the death of his sister Drusilla:

> Drusilla was married to Marcus Lepidus, at once the favorite and lover of the emperor, but Gaius [sc. Caligula] also treated her as a concubine. When her death occurred at this time, her husband delivered the eulogy and her brother accorded her a public funeral. 2 The Pretorians with their commander and the equestrian order by itself ran about the pyre and the boys of noble birth performed the equestrian exercise called 'Troy' about her tomb. All the honours that had been bestowed upon Livia were voted to her, and it was further decreed that she should be deified, that a golden effigy of her should be set up in the senate-house, and that in the temple of Venus in the Forum a statue of her should be built for her, 3 that she should have twenty priests, women as well as men; women, whenever they offered testimony, should swear by her name, and on her birthday a festival equal of the Ludi Megalenses should be celebrated, and the senate and the knights should be given a banquet. She accordingly now received the name Panthea, and was declared worthy of divine honours in all the cities. 4 Indeed, a certain Livius Geminius, a senator, declared on oath, invoking destruction upon himself and his children if he spoke falsely, that he had seen her ascending to heaven and holding converse with the gods; and he called all the other gods and Panthea herself to witness. For this declaration he received a million sesterces.

Take this as a benchmark and you could argue that the senators who proposed divine honours for Nero's baby-girl showed remarkable... restraint.[114]

pulvinar: A sacred couch on which the images of the gods were placed at a special celebration (the *lectisternium*) – the suggestion here is that the young baby's image be placed among them as a new goddess (*diva Claudia, Neronis filia*).

sacerdotem: The singular surprises in its conspicuous modesty: in contrast to the twenty priests and priestesses that Caligula appointed for the shrine of his sister, the temple of *diva Claudia* looks decidedly under-staffed.

atque ipse ut laetitiae, ita maeroris immodicus egit: Another very short and therefore emphatic sentence, in which Tacitus makes explicit how highly strung Nero was. The advanced position and parallelism of *ut laetitiae, ita maeroris* (both genitives are dependent on *immodicus*) highlight that Nero is prone to excess at either end of the emotional spectrum. The adjective *immodicus* ('excessive') carries strong negative connotations in traditional Roman morality, which regarded control of one's emotions as a sign of excellence; it correlates with the *ultra mortale* at 23.1, effecting a further bracketing of birth and death. Tacitus perhaps also invites us to evaluate Nero's emotional reaction to the arrival and departure of his baby daughter against the high infant mortality rate in antiquity. Valerie French provides some numbers:[115]

> If we retroject the worst mortality rates of the modern world back into the Greco-Roman one, we would estimate that about 5% of all babies born alive would die before they reached the age of one month, and that among every 20,000 women giving birth, five would die. If we include late fetal and in-childbirth deaths, the probability of infant mortality climbs from 5% to 8%.

---

114   As a further point of comparison one could cite Cassius Dio's account of the honours Augustus awarded to his nephew and son-in-law Marcellus after his death in 23 BC. It is indicative of an early stage of imperial honours, where the crossing of the divide between human and divine was still a taboo: 'Augustus gave him a public burial after the customary eulogies, placing him in the tomb he was building, and as a memorial to him finished the theatre whose foundations had already been laid by the former Caesar and which was now called the theatre of Marcellus. And he ordered also that a golden image of the deceased, a golden crown, and a curule chair should be carried into the theatre at the Ludi Romani and should be placed in the midst of the officials having charge of the games' (53.30).

115   French (1986) 69.

These figures help to explain the high level of anxiety (and the investment in religious supplications) as the date of birth was approaching – as well as the tangible sense of relief thereafter; but they also help to underscore the emotional excess of the emperor: in light of the rather high likelihood that the child would not survive, the degree to which Nero was buoyed with joy and struck down by grief generates the impression of an emotionally unbalanced individual.

23.4 adnotatum est, omni senatu Antium sub recentem partum effuso, Thraseam prohibitum immoto animo praenuntiam imminentis caedis contumeliam excepisse. secutam dehinc vocem Caesaris ferunt qua reconciliatum se Thraseae apud Senecam iactaverit ac Senecam Caesari gratulatum: unde gloria egregiis viris et pericula gliscebant.

The passage functions as a node that brings together various narrative threads. Tacitus here connects the last major event he recounted in his coverage of 62 (the speech of Thrasea on provincial government) with the first major event in his account of 63, i.e. the birth and death of Nero's baby daughter. At the same time, he takes the opportunity to recall via the figure of Seneca the early years of Nero's reign and to drop a hint about Seneca's and Thrasea's dire future. More precisely, the phrasing here stands in intratextual dialogue with the very end of the surviving portion of the *Annals*: at 16.21–35, Tacitus recounts the death of Thrasea Paetus and Barea Soranus (a respected elderly statesman), as the climax of Nero's killing spree – murdering them was to kill *virtus* personified: *trucidatis tot insignibus viris ad postremum Nero virtutem ipsam exscindere concupivit interfecto Thrasea Paeto et Barea Sorano* (21; 'After the slaughter of so many of the noble, Nero in the end conceived the ambition to shred Virtue herself by killing Thrasea Paetus and Barea Soranus'). The last image where the text breaks off is of Thrasea dying slowly in excruciating pain after opening his veins by order of the *princeps* (16.35). Thrasea's death was preceded by the death of Seneca in the wake of the Pisonian conspiracy, narrated as the climactic bookend sequence at 15.60–64, which followed a similarly gruesome pattern.

adnotatum est ... Thraseam prohibitum immoto animo praenuntiam imminentis caedis contumeliam excepisse: *adnotatum est* introduces an indirect statement with *Thraseam* as subject accusative and *excepisse* as infinitive. *contumeliam* – which is modified by the attribute *praenuntiam* (in predicative position and governing the genitive phrase *imminentis caedis*) – is the direct object of *excepisse*. *prohibitum* modifies *Thraseam* – it is Tacitus' condensed way of saying that Nero forbade Thrasea to attend his reception of the senate. Nero's decision to uninvite just him from the birth celebrations amounted to a *renuntiatio amicitiae* (renunciation of friendship) from the emperor, often a precursor to banishment or worse: this is what Tacitus refers to with *praenuntiam imminentis caedis contumeliam* (an affront which foreshadowed his impending murder). At 16.24, Tacitus notes that the emperor had prohibited Thrasea to join in the celebrations that greeted the arrival of Tiridates (the Parthian king) in Rome: *Igitur omni civitate ad excipiendum principem spectandumque regem effusa, Thrasea occursu prohibitus non demisit animum, sed codicillos ad Neronem composuit, requirens obiecta et expurgaturum adseuerans, si notitiam criminum et copiam diluendi habuisset* ('The whole city, then, streamed out to welcome the emperor and inspect the king, but Thrasea was ordered to avoid the reception. [Aptly named for 'Boldness'] He didn't lower his spirits, but drew up a note to Nero, asking for the allegations against him and stating that he would rebut them, if he was allowed cognizance of the charges and facilities for dissipating them').

omni senatu Antium ... effuso: Embedded within coverage of Thrasea occurs an ablative absolute in which Tacitus dispatches the rest of the senate. The whole (cf. the totalising *omni*) of the senate troop out to Antium to pay their homage to the newborn. The strong verb *effundo* (literally 'to pour out'; this picks up on the image of flux in the previous sentence: *quae fluxa fuere*) helps to convey how the senators were falling over themselves to be seen congratulating the emperor and his wife.

sub recentem partum: Immediately after the birth.

immoto animo: The contrast between Nero's wild emotions and Thrasea's unshaken spirit is pointed.

secutam [sc. *esse*] **dehinc vocem Caesaris ferunt qua reconciliatum** [sc. *esse*] **se Thraseae apud Senecam iactaverit ac Senecam Caesari gratulatum** [sc. *esse*]: The sentence introduces a surprising turn: after the reference to Thrasea's impending doom (and its Stoic acceptance), we now hear [the story] that Nero reconciled himself with his adversary and boasted about it to his old tutor Seneca. *ferunt* introduces an indirect statement with *vocem* and *Senecam* as subject accusatives and *secutam* (*esse*) and *gratulatum* (*esse*) as verbs. Within the relative clause *iactaverit* introduces an indirect statement with *se* as subject accusative and *reconciliatum* (*esse*) as verb. There is an interesting shift in grammatical position from the relative clause to the second part of the indirect statement dependent on *ferunt*: in the relative clause Nero is the subject of the main verb and the subjective accusative of the indirect statement (*se*), whereas Thrasea is in the dative; afterwards Nero is mentioned in the dative (*Caesari*), whereas Seneca becomes the subject accusative. It is another instance in which Tacitus uses evaluative syntax: he elevates Seneca to a more prominent syntactic position than the emperor and uses style to reinforce theme: as Furneaux puts it, 'the answer of Seneca implies that the friendship of Thrasea was worth more to Nero than Nero's to him.'[116]

apud Senecam: What we get here is a throw-back to the times when Seneca (c. 4 BC – AD 65) was Nero's tutor and tried to guide him in thought and practice, not least through his treatise *de Clementia* ('On Mercy'), which he addressed to his charge. At *Annals* 14.53–6, we were treated to an excruciating interview exchange when Seneca tried to let go his graduate and retire, only to run into a sample of the fancy rhetoric he had taught his prince pupil, and be refused.

ferunt: Tacitus often reports a story in this manner, neither mentioning his sources nor vouching for the story himself. Here, he tells the little tale to illustrate aspects of the intertwined characters of three major figures.

unde gloria egregiis viris et pericula gliscebant: *egregiis viris* refers to Seneca and Thrasea. Seneca won glory because of the fearless reaction to the emperor's vaunting, thus speaking an unwelcome truth to power (always a dangerous thing to do), whilst Thrasea won glory through the recognition of his status as a benchmark of political excellence and integrity – again a worrisome position to be in if the ruler is a tyrant who falls short of the standards set by some of his subjects. The position of *gloria* at the beginning suggests that the outcome of the event was as it should be, then the delayed and threatening *pericula* reminds us that the world of Neronian Rome was not so fair and just, and that something more sinister was awaiting them. Ultimately, both had to commit suicide. That the same action simultaneously brings glory as well as danger reveals the perverse nature of Nero's regime: qualities that ought to bring renown entail peril.

---

116   Furneaux (1907) 347.

et pericula: This is another instance of Tacitean style, what Oakley calls 'the pointed use of *et*.' He cites *Annals* 12.52.3 as an example: *de mathematicis Italia pellendis factum senatus consultum atrox et irritum* and translates: 'with regard to the expulsion of the astrologers from Italy, a decree of the senate was passed that was fearful – and ineffectual.'[117] The same effect is in play here: 'from this incident (*unde*) glory grew for these eminent men – and danger.'

gliscebant: This powerful metaphor gives the ominous sense of their futures: *glisco* is literally 'to swell up, blaze up.' Tacitus is fond of it: he uses it at the very beginning of the *Annals* to describe flattery and obsequiousness 'swelling' under Tiberius: *gliscente adulatione* (1.1). It belongs into the category of recherché or archaic words that Tacitus and other historiographers prefer over more common possibilities: 'The similarity exhibited by Sallust, Livy, Quintus Curtius Rufus (in his *History of Alexander the Great*) and Tacitus in their choice of vocabulary allows the generalisation that Latin historical style was marked by frequent employment of archaisms: e.g. the use of *cunctus* for the more mundane *omnis* ('all'), *glisco* for *cresco* ('grow') and *metuo* for *timeo* ('fear').'[118] Moreover, 'grow' is just what Nero's baby didn't manage to do. And with her went – the whole shooting-match. Soon. Poppaea and Nero, Seneca and Thrasea. The dynasty of Augustus, the *Annals* of Tacitus.

Section 2: *Annals* 15.33–45

15.33–45 can be divided as follows:

i.   33.1–34.1: Nero's coming-out party as stage performer

ii. 34.2–35.3: A look at the kind of creatures that populate Nero's court – and the killing of an alleged rival

iii. 36: Nero considers, but then reconsiders, going on tour to Egypt

iv. 37: To show his love for Rome, Nero celebrates a huge public orgy that segues into a (publicly consummated) mock-wedding with his freedman Pythagoras

v.   38–41: The fire of Rome

vi. 42–43: Reconstructing the Capital: Nero's New Palace

vii. 44: Appeasing the gods and Christians as scapegoats

viii. 45: Raising funds for buildings

---

117 Oakley (2009b) 200, with further examples in n. 23.
118 Oakley (2009b) 196.

(I) 33.1–34.1: NERO'S COMING-OUT PARTY AS STAGE PERFORMER

Chapter 33

33.1 C. Laecanio M. Licinio consulibus acriore in dies cupidine adigebatur Nero promiscas scaenas frequentandi. nam adhuc per domum aut hortos cecinerat Iuvenalibus ludis, quos ut parum celebres et tantae voci angustos spernebat.

As John Henderson points out to us, this paragraph initiates a narrative stretch in which a rhythmic pattern of 'ins-and-outs' (or '*es* and *ads*') bursts out all over through the to-and-fro of the storytelling, dancing attendance round Nero: [33] *adigebatur - adeptus - eliceret - e proximis coloniis - acciverat -* [34] *- evenit - egresso - adfuerat - edebatur - adsumptus...* [36] *edicto - adiit - aditurus - egressus - adversum - evenerat - acquireret - e terris - adstabant - ...*

C. Laecanio M. Licinio consulibus: As we have seen, this is the annalistic formula that indicates the beginning of the consular year (our AD 64). Gaius Laecanius Bassus outlived Nero and died during the reign of Vespasian (Pliny, *Natural Histories* 26.5). Marcus Licinius Crassus Frugi, however, was indicted for treason by the delator M. Aquilius Regulus and executed by Nero.[119] He thus followed in the footsteps of his parents, who died under Claudius.

acriore in dies cupidine adigebatur Nero promiscas scaenas frequentandi: The sentence is beautifully balanced: *acriore in-dies cupidine* [= 3 words] + *adigebatur Nero* [main verb and subject] + *promiscas scaenas frequentandi* [3 words]. At the same time, further syntactical aspects and relations generate the impression that Nero is carried away by disgraceful desire:

- the minor hyperbaton *acriore ... cupidine*, with the intervening phrase *in dies* generates the impression of an unstoppable escalation.

---

119 See Tacitus, *Histories* 4.42. Also: Pliny, *Letters* 1.5.3. For the practice of delation – a new development under the principate – see Introduction Section 2 and 6. Further literature includes Lintott (2001–2003) (including discussion of the republican background) and Rutledge (2001).

- the major hyperbaton *cupidine ... promiscas scaenas frequentandi* (the genitive of the gerund depends on *cupidine* and takes *promiscas scaenas* as accusative object) enmeshes and overpowers the emperor, who is caught in the middle.
- the passive verb *adigebatur* and the inversion of normal word order (verb – subject, rather than subject – verb) again suggests that Nero's rational agency is compromised: he is pushed along by his desires.
- the placement of verb and subject in the middle produces a powerful climax: we first get the ever-increasing desire, then the disconcerting intelligence that it has been overpowering the emperor, and, finally, the clarification of what the desire consists in: repeated (cf. *frequentandi*) appearances on stage in performances open to the public (cf. *promiscas*).

promiscas scaenas: *promiscas* refers to the fact that Nero's stage performances were now open to the public. He needed now to have indiscriminate access to the stage, no-holds-barred (cf. *immodicus* above).

nam adhuc per domum aut hortos cecinerat Iuvenalibus ludis, quos ut parum celebres et tantae voci angustos spernebat: Tacitus frequently supplies background information in a main clause in the pluperfect, set up by an adverb such as *adhuc* or *iam*, and followed by a subordinate clause situated in the narrative present. In terms of syntax, the sentence here recalls 23.2: *iam senatus uterum Poppaeae commendaverat dis votaque publice susceperat, quae multiplicata exolutaque*: (i) adverb (*iam*; *adhuc*); (ii) a main clause in the pluperfect (*commendaverat, susceperat; cecinerat*) providing background information; (iii) a relative clause that details actions in the narrative present (*quae ... exolutaque; quos ... spernebat*). Both sentences are perfect illustrations of Tacitus' habit of distributing information in surprising ways across main and subordinate clauses.

Iuvenalibus ludis: The reference is to the Juvenile Games that Nero celebrated in AD 59, at the occasion of his first shave as a 21-year-old. These games took place in Nero's palace and his gardens, i.e. were not open to the general public. Special festivities at this rite of passage were unremarkable. See Cassius Dio 48.34.3 on how Caesar Octavianus celebrated the occasion: 'For example, when Caesar now for the first time shaved off his beard, he held a magnificent entertainment himself besides granting all the other citizens a festival at public expense. He also kept his chin smooth afterwards, like the rest; for he was already beginning to be enamoured of Livia also, and for this reason divorced Scribonia the very day she bore him a daughter.' The future emperor Augustus, of course, did not contribute to the entertainment himself.

quos ut parum celebres et tantae voci angustos spernebat: The antecedent of *quos* is *hortos*, i.e. the gardens of the imperial estate. There is irony in Tacitus' voice as he says Nero felt these private performances did not attract the attendance figures (cf. *ut parum celebres*) he desired. Nero's talents as a singer and lyre-player are often derided in our sources, and the advanced position of *tantae* (such a great [voice]) has a sarcastic ring to it, especially since the appraisal of his *vox* as *tanta* is focalized for us through Nero himself. The vivid adjective *angustos* (literally, 'narrow', a ludicrous descriptor of the imperial gardens) suggests Nero feels restricted by his current opportunities to perform and wants 'more space.' Compare the account in Suetonius, *Nero* 20:

> Inter ceteras disciplinas pueritiae tempore imbutus et musica, statim ut imperium adeptus est, Terpnum citharoedum vigentem tunc praeter alios arcessiit diebusque continuis post cenam canenti in multam noctem assidens paulatim et ipse meditari exercerique coepit neque eorum quicquam omittere, quae generis eius artifices vel conservandae vocis causa vel augendae factitarent; sed et plumbeam chartam supinus pectore sustinere et clystere vomituque purgari et abstinere pomis cibisque officientibus; donec blandiente profectu, quamquam exiguae vocis et fuscae, prodire in scaenam concupiit, subinde inter familiares Graecum proverbium iactans occultae musicae nullum esse respectum.

> [Having gained some knowledge of music in addition to the rest of his early education, as soon as he became emperor he sent for Terpnus, the greatest master of the lyre in those days, and after listening to him sing after dinner for many successive days until late at night, he little by little began to practise himself, neglecting none of the exercises which artists of that kind are in the habit of following, to preserve or strengthen their voices. For he used to lie upon his back and hold a leaden plate on his chest, purge himself by the syringe and by vomiting, and deny himself fruits and all foods injurious to the voice. Finally encouraged by his progress, although his voice was weak and husky, he began to long to appear on the stage, and every now and then in the presence of his intimate friends he would quote a Greek proverb meaning 'Hidden music counts for nothing.']

33.2 non tamen Romae incipere ausus Neapolim quasi Graecam urbem delegit: inde initium fore, ut transgressus in Achaiam insignesque et antiquitus sacras coronas adeptus maiore fama studia civium eliceret.

Tacitus here takes a step back. Nero's desire to appear on stage may have been driving him on, but even he has not entirely lost a sense of decorum. He does not dare to inaugurate his career as a public performer in Rome but chooses a Greek city famous for its Greek entertainment culture instead. Tacitus presents this choice both as an avoidance of Rome and as an anticipation of Nero's trip to Greece, which would happen several years later (AD 66–67).

Romae: A locative: 'in Rome'.

Neapolim quasi Graecam urbem: Neapolis, modern Naples, was, as its Greek name (*nea* = new; *polis* = city, hence: 'New City') implies, originally a Greek foundation. The *quasi* here thus has causal force. Although it had long been part of Roman Italy, Neapolis seems to have retained much of its Greek character. Aristocratic norms were more flexible there, making it a more suitable place for Nero to inaugurate his career as a public performer. The antithesis between Greek and Roman is significant. Traditional Roman thinkers saw themselves as the guardians of great civilised Roman values (*mores maiorum*). They may have enjoyed and respected Greek art and literature, but Greek behaviour, morals and practices came with a stigma: Greekness was often tied up in Roman thought with luxury and immorality. Nero's desires are such that he has to leave Rome and find the nearest 'Greek city' to allow an outlet for his foreign, un-Roman, or, indeed, 'novel/ weird/ revolutionary', urges.

inde initium fore, ut transgressus in Achaiam insignesque et antiquitus sacras coronas adeptus maiore fama studia civium eliceret: *inde initium fore* is an indirect statement dependent on an implied verb of thinking. Tacitus slyly lets us partake of what he assumes were Nero's thoughts/ motivations at the time. According to him, the emperor already in AD 63 harboured grandiose plans of 'conquering' the Greek world with his showbiz talents, anticipating a triumphant return to Rome and an enthusiastic welcome from his fellow-citizens, not unlike those accorded to the military conquerors of old.

inde initium: The alliteration stresses that Nero envisages this performance as just a debut: an ominous sign! Both *initium* and *antiquitus* chime with/ against the 'newness' of Naples.

transgressus in Achaiam insignesque et antiquitus sacras coronas adeptus: The -*que* after *insignes* links *transgressus* and *adeptus*. The two participles (*transgressus; adeptus*) and the phrases they govern (*in Achaiam; insignesque et antiquitus sacras coronas*) are arranged chiastically.

transgressus in Achaiam: The Roman province of Achaea essentially covered mainland Greece. The participle *transgressus* carries an aggressive note, in a double sense: Nero is transgressing against Roman cultural norms; and he is invading Greece, reversing the cultural conquest of Italy famously noted by Horace at *Epistle* 2.1.156–57: *Graecia capta ferum victorem cepit et artis | intulit agresti Latio* ('Conquered Greece conquered/ captivated her wild vanquisher and brought her arts to rustic Latium').

insignesque et antiquitus sacras coronas adeptus: Winners in prestigious Greek competitions received wreaths (*coronae*) as prizes. Nero's thoughts here are designed to put across his devotion to and love of all things Greek: these wreaths are longingly described with the very positive adjectives *insignes* and *antiquitus sacras* (*lit.* 'anciently sacred'). Moreover, there is the arrogance and mindset of a tyrant here in the participle *adeptus* ('having won'): Nero does not doubt for one moment that he will be victorious – and why would he as emperor of the known world! This is Tacitus subtly showing us Nero's perversion of these competitions.

maiore fama: The word *fama* (fame) is an ambiguous word in Latin: it can mean 'fame' in the positive sense or, in a negative sense, 'disgrace', 'notoriety.' We are of course in Nero's thoughts, so 'he' means that he will win glory among the citizens; at the same time, we can hear Tacitus' cynicism and wonder whether the actual result will be Nero achieving disgrace and notoriety.[120]

---

120   On *fama* see now the magisterial treatment by Hardie (2012), with a discussion of rumour in Tacitus' historiographical works at 288–313. Flaig (2010a) offers an analysis of rumour in Roman politics from a sociological perspective, with specific reference to the reign of Nero.

studia civium eliceret: Nero imagines that his feats on stage will hit the spot, coax enthusiasm from the citizens.

33.3 ergo contractum oppidanorum vulgus, et quos e proximis coloniis et municipiis eius rei fama acciverat, quique Caesarem per honorem aut varios usus sectantur, etiam militum manipuli, theatrum Neapolitanorum complent.

The sentence features a series of subjects: (i) *vulgus*, which governs the perfect participle *contractum*; (ii) the implied antecedent of *quos*, i.e. *ei*; (iii) the implied antecedent of *qui*, i.e. *ei*; (iv) *manipuli*. They all go with the main verb at the end: *complent*. The *et* links *vulgus* and the first implied *ei*; the *-que* after *qui* links the two implied *ei*; Tacitus then continues, climactically, with *etiam* ('even'). The pronounced polysyndeton magnifies the list of those co-opted to swell the emperor's enormous retinue. Tacitus revels in the idea of so many men from so many different groups flooding into the theatre of Neapolis.

oppidanorum vulgus: The *oppidani* are the townsfolk of Neapolis, in contrast to the Roman citizens (*cives*) mentioned in the previous sentence. The word *vulgus* ('crowd', 'mob') suggests that Nero's local audience is made up of the lowest elements of society.

coloniis et municipiis: Although originally distinct forms of settlement (a *colonia* being a settlement of Roman citizens, a *municipium* an independent Italian town), by this period the distinction had lost some of its significance. Tacitus uses both to exaggerate Nero's recruitment to his fan-club, drawing from anywhere he could all over the country.[121]

eius fama: Here we meet that wonderfully ambiguous word *fama* again. Once again Tacitus uses it to imply (without explicitly saying) that these men were attracted by the *infamy* of what Nero was up to: in other words, he not only blackens Nero's character, but also suggests that the men who flocked to him were lowlifes, attracted to Nero's outrageous designs like flies round the proverbial canine ordure.

---

121 For the varying status of the cities in the Roman Empire see Edmundson (2006) 256–58.

quique Caesarem per honorem aut varios usus sectantur: In the midst of this unseemly rabble the words *Caesarem* and *honorem* seem incongruous. They help to give a sense of noble, devoted servants of the emperor caught up in this group. The impression is undone by the vague and promiscuous *aut varios usus* that follows it. Tacitus may have had in mind the so-called *Augustiani* – a special group of young men formed by Nero some years previously, to follow him, flatter him and applaud his performances: 'All great performers had their own claques (*fautores histrionum*) to cheer them on and to whip up the audience with elaborate rhythmic chants and hand-clapping. It was at his private Juvenile Games, celebrated in 59, that Nero first introduced his *Augustiani*, Roman knights in their prime who made both day and night ring with applause and praise of Nero's godlike beauty and voice. ... By the time Nero first appeared in public in Naples, in 64, these Roman knights were backed by some 5,000 hardy plebeian youths. They were divided into groups, *factiones*, to learn the different elaborate forms of clapping (imported from Alexandria) – "the buzzings," "the tiles," "the bricks" – by which Nero had been captivated and which they performed vigorously when he sang.'[122] (What, do you think, did 'the buzzings', 'the tiles', and 'the bricks' sound like?) They would have been amongst this group, and the frequentative verb *sectantur* ('keep following around', 'follow in the train of') suggests their fawning attendance on the emperor.

per honorem aut varios usus: The preposition *per* has a causal sense here. *honestum* ('the honourable') and *utile* ('the advantageous') are two key concepts in (philosophical) ethics, extensively discussed in (for instance) Cicero's *de Officiis*.

etiam militum manipuli: *etiam* ('even') and the delay of this group to the end of the long list, makes clear that the soldiers' presence was the most shocking: Nero has enlisted soldiers (most likely members of the Praetorian guard) to join his fan-club in the theatre and to cheer him on. The maniple was a company in the Roman army, numbering two centuries (i.e. about 120 men in total). Here it is plural (*manipuli*), indicating that Nero took a very sizeable number of soldiers with him. Their presence, stressed by the alliteration, the *etiam* and their final

---

122 Champlin (2003) 59–60. See Suetonius, *Nero* 20.3 and *Annals* 14.15.

position in the list, seems highly incongruous: these fighting men of Rome are there, not to invade, but to watch their emperor disgrace himself like a Greek on the stage.

theatrum Neapolitanorum complent: The object and verb come along at last after a long list of subjects, piling into the theatre. The verb *complent* makes abundantly clear the number of Nero's assembled supporters – they pack the house out.

Chapter 34

34.1 Illic, plerique ut arbitrabantur, triste, ut ipse, providum potius et secundis numinibus evenit: nam egresso qui adfuerat populo vacuum et sine ullius noxa theatrum collapsum est. ergo per compositos cantus grates dis atque ipsam recentis casus fortunam celebrans petiturusque maris Hadriae traiectus apud Beneventum interim consedit, ubi gladiatorium munus a Vatinio celebre edebatur.

illic, plerique ut arbitrabantur, triste, ut ipse, providum potius et secundis numinibus evenit: One could rephrase the sentence as follows, to bring out Tacitus' syntactic contortions: *illic res evenit tristis, ut plerique arbitrabantur, sed provida et secundis numinibus, ut ipse arbitrabatur*. In other words, we have:

- a hysteron proteron: Tacitus first gives us the evaluation, then the fact that is being evaluated (indeed, we have to wait until the next sentence to find out what actually happened – but the effect is already noticeable here with *arbitrabantur* preceding *evenit*);
- the use of adjectives (*triste, providum*) in the place of nouns; *triste* stands in antithetical contrast to *providum potius et secundis numinibus*;
- a parallelisms with twists: *plerique ut arbitrabantur* corresponds to *ut ipse*, but the subject *plerique* is pulled out of the first *ut*-clause for emphasis and in the second *ut*-clause the verb is elided.

The parallel structure and anaphora of *ut* renders the disparity between most people's judgment and Nero's apparent. A majority of right-thinking observers saw this event as *triste*, in contrast to the one man, Nero himself, who thought otherwise. Nero's opinion is not just different but the exact opposite. In addition the pleonastic *providum ... et secundis numinibus*, a prolix phrase designed to drown out the word *triste* with great, yet hollow triumphalist fanfare, suggests the bizarre amount of positive meaning Nero tried to read into the destruction of a theatre. The alliteration *providum potius* helps to stress the contrast.

illic: in Neapolis.

et secundis numinibus: An ablative absolute (with the verb – the non-existent present participle of *esse* – missing), awkwardly linked to *providum* with *et*.

nam egresso qui adfuerat populo vacuum et sine ullius noxa theatrum collapsum est: Tacitus now explains why Nero viewed the event as favourable – because the theatre was not destroyed while in use. Nevertheless, a theatre collapsing is not generally viewed as providential, and one can appreciate the challenge Nero faced in endowing it with positive meaning. Or, as John Henderson puts it: 'A failed building was a literal *ruina* – and everywhere outside Nero's nutcase spelled "ruination" (of social fabric, the universe, etc).'

egresso qui adfuerat populo: An ablative absolute that contains a relative clause within. The antecedent of *qui* is *populo*.

vacuum et sine ullius noxa: As in *providum potius et secundis numinibus*, Tacitus uses *et* very creatively here: 'the theatre collapsed [when it was] empty and [hence] without harm to anyone.'

theatrum collapsum est: After much delay Tacitus finally tells us what all the fuss is about. Suetontius, *Nero* 20.2, identifies an earthquake as the reason for the collapse, which, he claims, set in during one of Nero's performances: *Et prodit Neapoli primum ac ne concusso quidem repente motu terrae theatro ante cantare destitit, quam incohatum absolveret nomon* ('And he made his début at Naples, where he did not cease singing until he had finished the number which he had begun, even though the theatre was shaken by a sudden earthquake shock').

To understand Nero's reaction better, it is worth recalling Tacitus' account of a similar disaster at *Annals* 4.62, where he details the collapse of a *full* amphitheatre in the year AD 27 (i.e. in the reign of Tiberius):

[62] M. Licinio L. Calpurnio consulibus ingentium bellorum cladem aequavit malum improvisum: eius initium simul et finis exstitit. nam coepto apud Fidenam amphitheatro Atilius quidam libertini generis, quo spectaculum gladiatorum celebraret, neque fundamenta per solidum subdidit neque firmis nexibus ligneam compagem superstruxit, ut qui non abundantia pecuniae nec municipali ambitione, sed in sordidam mercedem id negotium quaesivisset. adfluxere avidi talium, imperitante Tiberio procul voluptatibus habiti, virile ac muliebre secus, omnis aetas, ob propinquitatem loci effusius; unde gravior pestis fuit, conferta mole, dein convulsa, dum ruit intus aut in exteriora effunditur immensamque vim mortalium, spectaculo intentos aut qui circum adstabant, praeceps trahit atque operit. et illi quidem, quos principium stragis in mortem adflixerat, ut tali sorte, cruciatum effugere: miserandi magis quos abrupta parte corporis nondum vita deseruerat; qui per diem visu, per noctem ululatibus et gemitu coniuges aut liberos noscebant. iam ceteri fama exciti, hic fratrem, propinquum ille, alius parentes lamentari. etiam quorum diversa de causa amici aut necessarii aberant, pavere tamen; nequedum comperto, quos illa vis perculisset, latior ex incerto metus.

[In the consulate of Marcus Licinius and Lucius Calpurnius, the casualties of some great wars were equalled by an unexpected disaster. It began and ended in a moment. A certain Atilius, of the freedman class, who had begun an amphitheatre at Fidena, in order to give a gladiatorial show, failed both to lay the foundation in solid ground and to secure the fastenings of the wooden structure above; the reason being that he had embarked on the enterprise, not from a superabundance of wealth nor to court the favours of his townsmen, but with an eye to sordid gain. Greedy for such amusements, since they had been debarred from their pleasures under the reign of Tiberius, people poured to the place, men and women, old and young, the stream swollen because the town lay near. This increased the gravity of the catastrophe, as the unwieldy fabric was packed when it collapsed, breaking inward or sagging outward, and precipitating and burying a vast crowd of human beings, intent on the spectacle or standing around. Those, indeed, whom the first moment of havoc had dashed to death, escaped torture, so far as was possible in such a fate: more to be pitied were those whose mutilated bodies life had not yet abandoned, who by day recognized their wives or their children by sight, and at night by their shrieks and moans. The news brought the absent to the scene – one lamenting a brother, one a kinsman, another his parents. Even those whose friends or relatives had left home for a different reason still felt the alarm, and, as it was not yet known whom the catastrophe had destroyed, the uncertainty gave wider range for fear.]

In the wake of the disaster, Tacitus goes on to report, the senate passed a decree that no one with a fortune of less than 400,000 sesterces should organize gladiatorial games and that amphitheatres had to be built on ground of tried solidity.

34.2 ergo per compositos cantus grates dis atque ipsam recentis casus fortunam celebrans petiturusque maris Hadriae traiectus apud Beneventum interim consedit, ubi gladiatorium munus a Vatinio celebre edebatur.

per compositos cantus: *compositos* implies that Nero wrote the songs himself.

grates dis atque ipsam recentis casus fortunam celebrans: One can either supply *agens* with *grates dis* or take both *grates* and *ipsam fortunam* as accusative objects of *celebrans* in what would be a zeugma. The zeugma gives the sentence a slightly strained feel, helping to convey the oddity of Nero's actions. *ipsam recentis casus* (= mis-fortune) *fortunam* (= luck, good fortune) *celebrans* amounts to a paradox.

grates: See above on **20.1**.

celebrans petiturusque: The *-que* links *celebrans* and *petiturus*. Note the *variatio* here, this time in terms of word order: the present participle *celebrans* comes at the end of its phrase, whereas the future *petiturus...* comes at the beginning. The juxtaposition of a present participle and future participle is striking: Nero has hardly finished dealing with one calamity before his mind is already set on the next outrage.

petiturusque maris Hadriae traiectus: Tacitus uses the poetic phrase *maris Hadriae* (*lit.* 'of the Sea of Hadria', i.e. the town of Adria, rather than plain adjectival 'of the Adriatic Sea'). *traiectus* is accusative plural. One wonders what evidence Tacitus can have had for the claim that already in AD 64 Nero had plans to go straight from his first public appearance on stage at Neapolis on a tour through Greece – two years before he actually did. At 36.1, at any rate, Tacitus reports that Nero had dropped the plan for unknown reasons and returned from Beneventum to Rome: *nec multo post omissa in praesens Achaia (causae in incerto fuere) urbem revisit* (see below). Now it is true that Beneventum, though situated to the north of Neapolis, would be a good stop on the way to Brundisium, especially if Nero wanted to honour Vatinius with his presence at the games: it was situated at the Via Appia (see *Map of Italy*); but for the same reasons, Nero might have gone there on his way back to Rome. Given that a tour of Greece by the emperor was a logistical challenge of the first order, it is rather unlikely that Nero opted for and against going at the spur of the moment. Possibly, Tacitus simply made this up, thereby anticipating Nero's actual trip to Greece two years later and illustrating the fickleness of the emperor on top. Support for this assumption comes from the etymology of Beneventum, which makes it an ideal place to ponder a sea voyage. As John Henderson points out, the story is that the auspicious Latin name 'Bene-ventum', 'Fair wind' (mildly in tension with *consedit*: see below), replaced the Latin rendering of the original nice Greek name, *Maloeis*, 'Appley' – 'Male-ventum', for portending a bad outcome for heedless voyagers.[123]

apud Beneventum interim consedit: Beneventum, a city located on the Via Appia, was the hometown of Vatinius, whom Tacitus introduces in the following clause. See previous note for its etymology. There is a mild pun in *consedit* as Nero, rather than setting sail, 'settled' – 'into his seat' to watch the gladiator show.

ubi gladiatorium munus a Vatinio celebre edebatur: For Vatinius, see Miller's colourful note: 'he was a native of Beneventum (Juvenal 5.46 [and therefore unrelated to the powerful foe of Cicero, whose family came from Sabine Reate]) and a new type of court character – the licensed buffoon. But such men, in Roman as in medieval times, could be powerful and dangerous. Tacitus recognises his importance, and his colour-value in the narrative.'[124] Gladiatorial games were a very Roman form of entertainment, unlike stage-plays, lyre-playing or athletics.

celebre: Tacitus delays the attribute that indicates the popularity of this form of entertainment – perhaps implying a contrast with the 'hired enthusiasts' that crowded Nero's performances? (Recall that at 33.1 Nero is presented as deeming his gardens *parum celebres* for his talents.)

(II) 34.2–35.3: A LOOK AT THE KIND OF CREATURES THAT POPULATE NERO'S COURT – AND THE KILLING OF AN ALLEGED RIVAL

In this stretch, Tacitus advances his narrative by loose associations: we move from Nero's own appearance at Neapolis (33) to the gladiatorial games organized by one of his courtiers, i.e. Vatinius (34.1). The mentioning of

123 See Maltby (1991) 78.
124 Miller (1975) 83.

Vatinius offers the occasion for a character-portrayal (or rather assassination) of malicious brilliance (34.2), before Tacitus claims that Nero *conceived* of the murder of his distant relative (and hence potential rival) Silanus Torquatus during the gladiatorial games put on by Vatinius (35.1). We then get an account of the events that led to Silanus' death: charge, pending trial, pre-emptive suicide, speech of regret by the emperor, announcing that he would have exercised mercy even though the defendant was guilty as charged (35.2). The entire sequence is held together by a 'factoid' for which Tacitus could not conceivably have had any evidence: that the *munus* of Vatinius was the moment at which Nero began to plot the murder of Silanus. The suspicion that Tacitus here exercises creative license thickens in light of the fact that Cassius Dio (62.27.2, cited below) dates Silanus' suicide to the following year. Again, one may wonder how best to explain this discrepancy in our sources. If Cassius Dio got it right, did Tacitus ride roughshod over chronological accuracy since he wished to plant a premeditated murder in Nero's mind during Vatinius' gladiatorial games, not least to blur the distinction between *voluptas* and *scelus*?

34.2 Vatinius inter foedissima eius aulae ostenta fuit, sutrinae tabernae alumnus, corpore detorto, facetiis scurrilibus; primo in contumelias adsumptus, dehinc optimi cuiusque criminatione eo usque valuit ut gratia pecunia vi nocendi etiam malos praemineret.

Here we get a little portrait of one of Nero's creatures – the parvenu Vatinius from Beneventum, who reputedly had a long nose (Juvenal, *Satire* 5.46–7, Martial, *Epigrams* 14.96) and made a fortune under the emperor as informer and 'sinister court-buffoon.'[125] In his *Dialogus de Oratoribus*, Tacitus mentions that Maternus eventually crushed the creature by means of some acid poetry (11.2).[126] The vocabulary of wickedness – *foedissima, sutrinae, detorto, scurrilibus, contumelias, criminatione, malos* – is densely packed here to give a very strong flavour of the corruption of Vatinius and of Nero's court.

Vatinius inter foedissima eius aulae ostenta fuit, sutrinae tabernae alumnus, corpore detorto, facetiis scurrilibus: After first establishing that Nero's entire court teemed with disgusting misfits – the implication of *inter*

---

125   Syme (1958) I 356.
126   For the (uncertain) text, translation, and discussion see Bartsch (1994) 103–4.

foedissima eius aulae ostenta is that there were many others who reached the same superlative degree of repulsiveness – Tacitus proceeds to specifics. They are presented in a punchy, asyndetic tricolon, with typical variation in construction and style: (i) *sutrinae tabernae alumnus*, (ii) *corpore detorto*, (iii) *facetiis scurrilibus*.

inter foedissima eius aulae ostenta: The superlative *foedissima*, a very powerful and negative word implying both moral and physical ugliness, gives an immediate sense of Vatinius' character. Tacitus further casts him as one of the *ostenta* (marvels, monstrosities) of the court, describing him like a freakish and horrifying object. *ostentum* is synonymous with *monstrum* and *prodigium* and refers to a *spectacularly* unnatural occurrence: Nero's entire court emerges as an abomination of what is normal and natural.

sutrinae tabernae alumnus: Tacitus reports scornfully his humble background, a sign for Roman readers of how unfitting it was for him to be in the emperor's court. Note the emphatic position of *sutrinae*, to stress the lowliness of his family.

corpore detorto: An ablative of quality. The adjective *detortus* ('twisted out of shape') gives a vivid evocation of his deformity. Tacitus, as many other classical authors, operates on the assumption that physical appearance offers insights into character. 'Physiognomy', as the procedure of deducing psychological traits from physical characteristics, was a pseudo-science with considerable traction in antiquity (and beyond).[127] We should therefore understand *detortus* both literally and metaphorically. In fact, Vatinius could be seen as the 'face' of Nero's regime – a twisted and ugly perversion of anything pleasing and natural. Under the Julio-Claudian emperors the 'body politic' is as deformed as Vatinius' appearance. Not coincidentally, Tacitus uses the verb at the very beginning of the *Annals* in his characterization of Tiberius (1.7.7): *postea cognitum est ad introspiciendas etiam procerum voluntates inductam dubitationem: nam verba vultus in crimen detorquens recondebat* ('It was realized later that his coyness had been assumed with the further object of gaining an insight into the feelings of the aristocracy: for all the while he was distorting words and looks into crimes and storing them in his memory').

---

127   See Swain et al. (2007).

facetiis scurrilibus: Vatinius' sense of humour was as deformed as his body. Again, the adjective *scurrilibus* is significant: it is a rare word and comes from the noun *scurra*, a buffoon or jester. 'Tacitus is giving him a basinfull of his own medicine: comically, the name Vatinius itself originated as one of those peasanty Roman nicknames for physical debility, "Knock-Knees". What for Nero's pet is presumably a 'trade-name' apes (and trashes) an inherited aristocratic badge of honour. Nero's next victim will go down for *his* pedigree name – and *bona fide* descent.'[128]

primo in contumelias adsumptus, dehinc optimi cuiusque criminatione eo usque valuit, ut gratia pecunia vi nocendi etiam malos praemineret: Vatinius was initially recruited to serve as an object of mockery, but managed to turn the victimization he suffered on account of his physical disabilities around by virtue of his sharp and evil wit. This structure *primo ... dehinc* ('first... then...') suggests the unexpected transformation of Vatinius from jester to power-figure.

primo in contumelias adsumptus: In other words, Vatinius was taken in as a member of the court as a jester (not exactly a sign of his nobility of character or eminence). Jesters were, as in mediaeval times, a feature of the Roman imperial court.

dehinc optimi cuiusque criminatione ... valuit: Tacitus was aware of the potential power and danger of the lowlier figures in the court. *optimi cuiusque* stands in implicit contrast to Vatinius himself, and there is evident disgust as Tacitus reports how a shoeshop-born, crippled jester from Beneventum brought about the downfall of noble Romans. The mention of *criminatione* (by accusing) tells us that Vatinius became a *delator* ('informer'): under the one-man rule of imperial Rome, many men found riches and favour by informing on their fellow citizens and having them condemned.[129] Informers populate Tacitus' *Annals* from 1.74 onwards.

eo usque valuit, ut...: The strongly-phrased result clause (to the point that...) makes clear how dramatically his power grew by his ignoble informing.

---

128   So Henderson; see further Henderson (2004) 77.
129   On the 'informer' see Introduction Section 2 and 6.

ut gratia pecunia vi nocendi etiam malos praemineret: The asyndetic tricolon, which consists of three ablatives of means, enumerates what Vatinius had gained under Nero: (i) *gratia*, by seeming to be particularly loyal to the emperor and by inspiring fear in the other courtiers; (ii) *pecunia*, because the confiscated property of the accused was often given in part to the informer; and (iii) *vi nocendi*, since influence at court and financial resources under Nero's regime yield great power to cause even further damage and harm. The punch-line comes at the end: Vatinius' influence at court is such that he stands out even among the *mali* – in Tacitus' imperial Rome that took some doing. The word ('bad men/crooks'), which refers to Nero's other courtiers, casts them as a thoroughly reprehensible lot, while the fact that Vatinius outdid 'even' (*etiam*) them makes clear how abysmal a character he was. Tacitus uses the verb *praeminere* ('to become pre-eminent over', 'to excel') with cutting sarcasm: like the English 'pre-eminent', it is usually a very positive word, implying superiority and nobility; but in the twisted world of Nero's court, Vatinius became 'pre-eminent' by being even more appalling and immoral than the rest. Turning physical impairment into a double plus, the jester turned informer rose to be a powerful – *towering* – strongman (*valuit, vi, praemineret*).

Chapter 35

35.1 Eius munus frequentanti Neroni ne inter voluptates quidem a sceleribus cessabatur. isdem quippe illis diebus Torquatus Silanus mori adigitur, quia super Iuniae familiae claritudinem divum Augustum abavum ferebat.

Nero, so Tacitus implies, was such an inveterate criminal that he planned his misdeed even during hours devoted to public entertainment. That he did not even cease from plotting murder while indulging in pleasure suggests that far from being mutually exclusive *voluptas* and *scelus* coincide in Nero's case, highlighting the emperor's savage and sadistic cruelty. The effect is enhanced by the use of the plural for both pleasures (*voluptates*) and crimes (*a sceleribus*): Nero is a perverse and criminal polymorph. Here the victim is Decimus Junius Silanus Torquatus, one of the consuls of AD 53 (at the end of the emperor Claudius' reign: see *Annals* 12.58). Like Nero, he was a great-great-grandson of Augustus – a lineage that turned him into a potential rival to the throne (see *Family*

Tree). The murder harks back to the very beginning of Tacitus' Nero-narrative, which poignantly starts with the death of Silanus' brother (Annals 13.1.1–2, cited in the Introduction, Section 5). Like mother, like son, who, now fully grown-up, no longer needs parental guidance to commit murder (having honed his skills by doing away with his own mother).

eius munus frequentanti Neroni ... cessabatur: *eius* refers back to Vatinius. *munus* is the gladiatorial games that Vatinius put on; it is the accusative object of the present participle *frequentanti*, which modifies *Neroni* (a dative of agency with the passive *cessabatur*).

isdem quippe illis diebus Torquatus Silanus mori adigitur: Cassius Dio has the following account (62.27.2): 'Junius Torquatus, a descendant of Augustus, was handed over for punishment on a remarkable charge. He had squandered his property rather prodigally, whether following his native bent or with the deliberate intention of not being very rich. Nero therefore declared that, as he lacked many things, he must be covetous of the goods of others, and consequently caused a fictitious charge to be brought against him of aspiring to the imperial power.' As discussed above, he places the enforced suicide in the following year. Notice the sardonic pseudo-parallelism between Nero 'driven by desire' and Silanus 'driven to death' (*adigebatur*, 33.1 ~ *adigit*, 35.1).

quia super Iuniae familiae claritudinem divum Augustum abavum ferebat: The Junian family was one of Rome's oldest and grandest patrician families (i.e. descended from Rome's original senate). Its most famous scions were the two Bruti, one of whom expelled the kings from Rome in 509 BC, the other who led the assassins of Julius Caesar in 44 BC. The immense nobility and antiquity of his lineage make him an especially dangerous threat to Nero.

[*Extra information:*

As John Henderson reminds us, 'the Junii Silani chapter in Syme's *Augustan Aristocracy* is maybe *the* most powerful performance of prosopography – and of death by prosopography, or sentencing-by stemma-under-tyranny.' And he elaborates: 'Rhetorically mixing Junius Silanus in with the sordid jester's fun and gladiatorial games gives Tacitus another chance to pump up the disgust: *as if* the bluest of blue nobles was not just liquidated but given the imperial thumbsdown – humiliated as star victim out in the arena among the condemned criminals and slaves. But this pathetically stark notice of elimination – earning no more coverage than that solo concert and those small beer games – *also* keeps the continuing story of the Silani (begun way back even *before* "great-great-grandfather" Augustus, and folding in the weight of the entire roll-call of Roman history since the republic began) as Nero's prime alternatives-and-targets stoked: where the reign (and *Annals'* Neronian hexad) began (*prima novo principatu mors Iunii Silanus* ..., 13.1.1), all but ceased (in the Pisonian Conspiracy, where Piso feared the next Silanus in line as *his* likely rival for the throne, 15.52), and plunged into non-stop purge (16.7-9, that next-in-line goes down valiantly fighting the emperor's hitmen): the nadir comes when a senator gets the three months April to *June* re-branded for Nero, Claudius and Germanicus, the last because the crimes of the Junii Torquati had made the name 'June-ius' unholy! (16.12) Finally, for the finale in our MSS, Thrasea Paetus provokes *his* martyrdom *inter alia* by public display of outrage for the Silani (16.22).']

35.2 iussi accusatores obicere prodigum largitionibus, neque aliam spem quam in rebus novis esse: quin inter libertos habere, quos ab epistulis et libellis et rationibus appellet, nomina summae curae et meditamenta.

iussi accusatores: The emphatic first position of *iussi* enacts Nero's decisive, unhesitating actions, ordering men to bring trumped-up charges against Torquatus.

obicere prodigum largitionibus: *obicere* introduces an indirect statement, with both the subject accusative (*eum*, sc. *Torquatum*) and the verb (*esse*) elided. *prodigum* stands in predicative position to the implied subject accusative: '...that he was excessively generous in his munificence.' As Miller points out, these two well-chosen words 'accuse him of being (*a*) poor, and so dangerous, as seeing in revolution his only hope of recouping his fortunes [cf. *neque aliam spem quam in rebus novis esse*], (*b*) responsible for his poverty, because of extravagance, and (*c*) over-generous, with overtones of bribery.'[130] Excessive munificence is one of the hallmarks of the tyrant since it secures willing followers who hope for more, so Torquatus' profligacy is

---

130   Miller (1975) 84.

turned into an implicit threat to Nero. Cassius Dio (cited above) suggests that Torquatus gave away his wealth as a safety measure, to pre-empt being murdered to fill the imperial purse. Under Nero, plain to see, it's damned if you do and damned if you don't.

quin inter libertos: We are still hearing the charges made against him. The use of *quin* ('moreover') here helps the accusers to magnify his treason. All large Roman households had freedmen in senior positions who managed the business and administrative responsibilities of their masters.

ab epistulis et libellis et rationibus appellet: Under the Republic, these titles would have been common in noble households. However, with the imperial household becoming the centre of power, these titles became essentially offices of state, which in turn meant that their use by anyone else but the emperor could be interpreted as a sign that this person harboured hopes of usurping the throne. The polysyndeton again exaggerates the number of Torquatus' crimes.

nomina summae curae et meditamenta: The genitive of quality *summae curae* ('of the highest, i.e. imperial, administration') goes with both *nomina* and *meditamenta* (a Tacitean neologism for *meditatio*). Nero's henchmen charge Torquatus with putting on a dress-rehearsal for his ascent to the throne, which implies that he is plotting Nero's overthrow.

35.3 tum intimus quisque libertorum vincti abreptique; et cum damnatio instaret, brachiorum venas Torquatus interscidit. secutaque Neronis oratio ex more, quamvis sontem et defensioni merito diffisum victurum tamen fuisse, si clementiam iudicis exspectasset.

intimus quisque libertorum vincti abreptique [sc. *sunt*]: Nero's henchmen go for Torquatus' key servants: *intimus quisque* (singular in form, but plural in sense – hence the verbs are in the plural) refers to those whom he held in closest confidence.

cum damnatio instaret, brachiorum venas Torquatus interscidit: Torquatus knew which way the wind was blowing and took the usual way out while the final verdict was still outstanding: 'Suicide was employed (A. 6,29) to anticipate condemnation, and to ensure an easier death, proper burial and the validity of the accused's will.'[131] For special effect, Tacitus again delays subject (*Torquatus*) and verb (*interscidit*) till the very end, though readers would have known what was coming after the accusative object (placed up front) *brachiorum venas*.

secuta [sc. *est*] **Neronis oratio**: *oratio* implies that Nero spoke in an official setting, perhaps in front of the senate. The inversion of normal word order, which gives special prominence to the verb *secuta*, makes clear the immediacy of Nero's statement, adding pathos and the irony that, straight after he all but forced Torquatus to suicide, the emperor claims that he would have spared his life if only he had waited.

ex more: This phrase is loaded with Tacitus' dark cynicism and despair: this, he says, was common practice under the emperors. In *Annals* 2.31, the emperor Tiberius did and said the same thing after forcing a senator called Libo to commit suicide: it seems this was a method the emperor could use to achieve what he desired and still maintain a pretence of clemency.

quamvis sontem et defensioni merito diffisum victurum tamen fuisse, si clementiam iudicis exspectasset: Tacitus summarizes Nero's oration in indirect speech: the subject accusative of the apodosis, sc. *Torquatum* (modified by *sontem* and *diffisum* in predicative position), is implied; the verb is *victurum fuisse*. Of course Nero does not concede that Torquatus was innocent; rather, he goes out of his way to stress that he was guilty. First, we have the emphatically placed *sontem*; then comes the comment that he was right to lose confidence in his defence (*defensioni merito diffisum*). Put differently, Nero here twists Torquatus' suicide into a confession of guilt. This serves him as foil to promote his mercy: he would have pardoned a man whom he knew to be plotting against him. After what has just been said, Tacitus is leading his reader to say, 'Yeah right!'

clementiam iudicis: Emperors liked to be able to boast mercy as one of their virtues (remember Nero's rapprochement with Thrasea at 15.23), and Nero's tutor Seneca had written a treatise entitled *de Clementia*, 'On Mercy', as a guide for Nero in his boyhood. The *iudex* Nero mentions is he himself, either because some trials of this type were held *intra cubiculum* (i.e. behind closed doors in the imperial palace): see *Annals* 11.2 for an example; or because he

---

131   Miller (1975) 84.

could have vetoed the capital punishment handed out by a senatorial jury (as he wished to do – but was pre-empted by Thrasea – in the case of Antistius: see *Annals* 14.49, cited in the Introduction, Section 6). That Tacitus presents Nero as referring to himself in the third person generates more of that ironic tone with which Tacitus has imbued this little story. 'Nero said that he would have been saved, if only he'd waited for a fair, merciful judge... like Nero!' At the same time, as John Henderson points out to us, Nero might well have acted on the principle *nomen est omen* ('the name is a portent') in driving Iunius Silanus *Torquatus* into suicide: 'Besides the hallowed/dangerous name of Iunius, our Silanus sports the legendary badge of honour "Torquatus" originally acquired by T. Manlius in solo victory over a champion Gaul (followed by decapitation and removal of his golden "torque", or "necklace" > hence "Torquatus"); besides the degradation of this pre-sentencing suicide, there is the force of the legend's sequel to reckon with, as marked by the Roman proverb *"imperia Manliana"*, where Torquatus now in command did not celebrate his son's copycat solo combat victory but instead had him executed for leaving the ranks without first asking permission (see Livy 8.7.8–22 for the gruesome details). Like everyone else, Nero knew perfectly well that "clemency" was *not* supposed to run in, or apply to, this family!'

(iii) 36: Nero considers, but then reconsiders, going on tour to Egypt

Chapter 36

36.1 Nec multo post omissa in praesens Achaia (causae in incerto fuere) urbem revisit, provincias Orientis, maxime Aegyptum, secretis imaginationibus agitans. dehinc edicto testificatus non longam sui absentiam et cuncta in re publica perinde immota ac prospera fore, super ea profectione adiit Capitolium.

nec multo post omissa in praesens Achaia: *nec* = *et non*, with the *non* negating the ablative of the measure of difference *multo*: 'not by much.' *multo* modifies the adverb post ('later', 'afterwards'). *omissa ... Achaia* is an ablative absolute, and *in praesens* another adverbial phrase of time ('for the moment'). The sentence harks back to 34.1 where Tacitus mentioned that Nero came to Beneventum on his way to Greece, at which point the narrative took a detour with the character portrayal of Vatinius and the Silanus affair. Nero returned to the idea of touring Greece in AD 66, but the part of the *Annals* that would have covered the tour is unfortunately lost. Tacitus here employs very vague temporal markers (what does *non multo post* mean, precisely?), arguably to obfuscate that he is playing fast and loose with facts and chronology – certainly to pretend to bracket off the (displaced) rubbing out of Silanus *as if* merely incidental to the chief narrative thread, storming the world of song. (Before 'revisiting' Beneventum.)

causae in incerto fuere: *fuere* = *fuerunt*. If the assumption is correct that Tacitus made up Nero's desire to tour Greece in AD 64 and then abandoning the plan, it hardly surprises that his reasons for not going remain obscure. At the same time, the phrase adds an air of intrigue to Nero's alleged change of heart. Did he hear about a conspiracy? Was the affair of Torquatus more serious? Was he more alarmed by events in Neapolis than he made out? The silence of this parenthesis adds drama, certainly. And by contrast it underlines that the reasons for getting rid of Silanus were unmistakeable, however nonchalantly Nero assured us otherwise.

urbem: Usually, as here, Rome.

provincias Orientis, maxime Aegyptum, secretis imaginationibus agitans: Tacitus here gives a standard idiom a lurid twist: *agitare aliquid/ de aliqua re* in the sense of 'to drive at a thing in the mind, to consider, meditate upon' often takes an ablative of place (with or without *in*), such as *in corde*, *in mente*, or *animo*. Here we get the highly suggestive *secretis imaginationibus* ('in his private delusions', 'in his secret fancies'). The rare, ponderous, noun *imaginatio*, to be sure, fits the object of Nero's obsession – in Rome's cultural imagination the Eastern part of the Mediterranean was associated with fables and fantasies as well as an elaborate culture of performance, from drama to music. But we may wonder how Tacitus could have had evidence of the day-dreams of the emperor. As with the abandoned trip to Greece, the historiographer here adopts a stance of impossible omniscience. The trip to the Near East, though, acquired a different degree of reality: as the following sentences make clear, Nero 'staged', in the most public fashion, his decision both to go – and not to go.

dehinc: Like *nec multo post*, this word ('then') keeps the action racing forward, presenting us with a picture of an extremely impulsive emperor leaping from one thing to another: first Greece, then not, then considering the East, then the plan is off.

edicto testificatus: Nero announces his plans to depart for the Near East in a public edict, combining the announcement of his absence from the capital with reassurances that he would not stay long and take measures to ensure the continued well-being of the capital. In other words, he counterbalances an action that could be interpreted negatively on the part of the people (departure from Rome, to honour another city with his presence) with declaring his abiding affection and concern for the urban populace even in his absence. All of this formed part of the elaborate system of symbolic communication between the emperor and the groups that sustained his reign. At the same time, Tacitus conveys something of Nero's egomaniac fantasizing: the imperial genius is frustrated in having to keep his talent close at home when he wants it to light up *his* world-empire.

non longam sui absentiam [sc. *fore*]: An indirect statement dependent on *testificatus*. This is Nero's first reassurance to the anxious (as Nero believes) people: he will not be gone long. The *sui* (his own) is not grammatically necessary, but is there to underscore Nero's realization that the people would be concerned to hear that he was going away. For a senatorial historiographer such as Tacitus, the proximity and affection between the people and the emperor would be grating. Horace, in an *Ode* addressed to Augustus while he was absent on campaign in Gaul, presents both the people and the senate as yearning for his return to the capital (4.5.1–8: *Divis orte bonis, optime Romulae* | *custos gentis, abes iam nimium diu:* | *maturum reditum pollicitus patrum* | *sancto concilio, redi.* | | *lucem redde tuae, dux bone, patriae.* | *instar veris enim vultus ubi tuus* | *affulsit populo, gratior it dies* | *et soles melius nitent*: 'Descended from the good divinities, excellent guardian of the Romulan race, you have been absent for too long: come back in haste as you promised the sacred council of senators. Bring back light to your country, good leader. When like springtime your face has shown upon the people, the day goes by more pleasantly and the rays of the sun shine more brightly.') Horace's harmonious *menage à trois* of *princeps*, senate, and people contrasts sharply with the dysfunctional relationships between these three constituencies of Roman imperial rule under Nero – as well as underscording the indispensability of the emperor's presence in Rome.

cuncta in re publica perinde immota ac prospera fore: Tacitus endows Nero's formulations with unintended irony: the great fire of Rome is only a paragraph away.

super ea profectione adiit Capitolium: The Capitoline Hill was the religious and ceremonial heart of the city and the empire. The temple of Jupiter Optimus Maximus Capitolinus, with the associated cults of Juno and Minerva, was the focus of Rome's official religion. There is something perverse about Nero's visit to the Capitol: in the 'old days', generals on the way to wars would have gone to pray to Jupiter, and it was also on the route of the triumphal procession for victorious generals; but now Nero goes there to pray for the help of the mighty Jupiter Optimus Maximus for his theatrical trip to the East.

super ea profectione: The preposition *super* here as a causal sense: 'on account of.'

36.2 illic veneratus deos, cum Vestae quoque templum inisset, repente cunctos per artus tremens, seu numine exterrente, seu facinorum recordatione numquam timore vacuus, deseruit inceptum, cunctas sibi curas amore patriae leviores dictitans.

veneratus ..., cum ... inisset, tremens ... seu numine exterrente ... seu ... numquam ... vacuus ... deseruit inceptum: The main verb of the sentence comes at last after the long build up of participles and subordinate clauses. The syntax conveys a sense of Nero's mounting anxiety until the breaking point, represented by the two-word clause *deseruit inceptum*.

veneratus deos: There were temples to many deities on the Capitoline, not just Jupiter.

Vestae ... templum: The temple of Vesta was in the Roman Forum just below the Capitoline Hill. Vesta was the goddess of the hearth and the Roman family: Nero is creating the image of a father leaving his family on his travels.

repente cunctos per artus tremens: Nero's fear manifests itself in physical symptoms. The sudden onset of Nero's panic is made clear by *repente*, and the extent of it by *cunctos* and the vivid verb *tremens*.

seu ... seu...: This technique of 'alternative motivation' is common in Tacitus.[132] When he provides two reasons for an event or phenomenon, the second one given is generally the one he wishes to stress. (It tends to be the more discreditable one as well.) This is the case here. The ploy also allows him to suggest things without affirming them, to force us to make up our minds as to which is more plausible, while also pushing one option as more likely. Tacitus' spin stands out particularly clearly if juxtaposed to the account of the incident in Suetonius' biography (*Nero* 19.1): *Peregrinationes duas omnino suscepit, Alexandrinam et Achaicam; sed Alexandrina ipso profectionis die destitit turbatus religione simul ac periculo. Nam cum circumitis templis in aede Vestae resedisset, consurgenti ei primum lacinia obhaesit, dein tanta oborta caligo est, ut dispicere non posset* ('He planned but two foreign tours, to Alexandria and Achaia; and he gave up the former on the very day when he was to have started, disturbed by a threatening portent. For as he was making the round of the temples and had sat down in the shrine of Vesta, first the fringe of his garment was caught when he attempted to get up, and then such darkness overspread his eyes that he could see nothing').[133] Suetonius reports an actual incident (Nero's garment getting caught) that could be interpreted as a sign from the gods; Tacitus construes divine agency differently – he raises the possibility that they addled his brain with fear *directly*, i.e. without an empirical sign that others could witness (cf. *numine exterrente*; the formulation does not exclude the portent that Suetonius reports, but it suppresses vital information), before suggesting that the reason might be the mental disturbance caused by Nero's prior crimes that come back to haunt him (again something that cannot be verified empirically). Put differently, Tacitus removes the incident from the sphere of empirical observation, explanation, and communication and locates it entirely in the psychology of Nero.

seu numine exterrente: Tacitus uses a (short) ablative absolute for the first option, suggesting that Nero's fear may be due to a terrifying experience at

---

132 Miller (1975) 85.

133 Caligula, too, was reported to have harboured plans to move to Alexandria after perpetrating mass slaughter among the Roman élite – a plot that Suetonius presents as the final straw that led to his assassination. See *Caligula* 49.2: *...periit, ingentia facinora ausus et aliquanto maiora moliens, siquidem proposuerat Antium, deinde Alexandream commigrare interempto prius utriusque ordinis electissimo quoque* ('... he perished, having dared great crimes and meditating still greater ones. For he had made up his mind to move to Antium, and later to Alexandria, after first slaying the noblest members of the two orders').

the hands of the divine power of the temple. The implied accusative object of *exterrente* is *eum/Neronem*. The strengthened verb <u>ex</u>terrente makes clear just how much the *numen* managed to frighten the emperor (if it did).

seu facinorum recordatione numquam timore vacuus: The second option is stressed by its length and its more complex syntax. The advanced position of *facinorum* draws attention to them as the likely cause of Nero's sudden trembling. The litotes of *numquam timore vacuus* stresses the power of the frightful memories lodged in his brain. It is an arresting image: Nero, as he looks upon the images of the gods, breaking down in terror as he remembers the crimes he has committed.

facinorum: Tacitus will be thinking especially of Nero's murder of his half-brother Britannicus in AD 55, whose drink he poisoned; of his mother Agrippina in AD 59, stabbed by his soldiers at his behest; and of the many senators whom he forced to die. (The murder of Silanus is still fresh in the mind of Tacitus' readers and, so Tacitus suggests, also stayed fresh in the mind of the emperor.) Tacitus emphasises Nero's fear elsewhere in the *Annals*. See, for instance, 14.10.1 (in the wake of the matricide): *Sed a Caesare perfecto demum scelere magnitudo eius intellecta est. reliquo noctis modo per silentium defixus, saepius pavore exsurgens et mentis inops lucem opperiebatur tamquam exitium adlaturam* ('But only with the completion of the crime was its magnitude realized by the Caesar. For the rest of the night, sometimes dumb and motionless, but not rarely starting in terror to his feet with a sort of delirium, he waited for the daylight which he believed would bring his end.').

*[**Extra information**:*

For Nero suffering from bouts of religious anxiety, see also Suetonius, *Nero* 46.1: *Terrebatur ad hoc evidentibus portentis somniorum et auspiciorum et omnium, cum veteribus tum novis. Numquam antea somniare solitus occisa demum matre vidit per quietem navem sibi regenti extortum gubernaculum trahique se ab Octavia uxore in artissimas tenebras et modo pinnatarum formicarum multitudine oppleri, modo a simulacris gentium ad Pompei theatrum dedicatarum circumiri arcerique progressu; asturconem, quo maxime laetabatur, posteriore corporis parte in simiae speciem transfiguratum ac tantum capite integro hinnitus edere canoros* ('In addition he was frightened by manifest portents from dreams, auspices and omens, both old and new. Although he had never before been in the habit of dreaming, after he had killed his mother it seemed to him that he was steering a ship in his sleep and that the helm was wrenched from his hands; that he was dragged by his wife Octavia into thickest darkness, and that he was covered with a swarm of winged ants, and now was surrounded by the statues of the nations which had been dedicated in Pompey's theatre and stopped in his tracks. A Spanish steed of which he was very fond was changed into the form of an ape in the hinder parts of its body, and its head, which alone remained unaltered, gave forth tuneful neighs').]

cunctas sibi curas amore patriae leviores dictitans: *amore* is an ablative of comparison after the comparative *leviores*. Nero stressed repeatedly (note the frequentative verb *dictito*) that love for this country outweighed any of his other concerns. But the way that Tacitus puts the point still makes Nero appear selfish: *sibi* is a dative of interest, whereas *cura*, in the parlance of politics, refers to the diligent management of state affairs, public duties, and civic responsibilities. The use of this term here in the basic sense of 'thought' or 'concerns' is thus disconcerting (not to say perverse), especially in contrast to the effusive and emotional term *amor*. It points up Nero as an incompetent regent of the empire, who oscillates between selfish interests and empty gestures of affection for his people.

36.3 vidisse maestos civium vultus, audire secretas querimonias, quod tantum itineris aditurus esset, cuius ne modicos quidem egressus tolerarent, sueti adversum fortuita aspectu principis refoveri. ergo ut in privatis necessitudinibus proxima pignora praevalerent, ita in re publica populum Romanum vim plurimam habere parendumque retinenti.

This and the next two sentences are in indirect speech, reporting what Nero said.

vidisse maestos civium vultus, audire secretas querimonias: The two asyndetic phrases are well balanced: two verbs of perceiving at the beginning (*vidisse, audire*; see end of note for the shift from perfect to present), followed by two accusative objects, consisting of an attribute (*maestos, secretas*) and a noun (*vultus, querimonias*), with the genitive *civium* best understood as modifying both. Despite the placement of *civium* in the first phrase, the second is slightly, climactically longer in terms of syllables: 3 + 2 + 3 + 2 vs. 3 + 3 + 5. Alliteration (*vidisse* – *vultus*) adds further stylistic colour to the first phrase and homoioteleuton (*-tas*, *-as*) to the second. Such rhetorical balance is very un-Tacitean, but remember that here we are hearing Nero's words – Tacitus imbues the speech with the sort of oratorical patterning that, for him, suggests hypocrisy. The change of tense of the infinitives is significant: the perfect *vidisse* tells us that the people's faces struck him in the past, but the present *audire* implies that the complaints of the people are still ringing in his ears, even though they are private. That Nero is partial to what people say 'off-record' as it were could be open to a sinister interpretation: he has spies everywhere.

tantum itineris aditurus esset: *itineris* is a partitive genitive dependent on *tantum*. Any absence of the emperor from Rome was a potential source of disquiet for the urban populace, and Nero's trip to Alexandria would have taken several months.

cuius ne modicos quidem egressus tolerarent: *cuius*, the genitive singular of the relative pronoun, refers to Nero and depends on *egressus* (accusative plural). The (implied) subject is the citizens. Nero, putting words into the mouths of his subjects, claims they cannot bear any absence of his: if they cannot even (*ne ... quidem*) endure his short (*modicos*) absences from the city, how are they to cope with a long one? Tacitus mischievously has Nero out himself here as someone with a tendency towards immoderate actions – recall 15.23 where he portrayed the emperor as *immodicus* in both joy and grief.

sueti adversum fortuita aspectu principis refoveri: *suetus* is the perfect participle of *suesco* ('accustomed'), here construed with the infinitive (*refoveri*). *fortuita* is an adjective used as a noun: it is a neuter accusative plural ('the contingencies of life') governed by the preposition *adversum*. Nero imagines the people consoled in the face of adversity by his presence. The vivid verb *refoveri* (literally, 'to be warmed up again' = 'to be revived') gives a sense of Nero's warming glow for his people, and this is caused not even by his actions but merely by being seen (*aspectu*). (It is tempting to take *refoveri* as a proleptic reference to the fire – Nero sure knows how to make the city glow...)

ergo ut in privatis necessitudinibus proxima pignora praevalerent, ita in re publica populum Romanum vim plurimam habere parendumque retinenti: The indirect speech continues: after the *ut*-clause we first have *populum Romanum* as the subject accusative and *habere* as the infinitive verb, to which Tacitus attaches a further clause, but with a change in construction: the *-que* links *habere* and the impersonal gerundive *parendum* [sc. *esse*]. *parere* takes a dative object, here an (elided) *ei*, referring back to *populum Romanum*, and governing the present participle *retinenti*. (One has to supply the accusative object for *retinere* – i.e. Nero.) In all, then, Nero is saying that 'the people, which are holding [him] back, must be obeyed.' Nero here makes a show of modesty, conceding that even the emperor must acquiesce to the wishes of the Roman people. Arguably, Tacitus here hints at the alternative scenario that we capture in Suetonius, namely that Nero was literally 'held back' (if momentarily) by a divine power in the temple of Vesta when his garment was caught (see *Nero* 19.1, cited above). Note the pronounced *p*-alliteration throughout by which Tacitus links – ominously for anyone harbouring republican sentiments – the private sphere (cf. *privatis, proxima, pignora, praevalerent*) with the public sphere (cf. *publica, populum, plurimam, parendum*), implying an assimilation of the two: under bad rulers such as Nero, who did not live up to the ideal of the *civilis princeps*, the *res publica* became for all intents and purposes coextensive with the household of the emperor.

privatis necessitudinibus: 'family obligations.'

proxima pignora: *pignora*, the subject of the *ut*-clause, here has the meaning of 'kin' – in the context of family obligations the closest kin has the greatest influence.

36.4 haec atque talia plebi volentia fuere, voluptatum cupidine et, quae praecipua cura est, rei frumentariae angustias, si abesset, metuenti. senatus et primores in incerto erant procul an coram atrocior haberetur: dehinc, quae natura magnis timoribus, deterius credebant quod evenerat.

haec atque talia plebi volentia fuere: *volentia* is the present participle in the nominative neuter plural of *volo* ('matters desirable' – *plebi*: to the people) and predicative complement to *haec atque talia*. It alliterates with *voluptatum*, suggesting that the people are slaves to desire.

voluptatum cupidine et, quae praecipua cura est, rei frumentariae angustias, si abesset, metuenti: Tacitus goes on to explain why the things Nero said pleased the people, linking, with *et*, an ablative of cause (*voluptatum cupidine*) and a participle with causal force (*metuenti*: it is in the dative since it modifies *plebi*). *angustias* is the accusative object of *metuenti* and the antecedent of the relative pronoun *quae*. Authors steeped in aristocratic ideology like Tacitus routinely mis-represent the people as motivated by base instincts and desires – a condition that Juvenal captures for ancient Rome in the pithy phrase *panem et circenses* ('bread and circuses'). See *Satire* 10.78–81:[134]

> nam qui dabat olim
>
> imperium, fasces, legiones, omnia, nunc se
>
> continet atque duas tantum res anxius optat,   80
>
> panem et circenses.

[The people that once used to bestow military commands, high office, legions, everything, now limits itself. It has an obsessive desire for two things only – bread and circuses.]

Tacitus, too, puts the emphasis on entertainment and food supply. The latter concern is expressed in much longer and more complex syntax, compared to the two words (*voluptatum cupidine*) dedicated to entertainment. The *variatio* lends more weight to the latter, not least because of the emphatic final position of *metuenti*, which renders it apparent that fear of corn shortage was greater than desire for games. We should note that these *real* reasons for the people's anxiety about Nero's absence bear no relation to Nero's speech: there's nothing here about Nero the father-figure or the consolation he gives in adversity; according to Tacitus, the people just care about being entertained and their bellies.

voluptatum cupidine: Tacitus here voices his (elitist) despair at the (perceived) pleasure-loving populace and the ease with which they are won over. The two words (desire for pleasures) are very negative words in Roman morality: *cupido* represents a strong lust or desire; and the plural of *voluptas* is a loaded word for moralising Roman historians – rather

---

134   We cite the text and translation of S. Morton Braund in the Loeb Classical Library (Cambridge, Mass. and London, 2004).

than the more neutral meaning of the singular ('pleasure', 'delight'), the plural often has the idea of sensual gratification or indulgence.

praecipua cura: Rome's huge population was dependent on corn from overseas, especially Egypt and Sicily. The populace were concerned that they be entertained, but even more so (*praecipua* = greatest, especial) that they be fed. Ensuring sufficient supply of free or highly subsidized grain to the urban populace was a major responsibility of the ruling élite, the designated officer, and, ultimately, the *princeps*. Neglect or failure could lead to riots.[135]

si abesset: The people feared that *if* he was absent, *then* there might be shortages in corn supply.

senatus et primores in incerto erant, procul an coram atrocior haberetur: After the plebs' reaction, Tacitus now tells us how the upper echelons responded to Nero's decision to remain in Rome. Their reaction is much more ambivalent, and their priorities rather different from the people's concern with the corn supply and games. They do not wonder whether he would be better near or far, but where he would be more dreadful (*atrocior*), implying of course that wherever he is, far or near (*procul an coram*), he is a horrendous prospect. The adjective *atrocior* is a very strong one, implying cruelty and savagery.

procul an coram atrocior haberetur: *an* introduces an indirect question, specifying two alternatives (*procul* or *coram*); *haberetur* = to be regarded as. The subject is Nero; *atrocior* is a predicative complement.

dehinc, quae natura [sc. *est*] **magnis timoribus, deterius credebant quod evenerat:** Being undecided as to whether Nero's absence or presence would result in the greater atrocities, they believed that worse which then actually happened (*quod evenerat*). Tacitus considers this psychological reaction a law of nature (cf. *quae natura magnis timoribus*). Do you agree?

---

135   See in general Garnsey (1988).

(IV) 37: TO SHOW HIS LOVE FOR ROME, NERO CELEBRATES A HUGE PUBLIC ORGY THAT SEGUES INTO A MOCK-WEDDING WITH HIS FREEDMAN PYTHAGORAS

Chapter 37

37.1 Ipse quo fidem adquireret nihil usquam perinde laetum sibi, publicis locis struere convivia totaque urbe quasi domo uti. et celeberrimae luxu famaque epulae fuere quas a Tigellino paratas ut exemplum referam, ne saepius eadem prodigentia narranda sit.

Tacitus suggests that even Nero knows deep down that the people don't believe he chose to stay in Rome for patriotic reasons, and feels the need to win the people's belief in his claims (*fidem adquireret*). The claim is made implausible, not just by his need to prove it but by the exaggerated nature of it. Nero's use of public places for his own private purposes is ominous and foreshadows the fact that eventually, after the Great Fire, Nero will build himself an enormous mansion in the centre of the city, the so-called *Domus Aurea* ('Golden House'). The emphatic position of *publicis*, and the arresting hyperbole of *tota urbe* (the whole city) being used like a private home (*quasi domo*) underline Nero's abuse of Rome's communal areas. The *domus* is the essence of private life, so *domo* is set in stark contrast to *publicis locis* to further stress the emperor's usurpation of Rome for his own personal uses. Tacitus' narrative then takes a subtle turn, gliding from a banquet staged with a specific rationale to a more general description of how Nero and his entourage carried on. He picks out the most notorious banquet (organized by Tigellinus, a freedman and Nero's Praetorian Prefect) as an illustrative example of the public debauchery rampant in Nero's Rome. Throughout the passage, Tacitus uses rare or unusual words or phrases to enhance the sense of exotic extravagance: see *prodigentia* (37.1), *superpositum* (37.2), *tractu* (37.2), *abusque* (37.2), *crepidinibus* (37.3), *lupanaria* (37.3), *obsceni* (37.3), and *tenebrae incedebant* (37.3). Cassius Dio, too, has a detailed description of the event (62.15):

> To such lengths did Nero's licence go that he actually drove chariots in public. And on one occasion after exhibiting a wild-beast hunt he immediately piped water into the theatre and produced a sea-fight; then he let the water out again and arranged a gladiatorial combat. Last of all, he flooded the place once more and gave a costly public banquet. 2 Tigellinus had been appointed director of the banquet and everything had been provided on a lavish scale.

The arrangements made were as follows. In the centre of the lake there had first been lowered the great wooden casks used for holding wine, and on top of these, planks had been fastened, 3 while round about this platform taverns and booths had been erected. Thus Nero and Tigellinus and their fellow-banqueters occupied the centre, where they held their feast on purple rugs and soft cushions, while all the rest made merry in the taverns. 4 They would also enter the brothels and without let or hindrance have intercourse with any of the women who were seated there, among whom were the most beautiful and distinguished in the city, both slaves and free, courtesans and virgins and married women; and these were not merely of the common people but also of the very noblest families, both girls and grown women. 5 Every man had the privilege of enjoying whichever one he wished, as the women were not allowed to refuse anyone. Consequently, indiscriminate rabble as the throng was, they not only drank greedily but also wantoned riotously; and now a slave would debauch his mistress in the presence of his master, and now a gladiator would debauch a girl of noble family before the eyes of her father. 6 The pushing and fighting and general uproar that took place, both on the part of those who were actually going in and on the part of those who were standing around outside, were disgraceful. Many men met their death in these encounters, and many women, too, some of the latter being suffocated and some being seized and carried off.

What makes Tacitus' handling of this incident special, however, is the way in which he links the orgy Nero celebrates at Rome to his abandoned plan to tour Egypt and the East. As Tony Woodman has shown in his seminal article 'Nero's Alien Capital: Tacitus as Paradoxographer (*Annals* 15. 36–7)', Tacitus suggests throughout this paragraph that Nero has managed to turn Rome *into* Alexandria, a cesspool of vice and sexual license.[136] By suggestively juxtaposing his report of Nero's desire to go East and the account of an 'eastern' orgy celebrated by the emperor in Rome, Tacitus subliminally turns Nero into a foreign pervert, who subverts Roman standards of civilization. Put differently, 'he others the emperor', drawing on the prejudices about oriental cultures (and in particular Egypt) that circulated in Rome. The centre that ought to hold the empire together thus emerges as alien and rotten at its core. (The practice of suggestive juxtaposition continues in the following paragraph, where Tacitus begins his account of the great fire of Rome; in other words, he goes from moral to physical chaos, from the metaphorical to the literal ruin of the capital under Nero. The sequence strongly suggests a *'post hoc ergo propter hoc'*, i.e. that the fire not only followed after Nero's debauchery but somehow resulted from it.)

---

136   Woodman (1998).

quo fidem adquireret: A purpose clause: *quo = ut eo*.

nihil usquam perinde laetum sibi: An indirect statement, with the verb (*esse*) elided. *nihil* is the subject accusative, *laetum* the predicative complement. *sibi* is in the dative of personal interest or reference. The adverb *perinde* ('equally', 'to the same degree') modifies *laetum*. Hence: Nero wanted to prove that 'nothing (*nihil*) was ever (*usquam*) to the same degree welcome (*perinde laetum*) to him (*sibi*) [sc. as Rome].'

publicis locis struere convivia totaque urbe quasi domo uti: *struere* and *uti* (linked by the *-que* after *tota*) are historic infinitives (i.e. infinitives used as main verbs). They serve to quicken the pace of the narrative as Nero's immorality spirals to new depths. The verb *struere* is especially interesting: whilst it is used here to mean 'to set up' banquets, it can often be used of 'contriving' or 'plotting' a crime. The word thus contains a hint of the sinister undercurrent to Nero's actions: they are paving the way for future outrages. The arrangement is chiastic: verb (*struere*) + accusative object (*convivia*) :: ablative object (*tota urbe*) + verb (*uti*).

celeberrimae luxu famaque epulae fuere: The superlative *celeberrimae*, qualified by the negative nouns *luxu* and *fama* (both ablatives of respect; *celeberrimae ... fama* is an 'almost tautological expression'[137]), paints a lurid picture of the immorality of the banquet. More generally, banquets in Tacitus are often used as the setting of profound immorality. In *Annals* 14, Nero's incest with his mother, Britannicus' murder, and part of the plot to kill his mother all occurred against the backdrop of a banquet. The decadence and corruption of Nero's court, of which Tacitus never ceases to remind us, make this an appropriate setting for the crimes of the regime and for demonstrations of his extravagance. Tacitus varies his vocabulary (*convivia*, *epulae*) and, with *luxu* (instead of the more common *luxuria*), chooses recherché diction to draw further attention to them and stress the number of degenerate feasts occurring.[138]

---

137 Woodman (1998) 172.
138 See more generally Woodman (2004) xxii: 'given a choice of synonyms, Tacitus often varies the linguistic norm by choosing the less common: *luxus* ("luxuriousness") for *luxuria* ("luxury"), *maestitia* ("sorrowfulness") for *maeror* ("sorrow"), *seruitium* ("servitude") for *seruitus* ("slavery").'

quas a Tigellino paratas [sc. *esse*] **ut exemplum referam, ne saepius eadem prodigentia narranda sit.** Tacitus here runs two sentences into one. Taken apart the Latin would be: *celeberrimae epulae ... fuere, quae a Tigellino [sunt] paratae; quas/ eas ut exemplum referam...* Put differently, the *quas* does double duty as both accusative object of *referam* and as subject accusative of the indirect statement dependent on *referam*. In English, this is impossible to reproduce and it is best to translate with two sentences: 'the most celebrated feasts were those that were arranged by Tigellinus; these I shall describe as an example...' Woodman notes on *quas ... ut exemplum referam*: 'This statement, with its combination of the noun *exemplum* and a first-person verb, is unique in the *Annals* and signals that the following description is digressive. The start of the digression is marked by *Igitur* (37. 2), which picks up *ut exemplum referam*, and its closure is marked by *denique* (37. 4).'[139]

Tigellino: Ofonius Tigellinus was prefect of the Praetorian Guard, the emperor's bodyguard, an extremely influential position under the Caesars. Here he is presented as the architect of an appalling display of imperial decadence.

ne saepius eadem prodigentia narranda sit: One banquet will serve Tacitus as representative of the rest. This approach will save him from having to detail all the other orgies that took place under Nero: *eadem* intimates that Tigellinus' banquet is nothing exceptional – though in reality, Tacitus has surely chosen an event of particular excess and debauchery. The feigned weariness in the *ne*-clause underscores Tacitus' contempt (and his skill in focused, economical exposition), though he also clearly revels in relating this sort of outrage and knows what his readers want, too.

prodigentia: The word seems to be a Tacitean neologism – it occurs nowhere else in Latin literature. Its meaning here is something akin to 'excessive extravagance or prodigality', but its etymological affinity with *prodigium* ('ominous, unnatural occurrence', 'portent') also hints at monstrosity.

37.2 igitur in stagno Agrippae fabricatus est ratem, cui superpositum convivium navium aliarum tractu moveretur. naves auro et ebore distinctae; remigesque exoleti per aetates et scientiam libidinum componebantur. volucres et feras diversis et terris at animalia maris Oceano abusque petiverat.

---

139   Woodman (1998) 171–72.

in stagno Agrippae: The general Agrippa was one of Augustus' closest companions and the architect of his victory at Actium. He also left his mark on the urban topography. Arguably the most famous building he sponsored was the Pantheon. The 'Lake of Agrippa' at issue here was a huge artificial reservoir, built on the Campus Martius in Rome, which supplied the 'Baths of Agrippa' with water and also served as an open-air swimming pool. The invocation of Agrippa – one of Nero's most famous ancestors – is significant: 'Tacitus no doubt relished pointing the contrast between the engineering of Agrippa, Nero's own great-grand-father, and that of Tigellinus, Nero's henchman: the one was intended for use and regular enjoyment, the other exclusively for irregular pleasures.'[140]

cui superpositum convivium navium aliarum tractu moveretur: The antecedent of *cui* is *ratem*. The subject of the relative clause is *convivium*. Tacitus says, literally, that the banquet was moving over the lake, pulled along by other ships (*navium aliorum tractu*).

navium ... naves: A rare repetition for Tacitus, the master of variation. Here the polyptoton helps to generate a picture of the number of boats and to emphasise the diverse uses to which they were put.

naves auro et ebore distinctae: Tacitus continues to describe the physical wonder of the spectacle: the boats were ornately decorated with the most precious materials.

remigesque exoleti per aetates et scientiam libidinum componebantur: Tacitus proceeds to paint his picture: we now see the rowers, usually hardy, strong men but here characterised by the highly derogatory *exoleti*, the perfect passive participle of *exolesco*: the rowers, apparently, were male (pathic) prostitutes. They are arranged according to age (*per aetates*) – and their sexual expertise (*scientiam libidinum*). The suddenness of this revelation is a big surprise after the purely choreographic description so far! So, with extra shock-value for its unexpectedness, the moral degeneracy of the party comes full into view.

volucres et feras diversis e terris et animalia maris Oceano abusque petiverat: The subject is Tigellinus. The accusative objects *volucres et feras* and

---

140 Woodman (1998) 172.

animalia maris are well balanced phrases that, with variation, cover animals of the air (*volucres*), land (*feras*), and sea (*animalia maris*). They come from far-flung and exotic habitats. Just like the phrases for the animals, those Tacitus uses for their location – *diversis e terris* and *Oceano abusque* – feature parallelism with variation: in each case, the preposition (*e*, *abusque*) that governs the ablative comes second (a phenomenon called 'anastrophe'); many words in this sentence are highly literary or poetic, and *abusque* (from *ab + usque*) especially. As Woodman points out, *Oceanoque abusque* 'is a most unusual phrase. The distance from which the creatures have been brought is underlined by the uncommon preposition *abusque*, which itself is further emphasized by being placed after its noun. And when Tacitus elsewhere refers to *Oceanus* in his own person (as opposed to in reported speech), he means a specific sea such as the English Channel or the North Sea; only here does he use *Oceanus* without qualification, evidently referring to the sea or great river which, according to ancient legend, encircled the world but about which even Herodotus expressed some scepticism on several occasions.'[141] For the idea that all the animals are called to the cosmopolis by the blessed world-ruler's magnetism, cf. Calpurnius Siculus 7, on Nero's showpiece. The shepherd Corydon reports that 'he saw every kind of beast' (57: *vidi genus omne ferarum*) during games in the amphitheatre sponsored by the emperor.

37.3 crepidinibus stagni lupanaria adstabant inlustribus feminis completa et contra scorta visebantur nudis corporibus. iam gestus motusque obsceni; et postquam tenebrae incedebant, quantum iuxta nemoris et circumiecta tecta consonare cantu et luminibus clarescere.

crepidinibus stagni: *crepido*, stressed further by its position, is a rare word (a more prosaic synonym would be *ripa*) and reinforces the sense of exoticism and flamboyance of the previous sentence. One could take it as a locative or, more likely, as dative with *adstabant*.

lupanaria adstabant inlustribus feminis completa: *lupanar, -aris* n. is, as Lewis & Short coyly put it in their entry, 'a house of ill-repute' – or, to use the vernacular, a brothel. The disgraceful incongruity of noble women (*inlustribus feminis*) manning brothels sums up the total disintegration of Roman morals. The piety, chastity and virtue of the noble Roman family woman (*matrona*) or maiden (*virgo*) was an essential part of idealised

---

141 Woodman (1998) 175.

Roman morality, and for noble women to be acting (in both senses…) as prostitutes is utterly appalling. Note how they appear in the midst of low, seedy vocabulary: *lupanaria* and, in the next sentence, *scorta* ('whores'). Also, Tacitus does not simply say that there were noble women in the brothel: they were *filled* (*completa*) with them.

et contra scorta visebantur nudis corporibus: *contra* is here used as an adverb, not a preposition; *scorta* is the subject of the sentence.[142] *nudis corporibus*, delayed emphatically to the end, paints a vivid and rude picture and completes the inversions of proper female conduct that Nero's orgy apparently celebrated: 'Facing each other on the banks of Agrippa's lake were upper-class women and low-class prostitutes (37. 3). Normally the former would be parading themselves, behaviour to which *inlustribus* perhaps partly alludes; but *scorta visebantur* suggests that the *feminae* are indoors, as the reference to their housing implies ('lupanaria adstabant … completa'). Conversely, the nakedness of the *scorta* would normally mean that they were out of sight; yet it is they who are on display (*visebantur*). These paradoxes and reversals lead to another. Since the *scorta* are naked (*nudis corporibus*), the suggestion is that the *feminae* are clothed; and, since the *feminae* are also *inlustres*, there is a contrast between their presumed *haute couture* and their incongruous surroundings (*lupanaria*).'[143] Put differently, in the topsy-turvey world Nero created what ought to be out is in, what out to be in is out; what should be in sight isn't, and what is oughtn't.

[*Extra information*:

With Tacitus' account, compare Suetonius, *Nero* 27.2–3, who sketches a general picture of debauchery: *Epulas a medio die ad mediam noctem protrahebat, refotus saepius calidis piscinis ac tempore aestivo nivatis; cenitabatque nonnumquam et in publico, naumachia praeclusa vel Martio campo vel Circo Maximo, inter scortorum totius urbis et ambubaiarum ministeria. quotiens Ostiam Tiberi deflueret aut Baianum sinum praeternavigaret, dispositae per litora et ripas deversoriae tabernae parabantur insignes ganea et matronarum institorio copas imitantium atque hinc inde hortantium ut appelleret. indicebat et familiaribus cenas, quorum uni mitellita quadragies sestertium constitit, alteri pluris aliquanto rosaria.* ('He prolonged his revels from midday to midnight, often livening

---

142   For Latin terms for 'prostitute' see Adams (1983).
143   Woodman (1998) 175–76.

himself by a warm plunge, or, if it were summer, into water cooled with snow. Sometimes too he closed the inlets and banqueted in public in the great tank in the Campus Martius, or in the Circus Maximus, waited on by harlots and dancing girls from all over the city. Whenever he drifted down the Tiber to Ostia, or sailed about the Gulf of Baiae, booths were set up at intervals along the banks and shores, fitted out for debauchery, while bartering matrons played the part of inn-keepers and from every hand solicited him to come ashore. He also levied dinners on his friends, one of whom spent four million sesterces for a banquet at which turbans were the theme, and another a considerably larger sum for a rose dinner').]

iam gestus motusque obsceni [sc. *erant*]: With the adverb *iam* ('already now', i.e. during the hours of daylight – the *iam* sets up the following *postquam tenebrae incedebant*) Tacitus moves from setting the scene to the action. A very short, punchy sentence, made more so by the ellipsis of the verb, draws our attention to what went on. The fact that the gestures and movements are the subjects of the sentence (one could have imagined Tacitus using verbs: 'they moved and gestured...') gives them extra impact and generates the proto-pornographic impression of impersonalized bodies in motion, an impression reinforced by the emphatic, final position of *obsceni*.

quantum iuxta nemoris et circumiecta tecta consonare cantu et luminibus clarescere: The subjects of the sentence are *quantum* and *circumiecta tecta*; *nemoris* is a partitive genitive dependent on *quantum*; *iuxta* is here used adverbially ('in close proximity'); the verbs are the historic infinitives *consonare* and *clarescere*. Stylistic features abound, conveying a sense of the sound level of the raucous party throughout Nero's movie-set pleasure park: note the song-like rhyme in *circumiecta tecta*, the *c*-alliteration *circumiecta – consonare – cantu – clarescere*, and the chiasmus (a) *consonare* (b) *cantu* (b) *luminibus* (a) *clarescere*. Tacitus reflects the sound and light of the party, its over-extravagance and ornateness, in his verbal design.

37.4 ipse per licita atque inlicita foedatus nihil flagitii reliquerat quo corruptior ageret, nisi paucos post dies uni ex illo contaminatorum grege (nomen Pythagorae fuit) in modum sollemnium coniugiorum denupsisset. inditum imperatori flammeum, missi auspices, dos et genialis torus et faces nuptiales, cuncta denique spectata quae etiam in femina nox operit.

With *ipse*, Tacitus introduces a shift in focus. So far, he has adopted a panoramic survey approach towards recording what happened at the party; now he zooms in on the emperor. After conveying a general sense of the proceedings, we get a detailed, close-up look at what Nero himself got up to. Apparently, the emperor indulged his depraved appetites without inhibition at the party, a factoid that Tacitus uses as a foil for something even more obscene, an account of his mock-marriage to Pythagoras. Nero's erotic license also attracted the attention of other writers. Suetonius, for instance, devotes two full chapters of his biography to the sexual transgressions of the emperor (28–29), including the tid-bit that Nero, when his aptly named freedman Doryphorus (Greek for the 'Spear-bearer' – Suetonius' equivalent to Tacitus' Pythagoras), 'finished him off' on his 'wedding night' went so far as 'to imitate the cries and lamentations of a maiden being deflowered.' Tacitus' reticence contrasts (favourably?) with the sensationalist gusto of the biographer who lovingly dwells on each unsavoury detail. Whereas Nero (and his biographers) glory in letting it all hang out, Tacitus abides by the principle, enshrined in his own name [Tacitus ~ *tacitus* = the perfect passive participle of *taceo*, 'I make no utterance, am silent, say nothing'], that some stuff is best shrouded in the veils of narrative obscurity. Put differently, Suetonius strips, Tacitus teases.[144]

per licita atque inlicita: Neronian vice covers the entire spectrum of possibilities, but Tacitus uses an oxymoron to articulate the comprehensive nature of his debauchery. In principle, it is difficult to defile oneself *per licita*, but Nero somehow manages the impossible. Conversely, Tacitus intimates that in Nero's perverse indulgence in public disgrace, even otherwise sanctioned forms of erotic activity become filthy and hideous.

foedatus: A very strong and ugly verb, suggesting how utterly Nero disgraced himself and sullied any sense of public morals.

nihil flagitii reliquerat: *flagitii* is a partitive genitive dependent on *nihil*. The pronounced hyperbole again makes clear Nero's degeneracy, suggesting that Nero saw this party as an opportunity to debase himself and made sure he left nothing out.

---

144 Cf. *Annals* 11.27 where Tacitus dismissively speaks of imperial Rome as a society in which there are no secrets and no topic is off-limits (*in civitate omnium gnara et nihil reticente*). His historiography is not least an attempt to establish a dignified voice within this sea of incessant, shameless chatter.

quo corruptior ageret: The antecedent of *quo* is *nihil*; *quo* is an ablative of means or instrument; *corruptior* is an adjective used instead of an adverb: 'through which he could have acted with greater depravity.'

paucos post dies: We move on from the party to its aftermath. As in 37.2 Tacitus uses anastrophe, with the preposition post-poned. The link involves the personnel – Pythagoras was among the perverted crowd that participated in the banquet of Tigellinus (*uni ex illo contaminatorum grege*). It is important to note, however, that the marriage was not part of the banquet. Put differently, Tacitus has his cake and eats it too: at the beginning of the chapter, he announced that he would pick out a particular egregious instance of Nero's debauchery *exempli gratia* – so as not to be compelled to cover the same stuff over and again (the implication being, of course, that Nero was a serial offender). At the same time, he indulges in the creative license to link up temporally distinct (but thematically related) episodes – in defiance of the annalistic principle. This condensation of material ensures that within this paragraph Tacitus reaches unprecedented heights on the imperial scandalometer.

uni ... in modum sollemnium coniugiorum denupsisset: Tacitus keeps his narrative dynamic and enthralling as we move from a general description, to a view of Nero specifically in that general setting, and now finally to a specific event. From a Roman point of view, Nero's same-sex marriage forms a shocking climax to the depravities committed during Tigellinus' banquet. Delivering on the heralded 'licit-and-illicit' headline, the emperor of Rome participates in a mockery of the sacred rite of marriage, and the perversion of this ancient ceremony is emphasised by the technical term for 'real' marriage, *coniugiorum*, and the adjective *sollemnium*. But the real shocker comes at the end: the verb *denubo* is specifically used of a woman marrying a man – so Nero is the bride here. It is therefore a savage comment on Nero's inversion of everything natural and normal (with acid overtones of his being the passive sexual partner). (In the cultural imaginary of ancient Rome, the distinction between 'active' and 'passive' was of far greater importance than the distinction between homosexual and heterosexual.)

ex illo contaminatorum grege: This refers to the perverts, who like the rowers and whores, fill the party. The *illo* adds a note of scorn and also presents them as infamous in Nero's reign. The word *grex* usually denotes animals, and thus dehumanises the men and emphasises their degeneracy. Finally, the powerfully pejorative adjective *contaminatorum* stresses the moral pollution of these men. The memorable and scything phrase sums up the company Nero kept: it is a paraded on-the-nail quotation from Horace's famous 'Cleopatra Ode' (*Ode* 1.37.6–10):[145]

> ... dum Capitolio
>
> regina dementis ruinas
>
> funus et imperio parabat
>
> *contaminato* cum *grege* turpium,
>
> morbo virorum.

> [... while the queen I was plotting mindless ruin for the I Capitoline and an end to Empire, I among her pervert company of disease- I polluted 'males.']

As Tony Woodman explains, this allusion to Horace clinches Tacitus' subliminal transformation of Rome into Alexandria: 'Horace was referring to the eunuchs who were conventionally associated with Egypt in the ancient world; and in his ode their leader, being a woman (*regina*), is an appropriate analogue to Nero, who in his wedding to Pythagoras adopts the female role. Yet Cleopatra was not only a woman but queen of, precisely, Alexandria.'[146] The allusion, then, achieves an identification of malicious ingenuity: Nero *is* Cleopatra, the king of Rome has turned into the queen of Egypt.[147] There is a further, sinister dimension to the Horatian intertext. His poem is, after all, a victory ode that celebrates a Roman triumph over an alien queen who *tried* to reduce Rome to ruins. Yet especially with the account of the fire coming up, Tacitus strongly implies that Nero succeeded where Cleopatra failed – Rome, in Horace's words, has become 'polluted', an empire has indeed come to 'an end.' We are, in other words, faced with another inversion, this time at the literary level: whereas Horace, writing under Augustus, composed a victory ode of joy, relief, and celebration that, in exorcising a threat from the East, looks forward to a bright future, Tacitus' narrative, which here chronicles the crimes of the last scion of the dynasty, who undoes or even reverses Augustus' victory of West over East, offers an obituary on Julio-Claudian Rome, which collapses in onto itself: in a monstrous spectacle of imperial history returning to its beginnings, Nero is Augustus, Antony, and Cleopatra all in one.

---

145 We cite the translation of Guy Lee, *Horace: Odes & Carmen Saeculare, with an English version in the original metres, introduction and notes*, Leeds 1998.

146 Woodman (1998) 181.

147 Woodman (1998) 184 further draws attention that Cleopatra's last Roman lover, Mark Antony – a distant ancestor of Nero no less! – was accused by Cicero of a homosexual marriage 'in very similar terms to those used by Tacitus about Nero': see *Philippic* 2.44.

nomen Pythagorae fuit: The name is Greek, conjuring ideas of effeminacy, homosexuality and loose morality. He is almost certainly also a eunuch – and a dreadful bringdown of a parodic return to life for the metempsychosis (and triangle and vegetarianism) guru.

flammeum ... auspices ... dos ... genialis torus ... faces nuptiales: All the ritual elements of genuine marriage are there in this disgraceful sham of a wedding, and Tacitus, by using the technical language of weddings, wants us to dwell on how totally Nero perverted the sacred ceremony:[148]

- The *flammeum* was the orange veil worn by the bride at her wedding (again, note that Nero assumes the female role).
- An *auspex* was a priest who foretold the future by observing the flight of birds. *Auspices* were sent to take their reading as part of the Roman wedding ceremony to gage the future prospects of the couple.
- The bride's dowry (*dos*) was officially transferred as part of the service.
- The bride and groom's marriage bed (*torus genialis*), on which the marriage would be consummated and which was a symbol of their union, was on prominent display during the ceremony.
- The wedding procession was accompanied by torch-bearers carrying the wedding torches (*faces nuptiales*), further symbols of wedlock.

inditum imperatori flammeum: Tacitus deliberately refers to Nero not by his name but by his most military title, *imperator* ('emperor', 'commander'). The appalling incongruity of this title inserted strategically in-between *inditum ... flammeum* (the word-order enacts the covering of the emperor in the bridal veil), brings dramatically and graphically to life Nero's distortion of both his office and the ceremony of wedlock. And his *passive* role in this play for today. Nero allegedly takes on a much more active role in the following chapter, which contains Tacitus' account of the fire of Rome – and Tacitus makes the connection via a verbal link: 'Nero's *flammeum* provides both a verbal and visual harbinger for the *flammae* that will sweep through the city of Rome in the next chapter (15.38.2).'[149]

---

148   The most recent study of the Roman wedding is Hersch (2010).
149   Santoro L'Hoir (2006) 248.

dos et genialis torus et faces nuptiales: The asyndeton of the previous two phrases, both containing verbs, turns into polysyndeton here, combined with the absence of any verb at all: this speeds up the list of sacred objects of marriage, which now pile up as Tacitus fires out the items Nero profaned. The perfect symmetry of the chiasmus (a) *genialis* (b) *torus* (b) *faces* (a) *nuptiales*, which features two adjectives meaning 'of marriage' in prominent position, brings details of the ceremonial part of the wedding to a mocking end – before Tacitus proceeds to recount its consummation.

cuncta denique spectata quae etiam in femina nox operit: Tacitus refers to the act of consummation. The culmination of a genuine wedding service came at night, when the bride was undressed by fellow women who had only ever had one man (*univirae*), before the groom was brought in and the marriage consummated in private, while friends and family sang wedding hymns outside. But Nero 'consummates' his 'marriage' by having intercourse with his 'groom' Pythagoras in full view of everyone. The *cuncta* (everything) suggests pretty graphically that there was no modesty here.

etiam in femina nox operit: In other words *even* (*etiam*) in heterosexual weddings decency requires the cover of night for the act of consummation. In contrast, Nero turns his wedding night experience into a public spectacle. And into the bargain, the way Tacitus makes it *sound*, right before their very eyes s/he pulled off a wizard feat of anatomical impossibility!

(v) 38–41: The fire of Rome

Tacitus' account of the fire of Rome can be divided as follows:

38: The outbreak of the fire and its devastation of the city
39: Nero's return to Rome and his counter-measures
40: Control of the initial conflagration and a new outbreak
41: Assessment of the damages

The fire is the last big event in Tacitus' account of AD 64 (*Annals* 15.33–47). The remainder of Book 15 (Chapters 48–74) covers the conspiracy of Piso in AD 65, which developed in part as a reaction to the rumour that Nero himself was responsible for setting the city on fire. Here is what Subrius Flavius, one of the conspiractors, allegedly said to Nero just before his execution (*Annals* 15.67):

'oderam te', inquit. 'nec quisquam tibi fidelior militum fuit, dum amari
meruisti: odisse coepi, postquam parricida matris et uxoris, auriga et histrio
et incendiarius extitisti.'

[He said: 'I hated you. No one of the soldiers was more loyal to you while
you deserved to be loved. I began to hate you after you became the murder
of your mother and your wife, a charioteer and actor, and an arsonist.']

To come to terms with Tacitus' account of the fire, it will be useful to begin
by establishing some background, which we will do under the following
four headings: (a) Emperors and fires in the *Annals*; (b) Other accounts
of the Neronian fire; (c) Tacitus' creative engagement with the *urbs-capta*
motif; (d) Nero's assimilation of the fire of Rome to the fall of Troy.

(a) Emperors and fires in the *Annals*

Tacitus mentions other significant fires elsewhere in his *Annals*; they had
been a staple item in the city of Rome's annual records from the year
dot: but now Tacitus makes sure each time to comment on the fact that
the event shaped the relation between the emperor and his subjects.
These passages provide telling foils and benchmarks for the way Nero
dealt with the challenge. Here is *Annals* 4.64 on events from AD 27 that
occurred right after that collapse of the amphitheatre at Fidena (see above
on 15.34.2):

Nondum ea clades exoleverat cum ignis violentia urbem ultra solitum
adfecit, deusto monte Caelio; feralemque annum ferebant et ominibus
adversis susceptum principi consilium absentiae, qui mos vulgo, fortuita
ad culpam trahentes, ni Caesar obviam isset tribuendo pecunias ex modo
detrimenti. actaeque ei grates apud senatum ab inlustribus famaque apud
populum, quia sine ambitione aut proximorum precibus ignotos etiam et
ultro accitos munificentia iuverat.

[The disaster had not yet faded from memory, when a fierce outbreak of
fire affected the city to an unusual degree by burning down the Caelian Hill.
'It was a fatal year, and the decision of the *princeps* to absent himself had
been adopted despite evil omens' – so men began to remark, converting,
as is the habit of the crowd, the fortuitous into the culpable, when the
Caesar checked the critics by a distribution of money in proportion to loss
sustained. Thanks were returned to him; in the senate, by the noble; among
the people, by a rise in his popularity: for without respect of persons, and
without the intercession of relatives, he had aided with his liberality even
unknown sufferers whom he had himself encouraged to apply.]

Tacitus here records a telling dynamic that also informs – *mutatis mutandis* – the Neronian fire. The people of Rome, he reports, are wont to ascribe responsibility for disasters to their leader, whom they charge with disregarding crucial pieces of supernatural intelligence that – so the assumption – could have averted the catastrophes if properly heeded. Tacitus, adopting the stance of enlightened and skeptical historiographer, mocks the people for positing causalities where there are none. Yet at the same time, both he (and the emperor) realize that these popular delusions about causal relationships between political and religious leadership on the one hand and general well-being or, conversely, suffering on the other are very real in their consequences. If the groundswell of negative opinion intensified, it could destabilize the political order, lead to riots, and cause a regime change (or at least a swap on top).[150] Tiberius achieves a mood-swing through some swift and decisive action: a well-orchestrated, public show of concern, combined with material generosity towards all and sundry. These measures are so effective that his popularity ratings rise again. Catastrophes, then, put leaders under pressure, not least in the court of public opinion: they can either be deemed to have risen to the challenge or to have failed to meet it. Tiberius proved adept in his crisis-management. He pulled off a similar stunt towards the end of his reign. Here is *Annals* 6.45.1–2 (AD 36, the year before his death):

> Idem annus gravi igne urbem adfecit, deusta parte circi quae Aventino contigua, ipsoque Aventino; quod damnum Caesar ad gloriam vertit exsolutis domuum et insularum pretiis. miliens sestertium in munificentia ea conlocatum, tanto acceptius in vulgum, quanto modicus privatis aedificationibus...

> [The same year saw the capital visited by a serious fire, the part of the Circus adjoining the Aventine being burnt down along with the Aventine itself: a disaster which the Caesar converted to his own glory by paying the full value of the mansions and tenement-blocks destroyed. One hundred million sesterces were invested in this act of munificence, the more acceptably to the multitude as he showed restraint in building on his own behalf...]

---

150   A fictional comparandum occurs in the first chapter of J. K. Rowling, *Harry Potter and the Half-Blood Prince*: 'The Other Minister', where the British (Muggle) Prime Minister is held responsible by his political opponents for a series of catastrophes (some nasty murders, the collapse of a bridge, a hurricane, the dismal weather): they gloatingly explain 'why each and every one of them was the government's fault'.

For future reference, more specifically Tacitus' account of the new palace that rose from the ashes of Nero's burnt-down Rome, what is important here is the distinction between personal and public investment on the part of the emperor. Tiberius gains the respect of his subjects for using his private purse for the public's benefit, while putting severe checks on his architectural self-aggrandizement. This approach reflects commitment to a norm that dates back to the republic. As Cicero says at *pro Murena* 76: *odit populus Romanus privatam luxuriam, publicam magnificentiam diligit* ('the Roman people loathe private luxury but they love public grandeur').

(b) Other accounts of the Neronian fire

Just like Tiberius in AD 27, Nero was not actually in Rome when the fire broke out. He returned to the capital to fund and oversee the relief efforts, though perhaps not as quickly as he could or should have done, at least according to popular opinion. Yet somehow, the urban rumour arose (and stuck) that Nero actually ordered the conflagration. Tacitus, as we shall see, is rather guarded on the question as to whether Nero was the culprit. Most of our other surviving sources, however, blame Nero outright. Here is Suetonius (*Nero* 38):

> Sed nec populo aut moenibus patriae pepercit. Dicente quodam in sermone communi: 'ἐμοῦ θανόντος γαῖα μειχθήτω πυρί', 'Immo', inquit, 'ἐμοῦ ζῶντος,' planeque ita fecit. nam quasi offensus deformitate veterum aedificiorum et angustiis flexurisque vicorum, incendit urbem tam palam, ut plerique consulares cubicularios eius cum stuppa taedaque in praediis suis deprehensos non attigerint, et quaedam horrea circum domum Auream, quorum spatium maxime desiderabat, ut bellicis machinis labefacta atque inflammata sint, quod saxeo muro constructa erant. Per sex dies septemque noctes ea clade saevitum est ad monumentorum bustorumque deversoria plebe compulsa. Tunc praeter immensum numerum insularum domus priscorum ducum arserunt hostilibus adhuc spoliis adornatae deorumque aedes ab regibus ac deinde Punicis et Gallicis bellis votae dedicataeque, et quidquid visendum atque memorabile ex antiquitate duraverat. Hoc incendium e turre Maecenatiana prospectans laetusque 'flammae', ut aiebat, 'pulchritudine' *Halosin Ilii* in illo suo scaenico habitu decantavit. Ac ne non hinc quoque quantum posset praedae et manubiarum invaderet, pollicitus cadaverum et ruderum gratuitam egestionem nemini ad reliquias rerum suarum adire permisit; conlationibusque non receptis modo verum et efflagitatis provincias privatorumque census prope exhausit.

> [But he showed no greater mercy to the people or the walls of his capital. When someone in a general conversation said: 'When I am dead, be earth

consumed by fire', he rejoined 'No, rather while I live', and his action was wholly in accord. For under cover of displeasure at the ugliness of the old buildings and the narrow, crooked streets, he set fire to the city so openly that several ex-consuls did not venture to lay hands on his servants although they caught them on their estates with tow and firebrands, while some granaries near the Golden House, whose room he particularly desired, were demolished by engines of war and then set on fire, because their walls were of stone. For six days and seven nights destruction raged, while the people were driven for shelter to monuments and tombs. At that time, besides an immense number of dwellings, the houses of leaders of old were burned, still adorned with trophies of victory, and the temples of the gods vowed and dedicated by the kings and later in the Punic and Gallic wars, and whatever else interesting and noteworthy had survived from antiquity. Viewing the conflagration from the tower of Maecenas and exulting, as he said, in 'the beauty of the flames', he sang the whole of the 'Sack of Ilium', in his regular stage costume. Furthermore, to gain from this calamity too all the spoil and booty possible, while promising the removal of the debris and dead bodies free of cost he allowed no one to approach the ruins of his own property; and from the contributions which he not only received, but even demanded, he nearly bankrupted the provinces and exhausted the resources of individuals.]

Unlike Suetonius, who specifies a pragmatic reason for setting the city on fire, Cassius Dio identifies sheer wanton destruction as Nero's principal motivation (62.16–18):

16 1 After this Nero set his heart on accomplishing what had doubtless always been his desire, namely to make an end of the whole city and realm during his lifetime. 2 At all events, he, like others before him, used to call Priam wonderfully fortunate in that he had seen his country and his throne destroyed together. Accordingly he secretly sent out men who pretended to be drunk or engaged in other kinds of mischief, and caused them at first to set fire to one or two or even several buildings in different parts of the city, so that people were at their wits' end, not being able to find any beginning of the trouble nor to put an end to it, though they constantly were aware of many strange sights and sounds. 3 For there was nothing to be seen but many fires, as in a camp, and nothing to be heard from the talk of the people except such exclamations as 'This or that is afire', 'Where?' 'How did it happen?' 'Who kindled it?' 'Help?' Extraordinary excitement laid hold on all the citizens in all parts of the city, and they ran about, some in one direction and some in another, as if distracted. 4 Here men while assisting their neighbours would learn that their own premises were afire; there others, before word reached them that their own houses had caught fire, would be told that they were destroyed. Those who were inside their houses would run out into the narrow streets thinking that they could

save them from the outside, while people in the streets would rush into the dwellings in the hope of accomplishing something inside. 5 There was shouting and wailing without end, of children, women, men, and the aged all together, so that no one could see anything or understand what was said by reason of the smoke and the shouting; and for this reason some might be seen standing speechless, as if they were dumb. 6 Meanwhile many who were carrying out their goods and many, too, who were stealing the property of others, kept running into one another and falling over their burdens. It was not possible to go forward nor yet to stand still, but people pushed and were pushed in turn, upset others and were themselves upset. 7 Many were suffocated, many were trampled underfoot; in a word, no evil that can possibly happen to people in such a crisis failed to befall them. They could not even escape anywhere easily; and if anybody did save himself from the immediate danger, he would fall into another and perish.

17 1 Now this did not all take place on a single day, but it lasted for several days and nights alike. Many houses were destroyed for want of anyone to help save them, and many others were set on fire by the very men who came to lend assistance; for the soldiers, including the night watch, having an eye to plunder, instead of putting out fires, kindled new ones. 2 While such scenes were occurring at various points, a wind caught up the flames and carried them indiscriminately against all the buildings that were left. Consequently no one concerned himself any longer about goods or houses, but all the survivors, standing where they thought they were safe, gazed upon what appeared to be a number of scattered islands on fire or many cities all burning at the same time. 3 There was no longer any grieving over personal losses, but they lamented the public calamity, recalling how once before most of the city had been thus laid waste by the Gauls. 18 1 While the whole population was in this state of mind and many, crazed by the disaster, were leaping into the very flames, Nero ascended to the roof of the palace, from which there was the best general view of the greater part of the conflagration, and assuming the lyre-player's garb, he sang the *Capture of Troy*, as he styled the song himself, though to the eyes of the spectators it was the Capture of Rome.

And Pliny the Elder, too, is convinced of Nero's guilt (*Natural History* 17.5, in a discussion of hugely expensive nettle trees):

duraveruntque, quoniam et de longissimo aevo arborum diximus, ad Neronis principis incendia cultu virides iuvenesque, ni princeps ille adcelerasset etiam arborum mortem.

[... and they lasted – since we have already also spoken of the limits of longevity in trees – down to the Emperor Nero's conflagration, thanks to careful tendance still verdant and vigorous, had not the emperor mentioned hastened the death even of trees.]

The author of the *Octavia* (a so-called *fabula praetexta* or 'historical drama' that features Nero's unfortunate first wife as protagonist) also blames Nero, but connects the fire with his outrageous treatment of Octavia, which happened two years earlier in AD 62 (831–33, Nero speaking):

> mox tecta flammis concidant urbis meis,
>
> ignes ruinae noxium populum premant
>
> turpisque egestas, saeva cum luctu fames.

> [Next the city's buildings must fall to flames set by me. Fire, ruined homes, sordid poverty, cruel starvation along with grief must crush this criminal populace.]

In the light of a tradition in which Nero is the culprit plain and simple, Tacitus' strategy is rather more subtle. He refrains from fingering Nero outright, relying instead on insinuation and a bag of further rhetorical tricks to associate the emperor with rendering his people, already adrift in a moral morass, 'Romeless' through the physical destruction of the capital. The most conspicuous ploy concerns his manipulation of the so-called *urbs-capta* topos, to which our last two sections are dedicated.

(c) Tacitus' creative engagement with the *urbs-capta* motif

The *urbs-capta* topos refers to the rhetorical representation of a city captured and destroyed by enemy forces.[151] The *Rhetorica ad Herennium*, an anonymous handbook on rhetoric from the first century BC, uses the topos as one of his examples to illustrate 'vivid description' (4.39.51):[152]

> Nam neminem vestrum fugit, Quirites, urbe capta quae miseriae consequi soleant: arma qui contra tulerunt statim crudelissime trucidantur; ceteri qui possunt per aetatem et vires laborem ferre rapiuntur in servitutem, qui non possunt vita privantur; uno denique atque eodem tempore domus hostili flagrat incendio, et quos natura aut voluntas necessitudine et benivolentia coniunxit distrahuntur; liberi partim e gremiis diripiuntur parentum, partim in sinu iugulantur, partim ante pedes constuprantur. Nemo, iudices, est qui possit satis rem consequi verbis nec efferre oratione magnitudinem calamitatis.

---

151 See the treatments by Paul (1982), who traces the literary topos and its thematic range back to Homer's *Iliad* and explores its subsequent career in 'tragic' historiography, and Ziolkowski (1993), who looks into the specifically Roman spin on it.

152 We cite the text and translation by H. Caplan in the Loeb Classical Library (Cambridge, Mass., 1954).

[For none of you, fellow citizens, fails to see what miseries usually follow upon the capture of a city. Those who have borne arms against the victors are instantly slain with extreme cruelty. Of the rest, those who by reason of youth and strength can endure hard labour are carried off into slavery, and those who cannot are deprived of life. In short, at one and the same time a house blazes up by the enemy's torch, and they whom nature of free choice has joined in the bonds of kinship or of sympathy are dragged apart. Of the children, some are torn from their parents' arms, others murdered on their parents' bosom, still other violated at their parents' feet. No one, men of the jury, can, by words, do justice to the deed, nor reproduce in language the magnitude of the disaster.]

And here is Quintilian's take, *Institutio Oratoria* 8.3.67–69:[153]

Sic et urbium captarum crescit miseratio. Sine dubio enim qui dicit expugnatam esse civitatem complectitur omnia quaecumque talis fortuna recipit, sed in adfectus minus penetrat brevis hic velut nuntius. At si aperias haec, quae verbo uno inclusa erant, apparebunt effusae per domus ac templa flammae et ruentium tectorum fragor et ex diversis clamoribus unus quidam sonus, aliorum fuga incerta, alii extremo complexu suorum cohaerentes et infantium feminarumque ploratus et male usque in illum diem servati fato senes: tum illa profanorum sacrorumque direptio, efferentium praedas repetentiumque discursus, et acti ante suum quisque praedonem catenati, et conata retinere infantem suum mater, et sicubi maius lucrum est pugna inter victores. Licet enim haec omnia, ut dixi, complectatur 'eversio', minus est tamen totum dicere quam omnia.

[This too is how the pathos of a captured city can be enhanced. No doubt, simply to say 'the city was stormed' is to embrace everything implicit in such a disaster, but this brief communiqué, as it were, does not touch the emotions. If you expand everything which was implicit in the one word, there will come into view flames racing through houses and temples, the crash of falling roofs, the single sound made up of many cries, the blind flight of some, others clinging to their dear ones in a last embrace, shrieks of children and women, the old men whom an unkind fate has allowed to live to see this day; then will come the pillage of property, secular and sacred, the frenzied activity of plunderers carrying off their booty and going back for more, the prisoners driven in chains before their captors, the mother who tries to keep her child with her, and the victors fighting one another wherever the spoils are richer. 'Sack of a city' does, as I said, comprise all these things; but to state the whole is less than to state all the parts.]

---

153   We cite the text and translation by D. A. Russell in the Loeb Classical Library (Cambridge, Mass., 2001).

The parallels between Quintilian's recommendations in particular of how to speak about a city captured and Tacitus' account of the fire of Rome are remarkable: they underscore the highly rhetorical (and hence conventional) nature of such descriptions. But Tacitus gives this material an interesting and innovative twist: he turns the fire from an instrument into the primary agent of destruction. In his narrative, it becomes a personified force that assaults the city of Rome like an external foe, reducing it to ashes and causing the same kind of human suffering as an enemy army.[154]

(d) Nero's assimilation of the fire of Rome to the fall of Troy

Now the archetype of 'the captured city' was none other than Troy, the sack of which stands behind the use of the motif – from Homer to Tacitus:[155]

> Its diffusion is owed in large measure, I believe, to the popularity of the theme of the destruction of Troy. The popularity of that theme is attested by the various treatments of the *Iliupersis* ['The Fall of Troy'] in poems of the Epic Cycle and by Stesichorus, who is credited with being the inspiration of the scene of Troy's destruction on a *Tabula Iliaca*. Various scenes from the sack of Troy frequently appear on vase-paintings. Scenes from the sack appear on the walls of Pompeian houses... The continuing popularity of the theme is indicated by Petronius' treatment of the *Halosis Troiae* ['The Capture of Troy'] (*Satyricon* 89); the poem, it will be remembered, is inspired by a wall-painting. Its possible relationship to Nero's *Troica* (Dio 62.29.1) need not be discussed here; Nero was, however, alleged to have sung of the *Troianum excidium* during the fire of Rome (Tac. *Ann.* 15.39). ... It is clear that the destruction of Troy and the resulting suffering and grief were firmly established as a literary and artistic theme.

Nero and Tacitus, then, stand in a tradition that stretches back to Homer – but for both the emperor and 'his' historiographer one account arguably surpasses all others in importance: that by Virgil in *Aeneid* 2. It assumes a special significance for both thematic and ideological reasons. As Richard Heinze remarks, 'in the whole course of the narrative..., it is striking how deliberately Virgil emphasizes the burning of the city.'[156] Austin observes that

---

154   Fans of J. K. Rowling's Harry-Potter saga may wish to compare Tacitus' passage with the 'Fiendfyre' that rages through the Room of Requirement in *Harry Potter and the Deathly Hallows*, Chapter 31: 'The Battle of Hogwarts': 'It was not normal fire..: as they turned a corner the flames chased them as though they were alive, sentient, intent upon killing them. Now the fire was mutating, forming a gigantic pack of fiery beasts... .'

155   Paul (1982) 147–48.

156   Heinze (1915/1993) 17. References to Troy engulfed in flames occur at *Aeneid* 2.311, 327, 329, 337, 353, 374, 431, 505, 566, 600, 632, 664, 705, 758, 764).

this thematic choice intertwines with issues in ideology by connecting the (unorthodox) emphasis on catastrophic conflagration *during* the sack to the apologetic subtext that runs through *Aeneid* 2: 'traditionally it was only when they finally left Troy that the Greeks fired the city..., and Heinze suggests that Virgil may be following some Hellenistic source. But there is no reason why the innovation may not be Virgil's own... And the stress laid upon the flames stresses also the uselessness of trying to serve Troy by remaining there.'[157] Let us recall, after all, that we get Virgil's account of the sack of Troy via his internal narrator Aeneas, who needs to justify why he abandoned his hometown in its greatest hour of need: the greater the destruction by fire, the less point there was for Aeneas to keep fighting, the less questionable his decision to turn tail. Within the plot of the *Aeneid*, of course, the phoenix fated to soar from the ashes of Troy is – Rome. The incineration of Troy in Book 2 is the radical point of departure of a teleological development that will see Rome founded as an alternative world-capital and in due course ascend to the status of Mediterranean top dog, ruling over a far-flung empire without end (or, in Jupiter's words, a world-wide *imperium sine fine*: see *Aeneid* 1.279). The principal agent of this 'transference of empire' (*translatio imperii*) from Troy to Rome was none other than the eponymous hero of the epic, Aeneas – the founding figure, via his son Ascanius or Iulus, of the *gens Julia*, to which Caesar, Augustus, and Nero also belonged. The 'Troy connection' – more specifically descent from Aeneas and thus divinity – already played a key role in Julius Caesar's self-promotion long before Virgil wrote the *Aeneid*.[158] And Virgil and Augustus together ensured that Troy acquired a central place in the imagination of imperial Rome more broadly: many events in Virgil's literary universe stand in creative, etiological dialogue with Augustan investment in Rome's Trojan ancestry. One of the best examples, not least for its relevance to Nero, is the so-called Game of Troy.[159] Its first, legenday celebration, so Virgil recounts in *Aeneid* 5, happened on Sicily during the funeral games for Aeneas' father Anchises; and he concludes his lengthy description by anticipating the future history of the Game (*Aeneid* 5.596–602):

---

157 Austin (1964) 135. See now also the discussion by Rossi (2004), Chapter 1: 'The Fall of Troy: Between Tradition and Genre', esp. 24–30: 'Flames'.

158 See Suetonius, *Caesar* 6, citing from Caesar's funeral speech for his aunt Julia, delivered in 68 BC (i.e. two year after Virgil's birth): 'The family of my aunt Julia is descended by her mother from the kings, and on her father's side is akin to the immortal Gods; for the Marcii Reges (her mother's family name) go back to Ancus Marcius, and the Julii, the family of which ours is a branch, to Venus.'

159 The following is based on O'Gorman (2000) 162–75 ('The Game of Troy').

hunc morem cursus atque haec certamina primus

Ascanius, Longam muris cum cingeret Albam,

rettulit et priscos docuit celebrare Latinos,

quo puer ipse modo, secum quo Troia pubes;

Albani docuere suos; hinc maxima porro

accepit Roma et patrium servavit honorem;

Troiaque nunc pueri, Troianum dicitur agmen.

[This manner of horsemanship, these contests Ascanius first revived when he surrounded Alba Longa with walls, and taught the early Latins how to celebrate them in the same way he had done as a boy and with him the Trojan youth. The Albans taught their children; from them in turn mighty Rome received and preserved the ancestral institution; and today the boys are called 'Troy' and the troop 'Trojan.']

Augustus, we learn from Suetonius, was particularly keen to sustain the tradition of the Game, following in the footsteps of Caesar (see Suetonius, *Caesar* 39.2) (*Augustus* 43.2):

Sed et Troiae lusum edidit frequentissime maiorum minorumque puerorum, prisci decorique moris existimans clarae stirpis indolem sic notescere.

[Besides he gave frequent performances of the game of Troy by older and younger boys, thinking it a time-honoured and worthy custom for the flower of the nobility to become known in this way.]

And it continued to be celebrated by his successors as well. In fact, a Game of Troy organized by Claudius provides the context for Nero's first appearance in Tacitus' *Annals* (11.11.2):

sedente Claudio circensibus ludis, cum pueri nobiles equis ludicrum Troiae inirent interque eos Britannicus imperatore genitus et L. Domitius adoptione mox in imperium et cognomentum Neronis adscitus, favor plebis acrior in Domitium loco praesagii acceptus est.

[During the presence of Claudius at the Circensian Games, when a cavalcade of boys from the great families opened the mimic battle of Troy, among them being the emperor's son Britannicus, and Lucius Domitius, – soon to be adopted as heir to the throne and to the designation of Nero, – the livelier applause given by the populace to Domitius was accepted as prophetic.]

For our purposes, however, it is crucial to note that genealogical and etiological connections between Troy and Rome do not amount to the *identity* of the two cities. In fact, in the course of the *Aeneid* Aeneas is forced to undergo the painful process of learning to turn his back on Troy (and the past) and to pursue Rome (and the future). He does not fully grasp this until about midway through the poem. Likewise, in the final meeting between Jupiter and Juno towards the end of *Aeneid* 12 up in cloud-cuckoo-land, Juno only agrees to desist from further opposing destiny once Jupiter has promised her that the Roman people will bear hardly any trace of Trojan cultural identity (such as speech or dress).[160] All of this is unsurprising: in a story that turns world-historical losers (the Trojans) into world-historical winners (the Romans), difference and differentiation from the catastrophic origins are just as important as legitimizing continuities.

Against this background, what happens in Tacitus' account of the fire of Rome acquires a fascinating intertextual and ideological complexion. As other sources, Tacitus records (though without committing himself to the truth of the rumour) that Nero, when the spirit moved him to comment on the conflagration in verse, allegedly assimilated the fire of Rome to the fall of Troy (15.39): ... *pervaserat rumor ipso tempore flagrantis urbis inisse eum domesticam scaenam et cecinisse Troianum excidium, praesentia mala vetustis cladibus adsimulantem* ('the rumour had spread that, at the very moment when Rome was aflame, he had mounted his private stage, and, assimilating the ills of the present to the calamities of the past, had sung the Destruction of Troy'). If he did, Nero would have activated a tragic outlook on Rome's prospects of eternity that contrasts sharply with the notion of an *imperium sine fine*. This outlook recalls, rather, Scipio Aemilianus Minor. Greek sources report the Roman general to have been stirred into a moment of tragic reflexivity after his sack of Carthage in 146 BC, when he apparently recited two verses from the *Iliad*, in which Hector recognizes the inevitability of the fall of Troy (6.448–49):

ἔσσεται ἦμαρ ὅτ᾽ ἄν ποτ᾽ ὀλώλῃ Ἴλιος ἱρὴ

καὶ Πρίαμος καὶ λαὸς ἐϋμμελίω Πριάμοιο.

[The day shall come when sacred Ilios will perish and Priam and the people of Priam with goodly spear of ash.]

Scipio here both thinks backwards in time (to Troy) as well as forward (to Rome), in anticipating the same future for Rome that Troy (and Carthage) have already suffered: destruction.[161] In so doing, he clearly *identifies* Troy and Rome, at least from the point of view of their ultimate destiny.

---

160 Virgil, *Aeneid* 12.791-842.
161 See O'Gorman (2000) 168–71 for possible affinities between Scipio and Nero (*via* Livy).

His (and Nero's) assimilation of destruction of Rome to the destruction of Troy invokes a cyclical notion of history at variance with Virgilian teleology, the phoenix rising from the ashes being reduced to it. But whereas Scipio simply ponders the ephemeral nature of human achievement at the moment of his greatest triumph, Nero's Trojan reminiscences, especially as represented by Tacitus in the *Annals*, are more specific. Nero undoes the achievement of his ancestors, in particular Augustus; under his reign the success story of Julio(-Claudian) Rome that Virgil celebrated in the *Aeneid* unravels; he destroys the Virgilian masterplot by reducing Rome to its origins: the ashes of Troy. And he sings about it. What Nero does in verse, Tacitus does in prose. By taking his inspiration from the emperor and casting the Neronian fire in terms of a city sacked in his own narrative, arguably in oblique dialogue with the 'Fiendfyre' of *Aeneid* 2, he positions himself as an ideological antipode to Virgil's *Aeneid*. If in Virgil the fall of Troy heralds the beginning of Rome and the inauguration of a history that has its positive end in Caesar and Augustus, i.e. the beginning of the Julian dynasty, in Tacitus the fire of Rome under Nero turns into a negative end to history, in which the new foundation that emerged from the ashes of Troy and found its culmination in Augustan Rome is itself reduced to rubble by the last representative of the Julio-Claudian lineage.

Chapter 38

Chapter 38 offers 'a splendid study of the chaos produced by calamity, and of the human suffering involved.'[162] Watch Tacitus keep his camera constantly on the move across different groups, using different signifiers for this purpose: *quique, alii, pars, quidam, multi* etc. This creates a complex and kaleidoscopic picture, with constant and varied activity all over his canvass. Key themes include: (i) The variety of constructions, complex syntax and winding sentences, evoking confusion; (ii) Personification of the fire, especially presentation of it as an invading army; (iii) Snapshot, impressionistic looks at different groups here and there; (iv) Moments of pathos and human suffering; (v) Speed of narrative and the progression of the fire. The structure of the opening paragraph is:

38.1: Introduction and general significance
38.2: Outbreak and causes
38.3: Power of the flames
38.4–7: The humans affected

---

162   Miller (1975) 90.

38.1 Sequitur clades, forte an dolo principis incertum (nam utrumque auctores prodidere), sed omnibus quae huic urbi per violentiam ignium acciderunt gravior atque atrocior.

sequitur clades: This very simple phrase, after the ornate language and structures of the previous passage, comes as a crashing shock, enacting the eruption of the fire. The inversion of verb (*sequitur*) and subject (*clades*) and the use of historic present make the opening highly dramatic. *sequitur* is also a quintessentially annalistic term, which should not obfuscate the fact that Tacitus, under the veneer of reporting events in chronological sequence, has engineered a highly effective juxtaposition. The sense of *sequitur* here is both temporal and causal: the fire 'follows' the abominations, but also 'follows from' them. The word *clades* points backwards as well as forwards, summing up Nero's perversion of Rome as a preliminary step towards the full-scale destruction of the city. As Syme puts it: 'another spectacle follows abruptly, the conflagration of the city.' Tacitus, of course, delays specifying what the *clades* comprised, slipping in an almost *en passant* reference to fire in the relative clause. We do not actually learn when precisely the fire broke out (19 July AD 64) until 41.2.

forte an dolo principis incertum: Another classic example of Tacitean 'alternative motivation', not explicitly favouring one version or the other (*incertum*), but giving clear weight to the less reputable option (*dolo principis*) by placing it in the emphatic second position. We still haven't heard what the matter at issue actually is.

nam utrumque auctores prodidere: Tacitus likes to record instances where the sources differ for a variety of reasons: (a) it shows him to be a diligent and analytic historian who takes several conflicting accounts into consideration; (b) it allows him to include colourful and dramatic yet perhaps also dubious elements under the protection of referencing other historians; and (c) it obliges us to pitch into the story and figure out what *we* think must have been going down.

In the light of the seemingly unanimous condemnatory tradition set out above, one also wonders which authors Tacitus refers to when reporting that opinion on Nero's guilt was divided in the sources he consulted. This question has yet to find a satisfying answer. What is at any rate noticeable is how guarded Tacitus is in formulating the options: he does not commit himself explicitly either way.

sed omnibus quae huic urbi per violentiam ignium acciderunt gravior atque atrocior [sc. *erat*]: *omnibus* picks up *clades*, i.e. *omnibus cladibus*, and is the antecedent of *quae*. Rome had suffered many fires in its history, as its location, layout and closely packed, frequently wooden buildings left it highly vulnerable. This Great Fire was remarkable only for the scale of its devastation. The hyperbaton of *omnibus* (an ablative of comparison dependent on *gravior atque atrocior*) emphasises the pre-eminent power of this fire, while *huic* helps to make the event more vivid for Tacitus' Roman readers – 'this city of ours.' Tacitus has already pulled out all the superlative stops in *Histories* 3.71–72 for the disaster of disasters, arson in civil war of the Temple of Capitoline Jupiter (see below).

38.2 initium in ea parte circi ortum quae Palatino Caelioque montibus contigua est, ubi per tabernas, quibus id mercimonium inerat quo flamma alitur, simul coeptus ignis et statim validus ac vento citus longitudinem circi corripuit. neque enim domus munimentis saeptae vel templa muris cincta aut quid aliud morae interiacebat.

initium ... ortum [sc. *est*]: This is technically a tautology ('the beginning began...'), and serves to give emphasis to the outbreak of the fire.

in ea parte circi ... quae Palatino Caelioque montibus contigua est: The Circus Maximus was Rome's great chariot racing track. It occupied the low land between the Palatine, Caelian and Aventine Hills (see *Map of Rome*). The part Tacitus refers to here is the south east corner of the Circus, in the vicinity of the Porta Capena.

ubi tabernas, quibus id mercimonium inerat quo flamma alitur: There was a huge mall of shops (*tabernas*) in the arches of the tiered seats of the Circus. The rare word *mercimonium* (wares) is an archaism, there for variation and interest as usual but also perhaps evoking the creaking old shops where the fire started. In addition, the flames are personified (not for the last time in this description): *quo flamma alitur* provides the image of the fire greedily devouring the flammable goods.

simul coeptus [sc. *est*] **ignis et statim validus ac vento citus longitudinem circi corripuit:** The two adverbs *simul* and *statim* make clear the immense speed with which the fire took hold. The fire's progression is rapid, from beginning (*coeptus*), to immediately gaining strength (*validus*) and speed (*citus*) to engulfing (*corripuit*) huge areas. The alliterations (*simul, statim; coeptus, citus, circi, corripuit; validus, vento*) help to stress the fire's speedy growth.

neque enim domus munimentis saeptae [sc. *sunt*] **vel templa muris cincta** [sc. *sunt*] **aut quid aliud morae interiacebat:** A list of three architectural elements which might have stopped the fire: large houses surrounded by walls, temples with a precinct, or – anything else. The polysyndeton helps to underscore the absence of anything that could have stopped the roaring inferno. Tacitus combines parallelism with variation: *domus munimentis saeptae* and *templa muris cincta* are virtually identical in construction, but the last colon of the tricolon breaks the pattern, setting aside measured and systematic exposition for a comprehensive expression of despair. *quid aliud morae* (*morae* being a partitive genitive dependent on *quid aliud*) suggests how utterly conducive this part of Rome was to fire.

domus ... templa: Miller explains the architectural significance of the absence of large residences and temples in this area of the city: 'self-contained houses, and temples, would have had walled grounds which might have stopped the flames: instead, there were only *insulae* (41,1), blocks of flats crowding narrow streets, which caught and spread the fire.'[163]

38.3 impetu pervagatum incendium plana primum, deinde in edita adsurgens et rursus inferiora populando, antiit remedia velocitate mali et obnoxia urbe artis itineribus hucque et illuc flexis atque enormibus vicis, qualis vetus Roma fuit.

The first part of the sentence (from *impetu* to *remedia*) traces the path of the conflagration, marked by the sequence *primum – deinde – rursus*, and fizzing on through *impetus-incendium-in-edita-inferiora*. The subject is *incendium*. The two main verbs are *pervagatum* (sc. *est*) with *plana* as accusative object and *antiit* with *remedia* as accusative object. In between comes the present participle *adsurgens* linked by *et* with the gerund *populando*. The second part of the sentence (*velocitate ... fuit*) specifies the reasons why the fire could spread so quickly. Here Tacitus links an ablative of cause (*velocitate mali*) with an ablative absolute of causal force (*obnoxia urbe*), to which he attaches two further ablatives of cause (*artis itineribus hucque et illuc flexis; enormibus vicis*).

---

163   Miller (1975) 88.

impetu: An ablative of manner, which amounts to more personification of the fire, and the first of several instances where it is presented as an assaulting army. The emphatic position here also draws our attention to this highly significant word. Its significance is manifold: (a) the metaphor of the fire as a sack of the city increases the drama and engages the reader in the savagery of the blaze; (b) Tacitus complained (very pointedly) at *Annals* 4.33 that such is the era he is writing about that he cannot write about great wars and battles but rather immorality and infighting: here he uses the fire to give outlet for the sort of narrative excitement usually reserved for war; (c) the idea of the city being sacked (it hadn't been sacked by an army since 390 BC) also raises questions about how low Rome had sunk under Nero.

pervagatum ... plana primum: Further personification – the verb *pervagor* usually means 'to range over' or 'rove about', with the *per*-prefix conveying the breadth of its spread and the alliteration adding further emphasis and colour.

plana primum ... deinde in edita ... rursus inferiora: The up-and-down, hither-and-thither surging of the uncontrollable fire is made very clear here with these simple phrases and the adverbs (first... then... again). As the following sentence makes clear, it thereby follows the narrow streets in this part of the city (cf. especially *hucque et illuc flexis*).

populando: More military personification: this verb means 'to plunder' and is usually used of troops ravaging enemy land.

antiit remedia: An emphatically placed verb for emphasis on the fire's speed and irresistibility. The word *remedia* is also a subtle medical metaphor, characterising the fire as an incurable disease.

artis itineribus hucque et illuc flexis atque enormibus vicis: The syntax here enacts the sense of the winding alleys of old Rome, their narrowness (*artis*), irregularity (*enormibus*) and winding nature (*hucque et illuc flexis*); the periphrastic *hucque atque illuc flexis* suggests the weaving back-streets; and the polysyndeton (*-que ... et ... atque*) keeps the sentence flowing onwards and adds to the labyrinthine impression.

qualis vetus Roma fuit: Of course Tacitus' readers, very few of whom would even vaguely have remembered pre-fire Rome, would be used to the more regimented building patterns which became the norm after this disaster. In fact, much of the Rome Tacitus knew was of Nero's creation; but Tacitus, as John Henderson reminds us, here also stands in dialogue with his historiographical predecessors: as he will go on to rub in (below), many readers would have been familiar with the historian Livy's (59 BC – AD 17) account of the rebuilding of Rome after near-total destruction by the Gauls, a nostalgic evocation of the citizens' higgledy-piggledy but faultlessly communitarian reconstruction work that draws to a close his first pentade and Rome down to Camillus, the 'august' saviour (and precursor for Augustus). Tacitus' phrase here virtually signals the intertextual reference.[164]

38.4 ad hoc lamenta paventium feminarum, fessa aetate aut rudis pueritiae, quique sibi quique aliis consulebat, dum trahunt invalidos aut opperiuntur, pars mora, pars festinans, cuncta impediebant.

With *ad hoc*, Tacitus moves from the physical destruction to the human cost.

lamenta paventium feminarum, fessa aetate aut rudis pueritiae: More pronounced *variatio* from Tacitus: first a noun/genitive combination (*lamenta paventium feminarum* – 'lamentations of frightened women'), then an ablative of quality (*fessa aetate* – '[those] of feeble age'), and finally a genitive of quality (*rudis pueritiae* – '[those] of tender childhood'). This syntactical variety helps to create interest, but also conveys a sense of the confusion and panic. Tacitus here focuses on the physically weaker and more vulnerable inhabitants (women, the old, children) in just the same way as he might describe the victims of a military attack on the city. This is pathos writ large.

quique sibi quique aliis consulebant: The anaphora *quique ... quique...* and polar contrast *sibi ... aliis* ('themselves... others') underlines how all groups, selfish and altruistic, were contributing to the mayhem.

dum trahunt invalidos aut opperiuntur: *trahunt* and *opperiuntur* form another polar contrast.

pars mora, pars festinans: *mora* (an instrumental ablative) and the circumstantial participle *festinans* form yet another polar contrast, further enhanced by the anaphora of *pars* and the asyndeton. The overall picture is one of panic.

---

164   See further Kraus (1994). Cicero, at *de Lege Agraria* 2.96, also mentions that Rome's roads 'are none of the best' and its side-streets 'of the narrowest'.

cuncta impediebant: After a long and twisting sentence revolving around contrasts, Tacitus sums it all up by blurring the distinctions – a ploy that further underlines the scale of the mayhem.

38.5 et saepe dum in tergum respectant lateribus aut fronte circumveniebantur, vel si in proxima evaserant, illis quoque igni correptis, etiam quae longinqua crediderant in eodem casu reperiebant.

The sentence begins with another conjunction, piling on more information about the panic. An arresting image follows: as people look behind them, the fire surrounds them to their front and side. The mention of all three directions (*tergum ... lateribus ... fronte*) in close succession, summarised by the verb <u>circum</u>*veniebantur*, depicts the fire all around these poor incinerated people.

si in proxima evaserant, illis quoque igni correptis: More language from the battle field: the vain efforts and hopelessness of fleeing from the fire is conveyed by the clause *si ... evaserant*, which suggests a successful escape, followed immediately by the fact that there was no safety even in the neighbouring districts (*proxima*), given the merciless pursuit of the fire.

etiam quae longinqua crediderant in eodem casu reperiebant: The subject of *reperiebant* is an (elided) *ea*, which is also the antecedent of the relative pronoun *quae*. The fire was everywhere: Tacitus' point here is that, whilst it might not be surprising that nearby neighbourhoods (*proxima*) are consumed by the fire, in this great fire even (*etiam*) districts which people believed to be far away from the fire (*longinqua*) are engulfed.

38.6 postremo, quid vitarent quid peterent ambigui, complere vias, sterni per agros; quidam amissis omnibus fortunis, diurni quoque victus, alii caritate suorum, quos eripere nequiverant, quamvis patente effugio interiere.

quid vitarent quid peterent ambigui: The anaphora, asyndeton, polar verbs, and delayed *ambigui* underline the utter bewilderment of the citizens who do not know which way to turn.

complere vias, sterni per agros: The historic infinitives *complere* and *sterni*, juxtaposed asyndetically, increase the pace of the narrative as the people take desperate action. *complere* implies a vast number of victims pouring into the streets, whereas *sternere* is another word often used in military contexts of 'laying someone low' or 'razing cities.' As John Henderson reminds us, in the human tragedy of the moment we ought not to forget the last pulsating throng that populated this very same cityscape but a chapter ago: *struere … completa*, 37.1, 3).

quidam amissis omnibus fortunis, diurni quoque victus, alii caritate suorum, quos eripere nequiverant, quamvis patente effugio interiere: The sentence begins with a bipartite structure that in the end converges in a picture of death fraught with pathos. We get:
Two subjects, juxtaposed asyndetically:

- *quidam*
- *alii*

Two ablatives, one an ablative absolute with causal force, the other an ablative of cause:

- *amissis omnibus fortunis* (followed by the further specification in the genitive to stress their appalling plight: *diurni quoque victus/* 'even of the daily bread' or 'down to the last penny')
- *caritate suorum, quos eripere nequiverant*

Another, concessive ablative absolute that applies to both groups:

- *quamvis patente effugio*

The main verb:

- *interiere*

Overall, the picture we end on is deeply moving – men refusing to abandon their loved ones even if they could not be saved. The final phrase *quamvis patente effugio interiere* is the most emotional as they refuse the option to save themselves. The last word *īntĕrĭērē* has a poetic rhythm (scanning like the fifth and sixth foot of a hexametric line), bringing the searing scene to a climax with death.

38.7 nec quisquam defendere audebat, crebris multorum minis restinguere prohibentium, et quia alii palam faces iaciebant atque esse sibi auctorem vociferabantur, sive ut raptus licentius exercerent seu iussu.

Tacitus now returns to the possibility that the fire began as arson; but again he refuses to take an unequivocal line. After the main sentence (*nec*

... *audebat*), he again continues with two different constructions indicating cause: an ablative of cause (*minis*) and a *quia*-clause.

defendere: The verb reinforces the impression that the fire acts like a hostile army bidding to sack the city.

(a) **crebris** (b) **multorum** (a) **minis restinguere** (b) **prohibentium:** The word-order is interlaced here: *crebris* goes with *minis*, *multorum* with *prohibentium*.

et quia alii palam faces iaciebant atque esse sibi auctorem vociferabantur: Tacitus first stresses the shamelessness of these men with *palam*, before finishing his account of the fire as he began it – with suggestion of a sinister and deliberate hand behind this disaster. The unnamed *auctorem* (instigator, mastermind) lends an air of supernatural mystery and suspicion.

sive ut raptus licentius exercerent seu iussu: Tacitus concludes with an 'alternative motivation', pondering the reality of Nero's hand in the whole disaster. He first mentions the possibility that looting was the cause (as it surely was to some extent), before adding the succinct, yet vague and ominous alternative *seu iussu*. The ablative of cause, rather than the purpose clause *ut ... exercerent*, continues to linger in the mind.

Chapter 39

39.1 Eo in tempore Nero Antii agens non ante in urbem regressus est quam domui eius, qua Palatium et Maecenatis hortos continuaverat, ignis propinquaret. neque tamen sisti potuit quin et Palatium et domus et cuncta circum haurirentur.

After his protestations of devotion to the city in chapter 36, it is not to Nero's credit that he is not in Rome at the time of the fire but staying in his luxury villa at Antium. As we saw earlier (15.23), Antium was the town of Nero's birth. While it does perhaps support the idea that Nero was not responsible for the fire, his nonchalance contrasts sharply with the efforts of his predecessors. Apart from the passages cited above, see also Suetonius, *Claudius* 18.1: *Cum Aemiliana pertinacius arderent, in diribitorio duabus noctibus mansit ac deficiente militum ac familiarum turba auxilio plebem per magistratus ex omnibus vicis convocavit ac positis ante se cum pecunia fiscis ad subveniendum hortatus est, repraesentans pro opera dignam cuique mercedem*

('On the occasion of a stubborn fire in the Aemiliana he remained in the Diribitorium for two nights, and when a body of soldiers and of his own slaves could not give sufficient help, he summoned the commons from all parts of the city through the magistrates, and placing bags full of money before them, urged them to the rescue, paying each man on the spot a suitable reward for his services'). Nor does it do Nero credit, especially after his great claims of patriotism, that he only returned when his own property (*domui eius*) was threatened. The emphatic position of *non ante* stresses that this was the only thing that motivated his return, and the delayed subject *ignis propinquaret* suggests he waited for the last possible minute.

qua Palatium et Maecenatis hortos continuaverat: This is the so-called *Domus Transitoria*: cf. Suetonius, *Nero* 31.1: *Non in alia re tamen damnosior quam in aedificando domum a Palatio Esquilias usque fecit, quam primo transitoriam, mox incendio absumptam restitutamque auream nominavit* ('There was nothing however in which he was more ruinously prodigal than in building. He made a palace extending all the way from the Palatine to the Esquiline, which at first he called the House of Passage, but when it was burned shortly after its completion and rebuilt, the Golden House'). Nero's palace lay between the site of the traditional imperial residence, Augustus' house on the Palatine (whence our word 'palace') and the great gardens of Maecenas on the Esquiline Hill, which he left to Augustus. The verb *continuaverat* exaggerates the scale of Nero's immense crosstown palace – but also skewers Nero's own hubristic wit in dubbing it 'Passageway.'

neque tamen sisti potuit quin et Palatium et domus et cuncta circum haurirentur: The emphatically placed *neque tamen* underlines again the impossibility of controlling the blaze, and the repetition of *Palatium* and *domus* from the previous sentence emphasises that nothing could be saved. The polysyndeton *et ... et ... et ...* and the alliterative cuncta circum both help to underscore the total devastation of the fire.

39.2 sed solacium populo exturbato ac profugo campum Martis ac monumenta Agrippae, hortos quin etiam suos patefecit et subitaria aedificia extruxit quae multitudinem inopem acciperent; subvectaque utensilia ab Ostia et propinquis municipiis pretiumque frumenti minutum usque ad ternos nummos.

The subject of *patefecit* and *extruxit* is Nero. *patefecit* takes three accusative objects, in a climactic tricolon: *campum Martis, monumenta Agrippae,* and *hortos suos.* (First we hit a public area of the city, then the building of one of Nero's ancestors, finally his own gardens.) *solacium* (also in the accusative) stands in apposition to all three.

sed solacium: Tacitus changes the tone, marked by the *sed,* from Nero's selfishness and failure to stop the fire to his more noble efforts at relief. His account is balanced, especially when compared to other historians of the event, presenting Nero's suspected arson in the same breath as his great energy in trying to help. What an actor! How to tell what's real in Nero's world?

populo exturbato ac profugo: Tacitus conveys the misery of the citizens with the powerful and strengthened adjective *exturbato* ('frightened out of their mind') and the fact that they are homeless refugees (*profugo*) in their own city. Given Tacitus' investment in aligning the fire of Rome with the sack of Troy (following in the footsteps of Nero, as the end of this paragraph makes clear), the term *profugus* may also gesture to Virgil's *Aeneid* and the most famous *profugus* in Roman history, Aeneas. See *Aeneid* 1.2, where Aeneas is introduced as *fato profugus* ('exiled by fate').

campum Martis: The 'Plain of Mars' had once been the mustering and training ground for soldiers just outside the boundaries of the old city walls. By this period, it was intensively developed, especially with imperial buildings such as the Pantheon and sporting facilities. It is usually referred to as the *Campus Martius* (see *Map of Rome*).

monumenta Agrippae: Agrippa, Augustus' right-hand man, had orchestrated much of the building on the *Campus Martius*, including the *Porticus Vipsania*, the Pantheon and the so-called Baths of Agrippa.

multitudinem inopem: This simple phrase suggests both the number of the impoverished Romans (*multitudinem*) and their ruin (*inopem*).

subvectaque utensilia: The emphatic position of the verb *subvecta* suggests Nero's speedy measures.

Ostia: The port of Ostia was located on the coast at the 'gateway' ('*ostium*') to the Tiber south west of Rome (see *Map of Italy*).

pretiumque frumenti minutum usque ad ternos nummos: This is a significant step: emperors did not usually intervene to set a maximum price for corn as it damaged the ability of merchants to make profit, so this marks a real emergency. With the price of corn at the time at around five sesterces per *modius* (about 16 pints of dry corn), this is a significant reduction, stressed by *usque ad* ('right the way down to').[165]

39.3 quae quamquam popularia in inritum cadebant, quia pervaserat rumor ipso tempore flagrantis urbis inisse eum domesticam scaenam et cecinisse Troianum excidium, praesentia mala vetustis cladibus adsimulantem.

quae ... popularia: *quae* is a connecting relative pronoun (= *ea*); it modifies *popularia*, which is an adjective used as a noun ('these popular measures').

quamquam: In a main clause: 'however'

pervaserat rumor: The rumour is personified as a force of its own, wandering around (*pervaserat*). The inversion of normal word order (verb + subject) adds emphasis to the power of this rumour and the extent of its spread. The pluperfect indicates that the damage had already been done.

rumor: Interestingly, it is again only Tacitus of the extant historians who reports that this was only a rumour: the others cheerfully record it as a fact. See Suetonius, *Nero* 38 and Dio 62.18.1, both cited above.

inisse eum domesticam scaenam et cecinisse Troianum excidium: An indirect statement dependent on *rumor*, with *eum* as subjective accusative and *inisse* and *cecinisse* as infinitives (note their front position and rhyme). This is where one of the most famous stories of Roman history comes from – Nero fiddling as Rome burns. Whatever its veracity (not counting the violin!), the plausibility of the rumour feeds on Nero's notorious obsession with dramatic performances.

domesticam scaenam: This harks back to 15.33, where Tacitus reports on Nero's desire to appear on stage before a larger public, in venues other than his house. This particular performance here, if it ever happened, took place within the confines of Nero's palace. There are no eye-witnesses Tacitus can rely on. So he reports a rumour – true to life, in the case of most such catastrophes?

---

165   On famine and food supply in ancient Rome see further Garnsey (1988).

Troianum excidium: The sack of the mighty city of Troy (on the western seaboard of modern Turkey) by the Greeks was one of the defining events of ancient mythology, told at length (above all) by Virgil in *Aeneid* 2. Nero opts for the grandest possible comparandum and must hint at the Trojan origins of Rome.

praesentia mala vetustis cladibus adsimulantem: The fact that Nero himself compared the fire to a (in fact *the*) military sack helps Tacitus' own subtle presentation of the fire as a battle. As our introduction to the section on the fire has tried to make clear, the rumour of Nero conflating in song Troy and Rome plays right into Tacitus' hands, enabling him to represent Nero, the last scion of the Julio-Claudian imperial lineage, as the 'anti-Augustus' of the principate: what started at Troy and climaxed with Augustus (as chronicled by Virgil) comes to an end with Nero (as chronicled by Tacitus).

Chapter 40

40.1 Sexto demum die apud imas Esquilias finis incendio factus, prorutis per immensum aedificiis ut continuae violentiae campus et velut vacuum caelum occurreret. necdum positus metus aut redierat plebi spes: rursum grassatus ignis, patulis magis urbis locis; eoque strages hominum minor, delubra deum et porticus amoenitati dicatae latius procidere.

sexto demum die: The fire lasted six days before it was extinguished. *demum* ('at last') suggests both the real length of the fire, and also how long the misery must have seemed.

apud imas Esquilias: The Esquiline hill was another of Rome's seven hills to the east of the city (see *Map of Rome*).

finis incendio factus, prorutis per immensum aedificiis: The phrase *finis incendio factus*, with its alliterative paronomasia (*finis ~ factus*) and its sequence of light and dark vowels, including all five (*i, i, i, e, i – o, a, u*), conveys a (premature) sense of closure. Through the demolition of buildings and clearance of the rubble, the fire was deprived of fuel. *prorutis ... aedificiis* is an ablative absolute. The emphatic adverbial phrase with preposition *per immensum* ('over a vast area') makes clear the enormous scale of the demolitions, which razed large sections of the city to the ground.

ut continuae violentiae [sc. *ignium* or *incendii*] **campus et velut vacuum caelum occurreret:** *continuae violentiae* is in the dative singular (with *occurreret*). The description of the city as a *campus* ('plain') suggests the utter eradication of buildings, as does the self-proclaimed hyperbole *velut vacuum caelum*, which evokes the desolation of the Roman skyline. (*continua violentia* recalls and replaces *continuaverat*, said of endless palace of Nero in 39.1.) Tacitus here mixes *c*- and *v*-alliteration (*continuae, campus, caelum; violentiae, velut, vacuum*), but does so indiscriminately across the two themes of 'conflagration' and 'counter-measures.' The emphatic position of *continuae violentiae* also conveys the constant threat of the fire.

necdum positus [sc. *erat*] **metus aut redierat plebi spes:** The text is corrupt here, and based on conjecture. Some editors prefer to read *levis* instead of *plebi*. It seems reasonably certain, however, that we are dealing with the expression of the same thought in two opposite ways ('still fear, no hope'), in each case with the verb coming first. The sentence stresses the despair that prevailed in the populace, with the elusive *spes* placed emphatically at the end.

rursum grassatus [sc. *est*] **ignis patulis magis urbis locis:** The verb (*grassatus*), once more placed first, is a very strong and evocative one, again personifying the fire in dramatic fashion: its basic meaning is 'to press on, march, advance', but it can also refer to brigands prowling around in the search for victims and carries connotations of lawlessness and violence. An inscription to commemorate the fire says *VRBS PER NOVEM DIES ARSIT NERONIANIS TEMPORIBVS* ('the city burned for nine days in Neronian times').[166] If the first fire was six days in duration, this implies the second blaze lasted three days. After *finis, prorutis,* and *aedificiis*, we now get five words in a row ending in -*is*: a striking series of thudding homoioteleuta. *patulis ... locis* is an ablative of place: this time it is the more open areas rather than the congested parts which burn.

eoque strages hominum minor [sc. *erat*]**:** The -*que* links *grassatus* [*est*] and [*erat*]. *eo* is an ablative of the measure of difference ('to the extent to which') that helps to coordinate the two comparatives *minor* and *latius*. The more open areas enabled people to avoid the flames better. The strong word *strages* ('slaughter', 'carnage') reminds us of the damage done by the first

---

166   See *Corpus Inscriptionum Latinarum* VI.1, 826.

conflagration; and given the number of casualties then, the fact that the second fire cost fewer lives is only a qualified relief.

delubra deum et porticus amoenitati dicatae latius procidere: Buildings remained vulnerable, and here Tacitus stresses the importance and beauty of those that fell victim to the flames in the second conflagration. The asyndetic juxtaposition of *minor [erat]* and *latius procidere* ensures that the bad news abruptly overpowers the good news, conveying the sense that the lower death-toll among the human population was amply compensated for by large-scale architectural damage (an impression reinforced by the length of the respective clauses). The alliterative *delubra deum* emphasises the ominous destruction of holy places, and is an epic (Ennian) phrase used in the awe-ful tableau of the last hours of Virgil's Troy (*Aeneid* 2.248), in a passage strongly intertwined with Livy's account of the fall of Veii (5.21.5, alluding to the same – Ennian – forerunner); and the description of the colonnades as *amoenitati dicatae*, with attention-drawing assonance, makes clear the beauty of the incinerated buildings. Note also the comparative adverb *latius*, presenting the destruction here as even worse than the one caused by the first fire. Finally, the verb *procidere* (an historic infinitive) once again evokes the power of the fire, and keeps the music going through to the final collapse (*por-* … *dic-* ~ *pro-cid-* …).

40.2 plusque infamiae id incendium habuit quia praediis Tigellini Aemilianis proruperat videbaturque Nero condendae urbis novae et cognomento suo appellandae gloriam quaerere. quippe in regiones quattuordecim Roma dividitur, quarum quattuor integrae manebant, tres solo tenus deiectae: septem reliquis pauca tectorum vestigia supererant, lacera et semusta.

plusque infamiae id incendium habuit: As Tacitus told us in Chapter 39, Nero attracted opprobrium because of the suspicion of arson in the first fire. Now he says there was more scandal. The comparative adverb *plus*, like *latius* before, conveys the escalation in destruction, both of the city and of Nero's reputation.

plusque infamiae: *infamiae* is a partitive genitive dependent on *plus*.

quia praediis Tigellini Aemilianis proruperat: *praedium* ('estate', 'land') is not to be confused with the more common/ familiar *praeda* ('booty'). *praediis*

... *Aemilianis* is an ablative of origin: apparently the second fire broke out at an estate that belonged to Tigellinus, the very same Praetorian Prefect who just stage-managed Nero's all-aboard floating orgy. The estate was probably located somewhere between the Campus Martius and the Capitol Hill, in the vicinity of what would become the Forum of Trajan.

videbaturque Nero condendae urbis novae et cognomento suo appellandae gloriam quaerere: The position of the verb *videbatur* straight after *proruperat* underscores how immediately the people leapt to conclusions and set the rumour mill spinning. Possibly, Nero or Tigellinus were responsible for the second fire, wanting to clear space for full-scale rebuilding. But it is equally possible that embers from a six-day blaze flared up again, and people acted without evidence on their desire to attribute blame, coming up with the rumour that all this was the emperor's doing. The chiastic arrangement of *condendae urbis novae et cognomento suo appellandae*, with the gerundives emphatic on the outside, exaggerates the shocking aims Nero was rumoured to have had. Suetonius, *Nero* 50, tells us that Nero intended to call the new city he wished to build Neropolis: a Greek name, and therefore yet another suggestion of Nero's Greek obsession. (Tacitus is careful not to mention the name, nor to report this as anything more than a rumour.)

gloriam quaerere: The implications of *gloria* are insidious: it is a quality that derives first and foremost from military conquest, and thus feeds into the latent characterization of the fire as a hostile army sacking Rome – with Nero as mastermind and general. Perversely, *gloria* here derives not from the triumph over a foreign enemy and the return to Rome with the spoils of victory, but death and destruction of his own capital. There is also unmistakable irony in Tacitus' use of *gloria* here: Nero desires glory for a re-foundation of the capital in his name, but what he acquires is notoriety for arson and hubris.

quippe in regiones quattuordecim Romam dividitur: The little word *quippe* introduces the final reckoning of the fire which Tacitus now gives, starting with a summary statement about the city: Augustus had divided Rome into fourteen administrative regions (see *Map of Rome*). Tacitus' readers would of course not have needed a reminder about Rome's administrative grid, especially since he already mentioned it at 14.12.2. And therefore many editors and commentators see this sentence as a marginal gloss by copyists that accidentally entered into the main text in the process of transmission.

But one could turn this around if one reads 14.12.2 as an anticipation of the fire: there Tacitus reports that in AD 59 there were several eclipses of the sun and all fourteen administrative districts of Rome were hit by lightning (*iam sol repente obscuratus et tactae de caelo quattuordecim urbis regiones*). Since no disaster happened immediately Tacitus goes on to dismiss the idea that this striking coincidence was a genuine prodigy (i.e. a meaningful sign of advanced warning of pending disaster sent by the gods): *quae adeo sine cura deum eveniebant, ut multos post ea annos Nero imperium et scelera continuaverit.* By taking an oblique look back to 14.12.2 here, by means of repeating basic information about the administrative layout of the city, Tacitus almost asks his readers to re-assess his own earlier (already ironic, in view of the upcoming, if somewhat belated, fire?) evaluation of divine efficaciousness.

quattuor [sc. *regiones*] **integrae manebant:** It is not entirely certain which four districts are meant. Here is Miller: 'these would be the districts farthest from the centre of the city and the fire, and would certainly include XIV (*Transtiberina*): as the fire stopped *apud imas Esquilinas* §1, V (*Esquiliae*) may have been another: the other possibilities are I (*Porta Capena*), VI (*Alta Semita*) and VII (*Via Lata*).'[167] Koestermann agrees on *regio XIV Transtiberina*, but disregards *V Esquiliae* and considers *I Porta Capena*, *VI Alta Semita*, and *VII Via Lata* as the other most likely candidates.[168]

tres [sc. *regiones*] **solo tenus deiectae** [sc. *erant*]: *tenus* is a preposition that takes, and follows, the ablative (*solo*). Again, the districts in question are in dispute: 'Of the three wholly destroyed, two must have been the 11th and 10th (Circus and Palatium), and the other is thought to have been the 3rd (Isis et Serapis, the Subura).'[169] Koestermann opts for *regio XI Circus Maximus, X Palatium* and *IV Templum Pacis*.[170]

septem reliquis [sc. regionibus] **pauca tectorum vestigia supererant, lacera et semusta:** The systematic account of the destruction continues: the dramatic description of *pauca vestigia* being left paints the picture of the unrecognizable wreckage of buildings. The adjective *lacer, -era, -erum,* which means 'mutilated' or 'mangled' tends to be used of corpses and

---

167 Miller (1973) 91.
168 Koestermann (1968) 242.
169 Furneaux (1907) 367.
170 Koestermann (1968) 242.

once more evokes the image of the city as a living being that fell victim to violent assault. Commentators draw attention to the fact that Tacitus here exaggerates. As he himself concedes later, the buildings on the Capitol remained intact and the Forum, too, was largely unaffected. See *Annals* 15.44.1 and 16.27. Even in the Campus Martius, buildings such as the Augustan portico of the Pantheon remained standing and, as Furneaux points out, 'the theatre of Pompeius was used for the Neronia [in AD 65] immediately after the conspiracy.'[171]

Chapter 41

41.1 Domuum et insularum et templorum quae amissa sunt numerum inire haud promptum fuerit: sed vetustissima religione, quod Servius Tullius Lunae et magna ara fanumque quae praesenti Herculi Arcas Evander sacraverat, aedesque Statoris Iovis vota Romulo Numaeque regia et delubrum Vestae cum Penatibus populi Romani exusta; iam opes tot victoriis quaesitae et Graecarum artium decora, exim monumenta ingeniorum antiqua et incorrupta, ut quamvis in tanta resurgentis urbis pulchritudine multa seniores meminerint quae reparari nequibant.

Tacitus takes stock of the damage. A good passage to compare this with is *Histories* 3.72, where Tacitus had described the impact of a later fire on the Capitol, which wrought similar devastation on ancient buildings and heirlooms. (This fire occurred in AD 69 as the result of violence among troops during the chaos surrounding the fall of Vitellius.)

> Id facinus post conditam urbem luctuosissimum foedissimumque rei publicae populi Romani accidit, nullo externo hoste, propitiis, si per mores nostros liceret, deis, sedem Iovis Optimi Maximi auspicato a maioribus pignus imperii conditam, quam non Porsenna dedita urbe neque Galli capta temerare potuissent, furore principum excindi. arserat et ante Capitolium civili bello, sed fraude privata: nunc palam obsessum, palam incensum, quibus armorum causis? quo tantae cladis pretio? stetit dum pro patria bellavimus. voverat Tarquinius Priscus rex bello Sabino, ieceratque fundamenta spe magis futurae magnitudinis quam quo modicae adhuc populi Romani res sufficerent. mox Servius Tullius sociorum studio, dein Tarquinius Superbus capta Suessa Pometia hostium spoliis exstruxere. sed gloria operis libertati reservata: pulsis regibus Horatius Pulvillus iterum consul dedicavit ea magnificentia quam immensae postea populi

---

171   Furneaux (1907) 367, with reference to *Annals* 16.4.2.

Romani opes ornarent potius quam augerent. isdem rursus vestigiis situm est, postquam interiecto quadringentorum quindecim annorum spatio L. Scipione C. Norbano consulibus flagraverat. curam victor Sulla suscepit, neque tamen dedicavit: hoc solum felicitati eius negatum. Lutatii Catuli nomen inter tanta Caesarum opera usque ad Vitellium mansit. ea tunc aedes cremabatur.

[This was the saddest and most shameful crime that the Roman state had ever suffered since its foundation. Rome had no foreign foe; the gods were ready to be propitious if our character had allowed; and yet the home of Jupiter Optimus Maximus, founded after due auspices by our ancestors as a pledge of empire, which neither Porsenna, when the city gave itself up to him, nor the Gauls when they captured it, could violate – this was the shrine that the mad fury of emperors destroyed! The Capitol had indeed been burned before in civil war, but the crime was that of private individuals. Now it was openly besieged, openly burned – and what were the causes that led to arms? What was the price paid for this great disaster? This temple stood intact so long as we fought for our country. King Tarquinius Priscus had vowed it in the war with the Sabines and had laid its foundations rather to match his hope of future greatness than in accordance with what the fortunes of the Roman people, still moderate, could supply. Later the building was begun by Servius Tullius with the enthusiastic help of Rome's allies, and afterwards carried on by Tarquinius Superbus with the spoils taken from the enemy at the capture of Suessa Pometia. But the glory of completing the work was reserved for liberty: after the expulsion of the kings, Horatius Pulvillus in his second consulship dedicated it; and its magnificence was such that the enormous wealth of the Roman people acquired thereafter adorned rather than increased its splendour. The temple was built again on the same spot when after an interval of four hundred and fifteen years it had been burned in the consulship of Lucius Scipio and Gaius Norbanus. The victorious Sulla undertook the work, but still he did not dedicate it; that was the only thing that his good fortune was refused. Amid all the great works built by the Caesars the name of Lutatius Catulus kept its place down to Vitellius' day. This was the temple that then was burned.]

domuum et insularum et templorum quae amissa sunt numerum inire haud promptum fuerit: The subject of the sentence is the infinitive *inire*, which governs the accusative *numerum* on which the genitive plurals *domuum*, *insularum* and *templorum* depend. (The relative pronoun *quae*, in the nominative neuter plural, corresponds grammatically to the closest of the nouns, i.e. *templa*, but clearly picks up all three.) The verb *fuerit* is in the perfect subjunctive, more specifically a 'potential subjunctive of modest assertion.'[172] For the distinction between *domus* and *insula*, see *Annals* 6.45.1,

---

172 Furneaux (1907) 368.

also in the context of a fire (cited above). Cf. Suetonius, *Nero* 38.2: *tunc praeter immensum numerum insularum domus priscorum ducum arserunt* ('at that time, besides an immense number of dwellings, the houses of leaders of old were burned'), who hands syntactical prominence to the aristocratic *domus*.

sed: The *sed* marks the contrast between the countless *domus* and *insulae* that fell victim to the flames, and the significant number of highly sacred temples and objects that perished – and which can be taken stock of, as Tacitus goes on to do.

sed vetustissima religione, quod Servius Tullius Lunae [sc. *sacraverat*]**, et magna ara fanumque, quae praesenti Herculi Arcas Evander sacraverat, aedesque Statoris Iovis vota Romulo Numaeque regia et delubrum Vestae cum Penatibus populi Romani exusta** [sc. *erant*]**:** In the previous sentence Tacitus explained that he would not enter into an itemized accounting of ordinary buildings (including temples) that fell victim to the flames. But (*sed*), he now lists those temples of most venerable age and religious import that burnt down. *vetustissima religione* is an ablative of quality or characteristic modifying the understood subject *templa*; the main verb comes at the end: *exusta*, sc. *sunt*. In-between we get a list of the sacred sites that were destroyed:[173]

- [*templum*], *quod Servius Tullius Lunae* (or *Lucinae*) [sc. *sacraverat*]
- *magna ara fanumque, quae praesenti Herculi Arcas Evander sacraverat*
- *aedes Statoris Iovis vota Romulo*
- *Numae regia*
- *delubrum Vestae cum penatibus populi Romani*

The delayed and strengthened verb (*ex-usta*), right at the end of the huge list, stresses the total destruction of these sites and how all of them shared one common fate.

sed ... et ... -que ... -que ... -que ... et ...: Tacitus uses a prolonged polysyndeton in his enumeration of the buildings, which is well-balanced between *et* and *-que* and helps to generate a good sense of the large number of buildings that burnt down – an effect further enhanced by the sheer length of the sentence,

---

173   Miller (1973) 92 regards *vetustissima religione* as 'a loosely attached abl. of attendant circumstances or quality.' Cf. *fessa aetate* (38.4).

and the variation in constructions and choice of words. To flesh out the special significance of the buildings under consideration Tacitus starts out with two relative clause (*quod ... Lunae; quae ... sacraverat*), then moves on to a perfect passive participle (*vota Romulo*), details one item without any further specification (*Numae regia*), and finishes with a prepositional phrase (*cum penatibus populi Romani*). To refer to holy sites, he piles up four different words, which are more or less synonymous with one another: *templum* (implied from the previous sentence), *fanum, aedes, delubrum*.

quod Servius Tullius Lunae [sc. *sacraverat*]: Servius Tullius was the sixth (and penultimate) king of Rome. This is the only place in which he is the founder of the temple of Luna on the Aventine, whereas other sources (Livy 1.45.2 and Dionysius Halicarnassus 4.26) have him as founder of the famous temple of Diana, also located on the Aventine. Since Diana was also goddess of the Moon, we may be dealing with a conflation of the two temples here. Koestermann prefers the alternative reading *Lucinae* (another name of Diana: see e.g. Catullus 34.13).[174] Irrespective of the textual problem and the identity of the temple, it is apparent that Tacitus wishes to insist on the heavy toll taken on the most ancient and religious edifices, and in so doing to suggest the corruption of modern Rome and its fall from its ancient roots.

et magna ara fanumque, quae praesenti Herculi Arcas Evander sacraverat: The *Ara Maxima*, situated towards the north west of the Circus, was an ancient sanctuary dedicated to Hercules. Evander was a pre-historic/ mythical hero who founded a settlement on the site of Rome after he came to Italy from Arcadia (hence *Arcas*) in Greece. He famously plays host to Aeneas in *Aeneid* 8. Virgil and other sources recount that Evander dedicated the altar after Hercules slew Cacus, the monster-in-residence at the future site of Rome. Again, the extreme antiquity of this shrine (which predates even the foundation of Rome) emphasises the loss.

aedes Statoris Iovis vota Romulo: Tacitus name-checks two of the greatest and most revered of figures: Jupiter, king of the gods, and the city's founder Romulus. Romulus was said to have dedicated this temple to Jupiter after he stopped the Romans from fleeing during their war with the Sabines – hence the epithet *Stator* ('the Stayer'). See, for instance, Livy 1.12.4–5. The

174 Koestermann (1968) 243.

temple stood in the Forum. Tacitus here arguably issues a subtle reminder of the indomitable military prowess of old, which in the inglorious present is literally burnt to cinders.

Numae regia: Numa, the second legendary king of Rome (way back in the eighth century BC), was especially famed for his religious devotion. His temple in the Forum was used as residence of Rome's chief religious official, the *pontifex maximus*. It housed many sacred objects of great antiquity, such as the shields of the priesthood of the Salii.

delubrum Vestae cum Penatibus populi Romani: The temple of Vesta, a distinctive circular building in the Forum, was where the Vestal Virgins tended to their sacred flame, symbolising the hearth of the Roman family (but we are also reminded of Nero's freak-out at Vesta's Capitoline temple in 37.1). The Penates, the household gods of Rome, were also kept here: these were said to have been brought to Italy by Aeneas on his flight from Troy, so are once again items of the utmost antiquity and sanctity. The destruction of these items, saved from Troy's fall but now ruined, is an extremely potent and ominous symbol of both the power of the fire and the reign of Nero. In placing a reference to the Penates last – the only object in a list of temples – Tacitus may even hint slyly at Nero's performance of the 'Sack of Troy' during the fire: everyone of his readers would know where they originally came from. The effect is enhanced by the following sentence, where Tacitus switches into a generic lamentation about the number of ancient and venerable objects that burnt, through which the Penates retrospectively gain even greater profile and significance.

iam opes tot victoriis quaesitae et Graecarum artium decora, exim monumenta ingeniorum antiqua et incorrupta [sc. *exusta sunt*], ut quamvis in tanta resurgentis urbis pulchritudine multa seniores meminerint quae reparari nequibant.

After a list of the shrines and temples (and the Penates) Tacitus proceeds to comment on the (again innumerable) objects that perished in the flames. The adverbs *iam* and *exim*, which give structure to the account, help to convey the seemingly endless list of items. The main sentence is designed as a tricolon: *opes – decora – monumenta*, the three subjects of the (elided) verb *exusta sunt*. But Tacitus, as is his wont, unsettles the design by linking the first and the second item with *et* and juxtaposing the first two (introduced by *iam*) and the last (introduced by *exim*) asyndetically.

opes tot victoriis quaesitae: The word *opes* ('riches'; cf. English 'opulence') makes clear the preciousness of the spoils destroyed, whilst the glory of their acquisition is represented by *victoriis* – in contrast to Nero's lavish use of riches and opulence, these were won in the proper Roman military manner.

Graecorum artium decora: *decora* refers to works of Greek art, which had been brought to Rome in the course of Rome's conquest (and plunder) of the Greek world. In fact, Nero was among the most avid collectors. The use of the word *decus*, which can designate both social and aesthetic value ('high esteem, honour, glory' – 'pleasing appearance, beauty, grace, splendour') conveys the magnificence of the artefacts lost.

monumenta ingeniorum antiqua et incorrupta: Tacitus is referring to destroyed works of literature. Although Rome's great Palatine Library was not damaged until its destruction in AD 363, many important texts may well have been burnt in temple records or private homes. The attributes *antiqua et incorrupta* contain an oblique and curious appraisal of the value of the works in question: Tacitus almost seems to be saying that these literary products were ancient *and hence* morally sound (i.e. untouched by the corruption that later set in), passing judgement on literary outputs in imperial times. The loss of this ancient, untainted literature is all the mere keenly felt given that his own times are no longer conducive to producing *monumenta incorrupta*. Alternatively, one could consider seeing here a rhetorical displacement of the attribute, with *incorrupta* modifying *monumenta* grammatically, but *ingeniorum* in terms of sense. The implications for Tacitus' view on literary production in imperial Rome are the same.

ut quamvis in tanta resurgentis urbis pulchritudine multa seniores meminerint quae reparari nequibant: Tacitus admits that the new city built by Nero was full of beauty, made clear by *tanta*, which modifies, in hyperbaton, *pulchritudine*. The phrase *in tanta ... pulchritudine* embraces the genitive *resurgentis urbis*, stressing the comprehensive beautification of the new Rome that rose after the conflagration. The vivid present participle *resurgentis* (*lit.* 'rising again') suggests that, even as the new beauty rose up, people realised the irreplaceable losses.

multa: Tacitus places the accusative object emphatically before the subject (*seniores*) to stress the enormity of the losses of ancient wonders.

quae reparari nequibant: Tacitus is explicit: although the new city was splendid, the likes of the great relics lost were never to be seen again.

41.2 fuere qui adnotarent XIIII Kal. Sextiles principium incendii huius ortum [sc. *esse*] [sc. *eo die*], **quo et Senones captam urbem inflammaverint. alii eo usque cura progressi sunt ut totidem annos mensesque et dies inter utraque incendia numerent.**

fuere qui...: As so often, Tacitus reports what some people said and thought without endorsing it himself. Here, this takes the form of some rather contrived observations about 'spooky' coincidences and parallels – not the sort of things the highly rational Tacitus thinks important or sensible, but he does titillate his readers by including them, even as he makes quite clear his own view on the matter.

adnotarent: The subjunctive is generic. *adnotarent* introduces an indirect statement with *principium* as subject accusative and *ortum* [sc. *esse*] as verb.

XIIII Kal. Sextiles: The Roman calendar had three marked days each month: the so-called 'Kalends' (always the first day of the month), 'Nones' (either the fifth or the seventh day of the month, depending on the number of days within), and 'Ides' (either the 13th or the 15th of the month, again depending on the number of days within). Dates that did not fall on the Kalends, Nones, or Ides (when the date would simply be 'on the Kalends, or Nones, or Ides of [name of the month]') were designated by looking *forward* to the next demarcation coming up and then counting *backwards*. This means that all the days in July *after* the Ides would be designated by looking ahead to the Kalends of August (1 August in our reckoning) and then counting backwards, and this is what is going on here. The day in question is (in our reckoning) 19 July, i.e. *ante diem quartum decimum Kalendas Sextiles* or, in the abbreviation Tacitus uses, *XIIII Kal. Sextiles*. There are fourteen days – *quartum decimum* = XIIII = XIV = 14 – since the Romans counted inclusively: both 19 July and 1 August contribute to the sum. In 8 BC, the Romans renamed *Sextilis* as *Augustus* (from which our August derives), but Tacitus pointedly ignores this re-branding.

quo et Senones captam urbem inflammaverint: The (Senonian) Gauls had captured and burned Rome in 390 BC on this same date. This is indeed a fascinating coincidence; but we must remember that there were a great number of fires in Rome, and that the dating of such earlier conflagrations may well have been both less than precise and open to a little massaging, way back in Rome's history. The sack of Rome by the Gauls was remembered fearfully throughout Rome's life as one of its lowest points, so the comparison here is an indication of how dire an event the Great Fire seemed to people. Notice how Tacitus stresses that the previous fire was during a military capture (*captam*), both reinforcing his imagery of the fire as an invading army and hinting further at the more inglorious causes attached to this modern fire (i.e. the emperor himself starting it – 'then it was our great enemies, now it is our own leader!'). (Conversely, the coincidence could well be mustered as an argument against the suspicion that Nero played arsonist, at least of the first fire: would he have chosen a date that would inevitably have associated him with one of Rome's worst enemies and nightmares?)

alii eo usque cura progressi sunt ut totidem annos mensesque et dies inter utraque incendia numerent: Miller has the following rather curious note here: 'from 390 B.C. to A.D. 64 is (on Roman inclusive reckoning) 454 years: this can be expressed as 418 years, 418 months (34 years, 10 months) and 418 days (14 months). The calculation has about as much real significance as have attempts to express the names of, e.g., Napoleon or Hitler in terms of the number of the Beast in *Revelation* 13,18, and Tacitus' comment indicates his opinion of such activities'[175] – curious since there are compelling scholarly arguments that the number of the Beast in *Revelation* in fact signifies – Nero![176] Given the apocalyptic anticipations in the run-up to the year 2000 (are you old enough to remember the hysteria caused by the 'Y2K bug' and the 'millennium doomwatch'?) or, more recently, the press coverage of the ancient Mayan calendar insofar as it predicted the end of the world on 21 December 2012, we are in a good position to appreciate the kind of anxieties caused by prophecies that circulated in Neronian Rome. Tacitus makes abundantly plain that he views this alleged coincidence as very contrived. The phrase *eo usque*, the strong verb *progressi sunt* (gone, advanced) and the result clause (*ut...*) all indicate that the men who made these calculations were stretching things rather. Nevertheless, he wants to

---

175   Miller (1973) 93.
176   Klauck (2003).

include it as a potentially amusing little nugget of information (and perhaps a derisive comment on how far some people go on these occasions to make supernatural sense of things). Cf. Cassius Dio 62.18.3: 'When some portents took place at this time, the seers declared that they meant destruction for him and they advised him to divert the evil upon others.' John Henderson recommends reading this passage with Livy in mind: 'Tacitus expects those who know the historian Livy's account of the Gallic Sack to remember how (well) Camillus underlines the count of years – 365, yes indeed: a significant number under the new Julian calendar! – that the gods looked after Rome since the foundation by Romulus: far too much to throw away ... (5.54.5: the religious arguments '*moved them*' most to stay put in their ruins, 5.55.1!).'

cura: An ablative of cause.

(vi) 42–43: Reconstructing the Capital: Nero's New Palace

Nero's architectural hubris attracted significant attention from litterateurs. Two voices that can usefully be compared with Tacitus' account in the following chapters are those of Suetonius and Martial. See Suetonius, *Nero* 31.1–3:

> Non in alia re tamen damnosior quam in aedificando domum a Palatio Esquilias usque fecit, quam primo transitoriam, mox incendio absumptam restitutamque auream nominavit. De cuius spatio atque cultu suffecerit haec rettulisse. Vestibulum eius fuit, in quo colossus CXX pedum staret ipsius effigie; tanta laxitas, ut porticus triplices miliarias haberet; item stagnum maris instar, circumsaeptum aedificiis ad urbium speciem; rura insuper arvis atque vinetis et pascuis silvisque varia, cum multitudine omnis generis pecudum ac ferarum. 2 In ceteris partibus cuncta auro lita, distincta gemmis unionumque conchis erant; cenationes laqueatae tabulis eburneis versatilibus, ut flores, fistulatis, ut unguenta desuper spargerentur; praecipua cenationum rotunda, quae perpetuo diebus ac noctibus vice mundi circumageretur; balineae marinis et albulis fluentes aquis. Eius modi domum cum absolutam dedicaret, hactenus comprobavit, ut se diceret quasi hominem tandem habitare coepisse. 3 Praeterea incohabat piscinam a Miseno ad Avernum lacum contectam porticibusque conclusam, quo quidquid totis Baiis calidarum aquarum esset converteretur; fossam ab Averno Ostiam usque, ut navibus nec tamen mari iretur, longitudinis per centum sexaginta milia, latitudinis, qua contrariae quinqueremes commearent. Quorum operum perficiendorum gratia quod ubique esset custodiae in Italiam deportari, etiam scelere convictos non nisi ad opus damnari praeceperat.

[There was nothing however in which he was more ruinously prodigal than in building. He made a palace extending all the way from the Palatine to the Esquiline, which at first he called the House of Passage, but when it was burned shortly after its completion and rebuilt, the Golden House. Its size and splendour will be sufficiently indicated by the following details. Its vestibule was large enough to contain a colossal statue of the emperor a hundred and twenty feet high; and it was so extensive that it had a triple colonnade a mile long. There was a pond too, like a sea, surrounded with buildings to represent cities, besides tracts of country, varied with tilled fields, vineyards, pastures and woods, with great numbers of wild and domestic animals. In the rest of the house all parts were overlaid with gold and adorned with gems and mother-of-pearl. There were dining-rooms with fretted ceilings of ivory, whose panels could turn and shower down flowers and were fitted with pipes for sprinkling the guests with perfumes. The main banquet hall was circular and constantly revolved day and night, like the heavens. He had baths supplied with sea water and sulphur water. When the edifice was finished in this style and he dedicated it, he deigned to say nothing more in the way of approval than that he was at last beginning to be housed like a human being. He also began a pool, extending from Misenum to the lake of Avernus, roofed over and enclosed in colonnades, into which he planned to turn all the hot springs in every part of Baiae; a canal from Avernus all the way to Ostia, to enable the journey to be made by ship yet not by sea; its length was to be a hundred and sixty miles and its breadth sufficient to allow ships with five banks of oars to pass each other. For the execution of these projects he had given orders that the prisoners all over the empire should be transported to Italy, and that those who were convicted even of capital crimes should be punished in no other way than by sentence to this work.]

And here is Martial, the second poem from his *Liber De Spectaculis*, a book of epigrams on the Flavian Amphitheatre (better known today as the Colosseum), which was begun by Vespasian and finished by Titus. In – deliberate – contrast to Nero's Golden House, this imperial building project was specifically designed to make a significant contribution to the civic life of Rome, thus restoring architectural order at the centre of the city, and it was recognized and hailed as such by Martial:[177]

Hic ubi sidereus propius videt astra colossus

    et crescunt media pegmata celsa via,

invidiosa feri radiabant atria regis

---

177 Text and translation by D. R. Shackleton Bailey in the Loeb Classical Library edition (Cambridge, Mass. and London, 1993).

unaque iam tota stabat in urbe domus;

hic ubi conspicui venerabilis Amphitheatri   5

    erigitur moles, stagna Neronis erant;

hic ubi miramur velocia munera thermas,

    abstulerat miseris tecta superbus ager.

Claudia diffusas ubi porticus explicat umbras,

    ultima pars aulae deficientis erat.   10

reddita Roma sibi est et sunt te preside, Caesar,

    deliciae populi, quae fuerant domini.

[Where the starry colossus sees the constellations at close range and lofty scaffolding rises in the middle of the road, once gleamed the odious halls of a cruel monarch, and in all Rome there stood a single house. Where rises before our eyes the august pile of the Amphitheatre, was once Nero's lake. Where we admire the warm baths, a speedy gift, a haughty tract of land had robbed the poor of their dwellings. Where the Claudian colonnade unfolds its wide-spread shade, was the outermost part of the palace's end. Rome has been restored to herself, and under your rule, Caesar, the pleasances that belonged to a master now belong to the people.]

Chapter 42

42.1 Ceterum Nero usus est patriae ruinis extruxitque domum in qua haud proinde gemmae et aurum miraculo essent, solita pridem et luxu vulgata, quam arva et stagna et in modum solitudinum hinc silvae inde aperta spatia et prospectus, magistris et machinatoribus Severo et Celere, quibus ingenium et audacia erat etiam quae natura denegavisset per artem temptare et viribus principis inludere.

ceterum: Not a strongly adversative 'but' (like *at*), but more expressing simultaneity: while others tried to probe into the deeper meaning of the catastrophe, Nero is busy taking advantage of it.

Nero usus est patriae ruinis et extruxit domum: A cuttingly short start as we return to Tacitus' narrative. *usus est* makes clear how Nero calculatingly saw the large-scale destruction as an opportunity, and Tacitus brings out the emperor's apparent lack of patriotism (we remember Chapter

36) in the striking phrase *patriae ruinis* and enhances the effect further by expressing one idea ('Nero used Rome's ruins to build a house for himself') in two separate clauses, each with a finite verb: 'he used Rome's ruins and built a house' (contrast his moonshine over the sideshow non-event at 34.1). The sentence acquires its punch owing to two interrelated contrasts: between *ruinis* and *extruxit*; and between *patriae* (the common fatherland) and *domus* (Nero's private house). These give the sentence real bite, developing the sense of Nero turning public misery into his own private gain. See further *Annals* 15.52.1, where we get a view of the building focalized by the conspirator Piso, who considers the palace a particularly apt location to assassinate the emperor: *in illa invisa et spoliis civium extructa domo* ('in that hated palace reared from the spoils of his countrymen'). The house in question is the so-called 'Golden House.' The enormous project was not yet completed at Nero's death, and Vespasian ordered it to be abandoned. He used part of the area to construct the Colosseum instead – which derives its name from the colossal statue of Nero mentioned by Suetonius in the passage cited above.

in qua haud proinde gemmae et aurum miraculo essent ... quam: The subjects of the relative clause are *gemmae et aurum*, with the latter hinting at the name of the house; the subjunctive *essent* expresses purpose (just as the dative *miraculo*). *haud proinde ... quam* goes together (*proinde ... quam*: 'in the same way or degree as'). Tacitus does not omit to mention that there was an abundance of precious metal and stones, but goes on to say that even these weren't the most amazing thing about the *Domus Aurea*.

solita pridem et luxu vulgata: The phrase, in the neuter nominative plural, stands in apposition to the subjects of the relative clause, i.e. *gemmae et aurum*. *solita ... vulgata* frame the further specifications of time (*pridem*) and of quality (*luxu*). Even the lavishness of the gold and gems of the palace were barely noteworthy in an age of such extravagance. The emphatic *solita* ('familiar') underlines how commonplace these riches were; *pridem* ('long since') suggests the long-term decline under emperors like Caligula and Nero; the moralising *luxu*, an ablative of respect, adds to this tone of decadence; and *vulgata* (coming from *vulgus*, the mob) implies even the common people were accustomed to such splendour (*luxu vulgata = vulgaria*). On Tacitus' preference for uncommon over common diction (in this case *luxu* instead of *luxuria*) see above on 37.1: *celeberrimae luxu famaque epulae fuere.*

quam arva et stagna et in modum solitudinum hinc silvae inde aperta spatia et prospectus [sc. *miraculo essent*]: A long, polysyndetic list of the rural elements of Nero's palace, with extra emphasis from the sibilant alliteration. The phrase *hinc ... inde...* conveys the extent of the estate, spreading out on all sides. Tacitus uses the striking noun *solitudo* ('lone wilderness') to make clear how the landscapers created the elements of wild nature in the centre of Rome. It was common for great Roman villas in the countryside to recreate aspects of nature ('improvements on Nature'); but Tacitus makes clear both the scale of Nero's efforts and the novelty of doing this in the heart of the city.

magistris et machinatoribus Severo et Celere: A nominal ablative absolute with *magistris et machinatoribus* in predicative position. We know nothing else about Severus and Celer. The alliteration and use of two nouns to describe them suggest the many skills and artistry of these men; *machinatoribus* especially implies great technical ability.

quibus ingenium et audacia erat etiam quae natura denegavisset per artem temptare et viribus principis inludere: The relative pronoun *quibus*, which is in the dative of possession, refers back to Severus and Celer. *ingenium* again underscores the talent of these men; *audacia*, however, is not necessarily a positive quality, and can hint at arrogance and recklessness, especially in this context. The architects and engineers are out to challenge the restrictions of nature. The antecedent of *quae* (and the accusative object of *temptare*) is an implied *ea*. The contrasts of this nicely wrought sentence stress how these men viewed nature's laws as no obstacle: *natura* (nature) opposes *artem* (human skill); and *temptare* challenges *denegavisset*.

et viribus principis inludere: Tacitus finishes with a cutting and unequivocally negative comment on these men. Their skills are not only in surpassing nature, but also in squandering money. The vivid verb *inludere* ('fool away'), from *ludo* ('play'), suggests the frivolity and vanity of the projects these men spent money on; and it is juxtaposed to *principis* to remind us powerfully of who is behind this (and whose resources are being wasted). *viribus* is dative with *inludere*.

42.2 namque ab lacu Averno navigabilem fossam usque ad ostia Tiberina depressuros promiserant squalenti litore aut per montes adversos. neque enim aliud umidum gignendis aquis occurrit quam

Pomptinae paludes: cetera abrupta aut arentia ac, si perrumpi possent, intolerandus labor nec satis causae. Nero tamen, ut erat incredibilium cupitor, effodere proxima Averno iuga conisus est; manentque vestigia inritae spei.

The idea of the canal was to link the bay of Naples, through Lake Avernus (there was already a canal from the sea to the lake), to Ostia (and hence Rome). It was not necessarily a hare-brained idea: the coastline from the Bay of Naples north to Rome was very dangerous to shipping, but vital for the corn supply to the capital. (Tacitus mentions wreckage of part of the corn fleet at 15.46.2.) An attempt to eliminate this danger was therefore sensible. It is just the scale of the project that is too vast: like Nero's planned canal through the isthmus of Corinth in Greece, and other gigantesque proofs of tyrant's megalomania à la Herodotus' Xerxes, the project was abandoned after Nero's death; but not forgotten — a *Nero* skit in Greek preserved in with the works of 2nd-century Lucian keeps the mockery alive.

namque [sc. *se*] **ab lacu Averno navigabilem fossam usque ad ostia Tiberina depressuros** [sc. *esse*] **promiserant:** The subjects are still Nero's architects Severus and Celer. *promiserant* introduces an indirect statement, with an implied subjective accusative (*se*) and the future infinitive *depressuros* (*esse*) as verb; it takes *fossam* as accusative object.

ab lacu Averno ... ad ostia Tiberina: Tacitus separates the two ends of the canal in the sentence to enact the immense length of it, further made clear by *usque ad* ('all the way to') – Suetonius, in the passage cited above, estimates the length as about 160 miles.

squalenti litore aut per montes adversos: Tacitus stresses the (insurmountable) difficulties of the project through: (i) the emphatic position of the entire phrase at the end of the sentence; (ii) the *variatio* of the ablative phrase and the prepositional phrase; (iii) the highly poetic and vivid adjective *squalenti* (barren, rough); (iv) the chiastic arrangement; (v) and climactic, final *adversos*.

neque enim aliud umidum gignendis aquis occurrit quam Pomptinae paludes: Tacitus continues to list problems to do with the building of the canal. The absence of water is strongly emphasised by the litotes *neque ... aliud umidum* (*lit.* 'not anything moist'), which suggests utter aridity.

gignendis aquis is a gerundive in the dative (expressing purpose). Already Caesar had tried to drain the (malarial) marshes behind Cape Circeo in Latium.[178] Mussolini managed to make some headway in the 1930s.

cetera abrupta aut arentia [sc. *erant*] **ac, si perrumpi possent, intolerandus** [sc. *erat*] **labor nec satis causae** [sc. *erat*]: Assonance emphasises the unsuitability of the land, made clear by the two graphic adjectives *abrupta* and *arentia*. Tacitus finishes with a scything comment on the futility of the operation. Even if the alternative route were feasible in principle, the work would be too much (*intolerandus*), and the positives would not outweigh the problems (*nec satis causae*). Tacitus delays this phrase in particular to finish off the description.

nec satis causae: *causae* is a partitive genitive dependent on *satis*.

Nero tamen, ut erat incredibilium cupitor, effodere proxima Averno iuga conisus est; manentque vestigia inritae spei: Despite all of what Tacitus has said, Nero still went ahead with the project. The *tamen* stresses how Nero is at odds with all logic.

ut erat incredibilium cupitor: A wonderfully succinct characterisation of Nero's attitude. The *-tor* ending in Latin indicates a profession (as in *mercator, imperator, machinator* etc), and so the word *cupitor* or, according to another reading, *concupitor* represents Nero's love of the impossible as something he does for a living. This is also a very rare word, coined by Tacitus, and thus conveys in and of itself something of Nero's love of the unusual.

effodere proxima Averno iuga conisus est: The hyperbaton *effodere ... conisus est* stresses the manifold difficulties that Nero dismissed: he pushed on regardless.

manent vestigia inritae spei: Tacitus finishes off his account of the canal by revelling in the folly of the undertaking, pointing to the traces of the failure which are still visible even today. The emphatic position of the verb *manent*, and the dismissive last words *inritae spei*, leave us with a picture of a vainglorious emperor with no understanding of practicalities.

---

178   See Plutarch, *Julius Caesar* 58.

Chapter 43

43.1 Ceterum urbis quae domui supererant non, ut post Gallica incendia, nulla distinctione nec passim erecta [sc. *sunt*]**, sed dimensis vicorum ordinibus et latis viarum spatiis cohibitaque aedificiorum altitudine ac patefactis areis additisque porticibus quae frontem insularum protegerent.**

Tacitus frames this sentence with an initial and a final relative clause: *urbis quae domui supererant – quae frontem insularum protegerent*. In between he gives details on the architectual principles that informed the rebuilding of Rome, revolving around the main verb: *erecta* [sc. *sunt*]. (The subject, which is also the antecedent of the first relative pronoun, i.e. *ea*, is elided.) Tacitus first lists two modes in which the city-planners (unlike their predecessors after similar catastrophes) did *not* proceed: *nulla distinctione nec passim*; then, in antithesis, he enumerates the principles that were applied, not least as precautionary measures against future fires:

- *dimensis vicorum ordinibus*
- *latis viarum spatiis*
- *cohibita aedificiorum altitudine*
- *patefactis areis*
- *additis porticibus*

Tacitus' verbal design emulates the layout of the new Rome: the adjectives or participles *dimensis, latis, cohibita, patefactis, additis*, which give a sense of careful planning and a desire to create a beautiful city stand in stark contrast to *nulla distinctione* and *passim* before; they also all come first in their phrases. Likewise, the first three phrases *dimensis vicorum ordinibus* || *latis viarum spatiis* || *cohibita aedificorum altitudine* are of identical construction (ablative phrases sandwiching a genitive plural).

ceterum: This is the second chapter in a row that Tacitus begins with the adverb *ceterum*.

urbis quae domui supererant: The partitive genitive *urbis* depends on the elided *ea*. With the relative clause, Tacitus makes a savagely ironic comment on the inordinate size of Nero's new palace – as if it left marginal space for reconstructing the rest of the city that had burned down. Koestermann thinks the phrase *quae domui supererant* is 'suspicious', but cites a two-line poem (a 'distich') transmitted by Suetonius, *Nero* 39.2 (*Roma domus fiet: Veios migrate, Quirites,* | *si non et Veios occupat ista domus* – 'Rome is becoming one house; off with you to Veii, Quirites! If that house does not soon seize upon Veii as well') and Martial, *Liber de Spectaculis* 2.4 (cited above) as two other sources that crack the same joke.[179] In further support, one could point to the fact that Tacitus concluded his stock-taking of the destruction wrought by the fire in Chapter 40 by using the same verb as here: *septem reliquis pauca tectorum vestigia supererant, lacera et semusta.* The lexical coincidence seems to intimate that the large-scale devastation inflicted on the cityscape by the fire are similar in kind to those inflicted by Nero's palace.

ut post Gallica incendia: Another reference to the torching of Rome by the Gauls in 390 BC. In Livy's account (as we saw above), when the Gauls sacked Rome, a proposal to move Rome to the site of Veii was flattened by the re-founding hero Camillus with the rhetorical question (5.54):

> Si fraude, si casu Veiis incendium ortum sit, ventoque ut fieri potest, diffusa flamma magnam partem urbis absumat, Fidenas inde aut Gabios aliamve quam urbem quaesituri sumus quo transmigremus?

> [If by crime or chance a fire should break out at Veii, and that the wind should spread the flames, as may easily happen, until they consume a great part of the city – are we to quit it, and seek out Fidenae, or Gabii, or any other town you like, and migrate there?]

nulla distinctione nec passim erecta: Livy tells us that, after the Gauls, the city was rebuilt in a rushed and haphazard way (5.55):

> ... promisce urbs aedificari coepta. tegula publice praebita est; saxi materiaeque caedendae unde quisque vellet ius factum, praedibus acceptis eo anno aedificia perfecturos. festinatio curam exemit uicos dirigendi, dum omisso sui alienique discrimine in vacuo aedificant...

> [... people began in a random fashion to rebuild the city. Tiles were supplied at public expense, and everybody was granted the right to quarry stone and to hew timber where he liked, after giving security for the completion of the structures within that year. In their haste men were careless about making the streets straight and, paying no attention to their own and others' rights, built on the vacant spaces...]

---

179 Koestermann (1968) 248.

In Tacitus, the emphatic *nulla* and the vivid *passim* ('all over the place') evoke the weaving, irregular streets that resulted.

latis viarum spatiis: Remember the narrowness of the streets before, mentioned in Chapter 38 as a cause of the fire's rapid progress and one of the reasons for the high death toll. Nero's vision is for wide boulevards.

porticibus: Colonnades to walk and talk in. Here, the stone colonnades also have the extra advantage of protecting the jerry-built blocks of flats from fire, from passing traffic and from the sun.

quae frontem insularum protegerent: The subjunctive in the relative clause expresses purpose. Cf. Suetonius, *Nero* 16.1: *Formam aedificiorum urbis novam excogitavit et ut ante insulas ac domos porticus essent, de quarum solariis incendia arcerentur; easque sumptu suo exstruxit* ('He devised a new form of buildings of the city and in front of the houses and apartments he erected porches, from the flat roofs of which fires could be fought; and these he put up at his own cost').

43.2 eas porticus Nero sua pecunia extructurum purgatasque areas dominis traditurum pollicitus est. addidit praemia pro cuiusque ordine et rei familiaris copiis finivitque tempus intra quod effectis domibus aut insulis apiscerentur.

Tacitus now details measures undertaken by the emperor to relieve the stricken city. This was expected – it was the standard way to restore confidence among the population after the catastrophe. Apart from the instances of rapid response by Tiberius and Claudius cited above, see Suetonius, *Augustus* 30, who reports that Augustus gained renown by putting in place proactive measures and taking general care of intelligent town planning:

> Spatium urbis in regiones vicosque divisit instituitque, ut illas annui magistratus sortito tuerentur, hos magistri e plebe cuiusque viciniae lecti. Adversus incendia excubias nocturnas vigilesque commentus est; ad coercendas inundationes alveum Tiberis laxavit ac repurgavit completum olim ruderibus et aedificiorum prolationibus coartatum. Quo autem facilius undique urbs adiretur, desumpta sibi Flaminia via Arimino tenus munienda reliquas triumphalibus viris ex manubiali pecunia sternendas distribuit.

[He divided the area of the city into regions and wards, arranging that the former should be under the charge of magistrates selected each year by lot, and the latter under 'masters' elected by the inhabitants of the respective neighourhoods. To guard against fires he devised a system of stations of night watchmen, and to control the floods he widened and cleared out the channel of the Tiber, which had for some time been filled with rubbish and narrowed by jutting buildings. Further, to make the approach to the city easier from every direction, he personally undertook to rebuild the Flaminian Road all the way to Ariminum, and assigned the rest of the highways to others who had been honoured with triumphs, asking them to use their prize-money in paving them.]

It would be interesting to compare the reaction of the Berlusconi government to the earthquake that flattened the Italian city of L'Aquila (in Abbruzzo) in April 2009 or the people of Japan to the 2011 tsunami. Tacitus, like other Roman historians, lets his emperor play one-man rescue team and take all plaudits and complaints as if he has no advisers behind him: for a while he suspends his 'it's all a[nother] big act' rhetoric of suspicion.

eas porticus Nero sua pecunia extructurum purgatasque areas dominis traditurum pollicitus est: The subject is *Nero*, the verb is *pollicitus est*, which introduces an indirect statement. The subject accusative (*se*, i.e. Nero) is only implied. Tacitus does not say that Nero *did* do these things, only that he *promised*. We never find out if he delivered on this promise. But Suetonius (*Nero* 16.1: see above), too, reports that Nero built the colonnades at his own expense. In addition, he took on the expense of clearing away the rubble, so that those who lost their property in the fire had a clean construction site on which to rebuild their houses.

addidit praemia pro cuiusque ordine et rei familiaris copiis finivitque tempus intra quod effectis domibus aut insulis apiscerentur: Nero also provided financial support for the rebuilding effort, correlating the amount according to the rank (*pro ... ordine*) and wealth (*pro ... rei familiaris copiis*) of each individual (*cuiusque*); he also specified a deadline by which the reconstruction had to be completed if the owners wished to cash in on the reward-scheme. The house-owners are the subject of the deponent verb *apiscerentur*; its (implied) accusative object is *ea* (= *praemia*). *effectis domibus aut insulis* is an ablative absolute. Despite the fact that landlords received a sum of money on timely completion of houses or flats which complied with the regulations, the rebuilding nevertheless proceeded slowly, as Suetonius notes in his biography of Vespasian (8.5): *Deformis urbs veteribus incendiis ac* *ruinis erat; vacuas areas occupare et aedificare, si possessores cessarent, cuiusque* *permisit* ('As the city was unsightly from former fires and fallen buildings, he allowed anyone to take possession of vacant sites and build upon them, in case the owners failed to do so').

43.3 ruderi accipiendo Ostienses paludes destinabat utique naves quae frumentum Tiberi subvectassent onustae rudere decurrerent; aedificiaque ipsa certa sui parte sine trabibus saxo Gabino Albanove solidarentur, quod is lapis ignibus impervius est;

ruderi accipiendo Ostienses paludes destinabat utique...: This verb has two objects, connected by the *-que* after *uti*: the accusative *Ostienses paludes*; and the *uti*-clause. Nero and his advisers came up with a smart scheme, by which the boats that brought corn up the Tiber returned loaded with rubble, to be deposited at Ostia, where the Tiber reached the sea. On previous occasions, people apparently dumped the rubble straight into the Tiber, which caused blockages: see Suetonius, *Augustus* 30.1, cited above.

ruderi ... rudere: The position of this word (rubble) at the beginning and end of the sentence enacts the sense of the conveyer-belt system Nero is trying to achieve.

subvectassent: The syncopated form of *subvectavissent*.

aedificiaque ipsa certa sui parte sine trabibus saxo Gabino Albanove solidarentur: The Latin reflects the building blocks under discussion: *aedificia ipsa – certa sui parte – sine trabibus – saxo Gabino Albanove* + the verb that indicates the aims and objectives of the effort: *solidarentur*.

aedificia ipsa: The *ipsa* helps to stress Nero's attention to detail in the reconstruction of the city.

certa sui parte: *sui* refers back to *aedificia*. The lower part of the buildings was to be made out of stone only.

saxo Gabino Albanove: An instrumental ablative. Its position next to *sine* *trabibus* helps to emphasise the replacement of wooden beams with fire-proof rock. Gabian rock was quarried in Gabii, ten miles east of Rome; Alban rock came from the shores of the Alban Lake, 15 miles south-east of Rome.

quod is lapis ignibus impervius est: These types of rock were of volcanic origin and hence known for their fire-resistant qualities. But, as Miller points out, 'they are also rough and not very decorative: hence the regulation to ensure their use.'[180]

43.4 iam aqua privatorum licentia intercepta quo largior et pluribus locis in publicum flueret, custodes; et subsidia reprimendis ignibus in propatulo quisque haberet; nec communione parietum, sed propriis quaeque muris ambirentur.

Tacitus here enumerates three further measures undertaken by Nero for the benefit of the Roman citizens, as precautions against future fires. They are designed to ensure (a) a good supply of water; (b) means of fighting fires at the moment they break out; (c) measures to prevent fires from spreading. The syntax of this chapter still depends, in a loose way, on the *destinabat* of 43.3. Thus *custodes* could be taken either as a direct object ('he designated guardians') in parallel to *Ostienses paludes* or as the subject of an elliptical *ut*-clause in parallel to the *uti*-clause ([*ut*] *custodes essent*). *custodes* is preceded by a long purpose clause introduced by *quo*, but with the subject, i.e. *aqua*, which agrees with *intercepta*, placed in front for emphasis. Tacitus elides the *ut* in the two following clauses as well: *et ... haberet*; *nec ... ambirentur*.

aqua privatorum licentia intercepta: Tacitus begins with the problem – irresponsible citizens diverting Rome's water supply for their own use (often only for ornamental fountains). The prominent position of *aqua* (a long way from its verb *flueret*) stresses the need to address this problem; and the pejorative *licentia* (an ablative of cause) heaps condemnation on the Romans who thieve from their fellows.

privatorum ... in publicum: The contrast between private and public also dominated Tacitus' account of Nero's *Domus Aurea*. It is almost as if the emperor here seems to make some amends for his own encroachment of civic space by stopping the private theft of public resources.

custodes: Nero's arrangements here build on the public administration of a vital resource (water) first put into place by Augustus.[181] Nero's custodians

180   Miller (1973) 95.
181   Eck (2009) 238–39.

were meant to patrol the aqueducts to ensure individuals could not siphon water off for themselves.

subsidia reprimendis ignibus: A remarkably modern, 'health and safety'-style idea.

quisque haberet ... quaeque ... ambirentur: The *quisque* and the *quaeque* (which refers back to *aedificia*) emphasise the attempt to achieve universal fire protection.

nec communione parietum, sed propriis quaeque muris: There is classic Tacitean *variatio* at play here: firstly in the two different words for wall (*parietum ... muris*); and secondly in the change of construction from 'noun + genitive' to 'noun + adjective attribute.' This not only keeps the narrative from becoming monotonous, but also enacts the change of the regulations itself. Clearly detached houses are much less conducive to the spread of fire than semi-detached buildings. As Koestermann points out, already the 12 Tables (Rome's most ancient code of law) specified a distance of 2.5 feet between housing blocks (*insulae*).[182]

43.5 ea ex utilitate accepta decorem quoque novae urbi attulere. erant tamen qui crederent veterem illam formam salubritati magis conduxisse, quoniam angustiae itinerum et altitudo tectorum non perinde solis vapore perrumperentur: at nunc patulam latitudinem et nulla umbra defensam graviore aestu ardescere.

ea ex utilitate accepta decorem quoque novae urbi attulere: *attulere* = *attulerunt*. The pronoun *ea* (nominative neuter plural) sums up the measures Nero put in place. Motivated in the first place by utilitarian considerations, they also (*quoque*) helped to beautify the city. *decus* is a very positive word, implying glory and achievement as well as purely aesthetic qualities. In addition, *novae urbi* gives a flavour of what post-conflagration Rome must have looked like, a city renewed, with a different outlook than before.

erant tamen qui...: Even after such a positive passage on Nero's work, Tacitus reports the comments of some more sceptical voices (although, as usual, he refrains from indicating whether he shares their opinion). This

---

182   Koestermann (1968) 251.

finish to the chapter helps to convey Nero's unpopularity: even when he did well, there were plenty of critics. Miller, following Koestermann, notes that 'there always are such people: and they sometimes (as here) have a point.'[183] Perhaps, though the open streets, even if affording less shade, may well have been healthier in terms of preventing disease and ensuring a supply of fresh air. (Contrast Livy's affectionate nostalgia for the rabbit warren of Rome as shoved up after the Gallic wipe-out, above.)

qui crederent: The subjunctive in the relative clause is generic.

angustiae itinerum et altitudo tectorum: Tacitus had occasion to mention the (notorious) narrowness of the Roman streets in Chapter 38 as one of the key causes of the fire's rapid spread. So one wonders whether he is making a point here about Nero's no-win position and the intractability of some of his critics. You may reflect on how sensitive the handling of disasters such as the New Orleans floods has proved for the standing of American presidents.

non perinde solis vapore perrumperentur: *perrumperentur* is in the (oblique) subjunctive: this is not Tacitus' own explanation but the argument of the critics who exaggerate the power of the sun's rays so as to be able to harp about the new layout of the city. Put differently, this sentence does not mean 'since the narrowness of the streets etc. were not so easily penetrated', but 'since *they argued that* the narrowness of the streets etc. were not so easily penetrated.' This subtlety keeps the historian at an arm's length from the comments of these men.

solis vapore: A metaphorical expression for 'the heat of the sun' – Tacitus here stays within the idiom used by Nero's critics.

patulam latitudinem et nulla umbra defensam graviore aestu ardescere: Tacitus continues to reproduce the exaggerated language of the critics: note the metonymic expression *patula latitudo,* picking out for emphasis the offending feature of the new streets (they are broad and open); the hyperbole in *nulla umbra*; the powerful phrase *graviore aestu*; the almost-military idea of *defensam*; and the emphatic metaphor in *ardescere*. At *Annals* 4.67.2 Tacitus calls the volcano Vesuvius a *mons ardescens.* The verb also ominously recalls the fire and anticipates the burning of the Christians.

---

183 Miller (1973) 95.

(VII) 44: Appeasing the Gods, and Christians as Scapegoats

Chapter 44

44.1 Et haec quidem humanis consiliis providebantur. mox petita dis piacula aditique Sibyllae libri, ex quibus supplicatum Vulcano et Cereri Proserpinaeque ac propitiata Iuno per matronas, primum in Capitolio, deinde apud proximum mare, unde hausta aqua templum et simulacrum deae perspersum est; et sellisternia ac pervigilia celebravere feminae quibus mariti erant.

haec refers back to the measures covered in the previous chapters. In addition to efforts that relied on human skill and ingenuity, Nero and his advisers looked into the perceived supernatural dimension of the fire. The Romans had the option of ascribing catastrophic events at least in part to the will of the gods, as an expression of their wrath with human failings in religious observance. In the aftermath of natural or military disasters, they therefore tried to figure out what had gone wrong and what they needed to do to make amends, to re-establish good relations with the divine sphere. The chapter is therefore replete with technical words from Roman ritual and cult: *piacula, Sibyllae libri, supplicatum, propitiata, templum et simulacrum deae, sellisternia, pervigilia*. The persistent use of perfect passives (*petita, aditi, supplicatum, propitiata, perspersum*, with *sunt/est* systematically elided except in the last item) conveys a sense of the formality characteristic of ritual proceedings – as does the pronounced p-consonance *petita ... piacula ... supplicatum ... Proserpinae ... propitiata ... primum ... apud proximum ... templum ... perspersum ... pervigilia*.

mox petita [sc. *sunt*] **dis piacula:** A *piaculum* is an expiatory offering to an offended divinity, though it can also refer to an act or event (such as a natural disaster) that requires expiation. *dis* [= *deis*] is in the dative. The Romans looked into making atonements to the gods they held responsible for the fire.

aditique Sibyllae libri: Tacitus uses noun + genitive (*lit.* 'the books of the Sibyl') rather than the more usual *Sibyllini libri* ('Sibylline books'). These were a collection of prophecies consulted by the Romans in times of dire national crisis (hence Tacitus' stress on them). The greatest sibyl (a female priestess struck by divine inspiration) of the ancient world was the Cumaean Sibyl, and it was works from her that were said to have been brought to Rome by the fifth king, Tarquinius Priscus. The original collection, housed in the temple of Jupiter Optimus Maximus, was destroyed in the fire that ravaged the Capitol Hill in 83 BC, but the collection was re-constituted. Augustus vetted the holdings (burning many prophecies that were ruled apocryphal) and transferred the collection to the temple of Palatine Apollo (which apparently survived the fire more or less unscathed). The priesthood in charge of the books and their interpretation were the so-called *quindecimviri sacris faciundis*. At *Annals* 11.11.1 Tacitus tells his readers that he, too, was elected into this priesthood (see the Introduction for further details).

ex quibus supplicatum [sc. *est*] **Vulcano et Cereri Proserpinaeque ac propitiata** [sc. *est*] **Iuno per matronas, primum in Capitolio, deinde apud proximum mare, unde hausta aqua templum et simulacrum deae perspersum est:** *ex quibus* (the antecedent being *Sibyllae libri*) refers to the recommendations extrapolated (cf. *ex*) from the books. They included: (i) appeasing sacrifices to the god of fire, Vulcan; (ii) appeasing sacrifices to the goddess Ceres and her daughter Proserpina (their temples stood in the vicinity of the Circus Maximus near the Aventine Hill, i.e. close to where the fire broke out); (iii) appeasing sacrifices to Juno, first in her temple on the Capitol, then in Ostia at the sea, from where they brought ritually purified sea-water back to Rome for the cleansing of the temple and the cult-statue in the city.

Iuno per matronas: Juno, goddess of marriage, is appropriately appeased by married women.

sellisternia: A *sellisternium* was a sacred banquet at which the (female) divinities sat on chairs.[184] (It is a subcategory of the *lectisternium* – from *lectum sternere*, i.e. 'to spread out a couch' – during which the images of the gods in attendance were placed on couches.) A *sellisternium* was usually offered by women. See e.g. Valerius Maximus, *Memorable Doings and Sayings*, in a section on 'Ancient Institutions' (2.1.2): *Feminae cum viris cubantibus sedentes cenitabant. quae consuetudo ex hominum convictu ad divina penetravit: nam Iovis epulo ipse in lectulum, Iuno et Minerva in sellas ad cenam invitabantur. quod genus severitatis aetas nostra diligentius in Capitolio quam in suis domibus conservat, videlicet quia magis ad rem <publicam> pertinet dearum*

---

184   See Linderski (1996) 1382.

quam mulierum disciplinam contineri ('Women used to dine seated with their reclining menfolk, a custom which made its way from the social gatherings of men to things divine. For at the banquet of Jupiter he himself was invited to dine on a couch, while Juno and Minerva had chairs, a form of austerity which our age is more careful to retain on the Capitol than in its houses, no doubt because it is more important to the commonwealth that discipline be maintained for goddesses than for women.')[185]

feminae quibus mariti erant: This is virtually identical in meaning to *matronas*, but Tacitus' *variatio* here helps to exaggerate the number of means (and people) mustered in the appeasement process. The passage here stands in striking contrast to the prostituted *illustres feminae* at the sex pageant (37.3).

44.2 sed non ope humana, non largitionibus principis aut deum placamentis decedebat infamia quin iussum incendium crederetur. ergo abolendo rumori Nero subdidit reos et quaesitissimis poenis adfecit quos per flagitia invisos vulgus Christianos appellabat.

The clause introduced by *sed* brings out the tremendous effort Nero invested to make up for the loss of confidence in his reign caused by the fire and to combat the pernicious rumour that he was responsible for it – all to no avail. The sentence is designed as a scale, with the verb (*decedebat*) at the centre. On one side, we have three phrases that summarily rehearse Nero's measures in the wake of the fire, in syntactical variation: ablative noun + adjective (*ope humana*), ablative noun + genitive singular (*largitionibus principis*), genitive plural + ablative noun (*deum placamentis*); on the other side, the simple noun (and subject of the sentence), i.e. *infamia*, which finds further elaboration in the *quin*-clause. The anaphora of *non ... non...* underlines the failure of the efforts, which cover the human sphere more generally (*ope humana* harks back to *humanis consiliis* in 44.1), the emperor (specifically the *praemia* mentioned in 43.2 and his other forms of aid), and the gods (the large-scale campaign of appeasement Tacitus just recounted). These were not sufficient to quell the rumours, and hence Nero decided on more drastic measures – he needed a scapegoat to detract attention

185 Text and translation are taken from D. R. Shackleton Bailey's Loeb edition (Cambridge, Mass. and London, 2000). With reference to the last sentence he comments in a footnote: 'A rare touch of humour'.

from his own perceived culpability. For this purpose, the Christians came in handy: Christianity was spreading through the Roman empire at the time, with two of its founding figures, Peter and Paul, still active. Legend even had them perish in Nero's persecution. The sect quickly acquired a foul reputation because of its secrecy and idiosyncratic rites, such as the holy communion, during which worshippers consumed the body and blood of Christ, which an uncomprehending public turned into lurid and slanderous charges of ritual infanticide and cannibalism. This is the earliest reference to Christians in Roman historiography.

Nero's persecution set a dangerous precedent. Rives draws out the implications of this incident for the fate of Christians in imperial times: 'This episode provided a very clear precedent that being a Christian was in itself enough to justify condemnation to death. Thereafter, if anyone came before a Roman governor with a charge that someone was a Christian, the governor would have been fully justified in following this precedent and condemning that person, provided that he or she did nothing to disprove the allegation.' At the same time, 'Roman officials nevertheless had considerable leeway in how they responded to particular situations.'[186]

decedebat infamia: The delayed subject is greatly emphasised after the long list: all of the methods Nero tried to crush this *infamia* (scandalous rumour) were to no avail, there it is still.

quin iussum [sc. *esse*] **incendium crederetur:** *quin = ut non*. A very compact, Tacitean expression of the belief that persisted. The position of *iussum* adds emphasis, whereas the passive construction leaves it open who actually gave the order, though the rumour under discussion clearly fingered Nero as the culprit.

abolendo rumori: The advanced position of this phrase underlines Nero's desperation to eliminate the suspicions which fell upon him. The verb *aboleo* ('to demolish, destroy') is very powerful, conveying Nero's desperation to crush the rumour.

subdidit reos: This verb, here meaning 'to put someone up on a false charge' leaves us in no doubt as to Nero's unscrupulous and hypocritical conduct,

---

186   Rives (2007) 198–99.

offering up scapegoats to cover his own perceived responsibility for the fire. The legal term *reos* ('defendants') is an ironical comment on Nero's perversion of justice. Remember Tacitus' preoccupation with pretence, hypocrisy and reality here as Nero happily massacres innocent people as a diversion. Or is this still sensible 'damage-limitation' within an effective crisis management?

quaesitissimis poenis adfecit: The superlative *quaesitissimis* makes clear the savage ingenuity Nero applied to the task. Although Tacitus shares his compatriots' suspicion of the Christians, he shows palpable sympathy for the victims of Nero's cruelty throughout this section.

quos per flagitia invisos vulgus Christianos appellabat: The antecedent of *quos* is *reos*, the subject of the relative clause is *vulgus*. Nero picked on a group already unpopular with the people (cf. *invisos*). The *-iani* suffix in the term *Christiani* is 'somewhat contemptuous',[187] suggesting the mob's feeling towards this new, little-known sect. The strongly moralising *flagitia* ('outrages') denotes the abhorrence felt towards the Christians: 'their crimes were those (like incest and infant cannibalism, cf. Tert. *Apol.* 7) which a lurid imgination attributed to an apparently peculiar and secretive group, and of which members of that group were automatically presumed to be guilty (cf. *flagitia cohaerentia nomini* Pliny, *Epp.* 10.96.2).'[188] Miller's references are to Pliny the Younger, *Epistle* 10.96.2 (cited in the next note) and the *Apologeticum* of Tertullian, a Christian living around AD 200. In this work, Tertullian offers a defence of Christians against charges of (i) taking part in crimes like ritual incest, infanticide, and cannibalism of the babies killed; (ii) high treason and contempt for the Roman state religion.

Christianos: There is some dispute as to whether Tacitus wrote *Christianos* or *Chrestianos* and, if (as seems now consensus) the latter, whether he meant to refer to Christians or, as some have argued, Jewish followers of an agitator called Chrestus, who is mentioned by Suetonius, *Claudius* 25.4,[189] and whose Greek name, or title, 'Useful, Good Guy', would make a usefully sardonic point here, unlike 'The Anointed One'; all the same, as Lichtenberg puts

---

187   Miller (1973) xxviii.
188   Miller (1973) xxviii.
189   For a discussion of the paleographical evidence see e.g. http://www.textexcavation.com/documents/zaratacituschrestianos.pdf

it, 'there is no question that the Christians are to be understood under the name *Chrestiani*, for in what follows Tacitus traces them back to their founder Christus.'[190]

appellabat: As Miller points out, the imperfect *appellabat* is perhaps best translated as 'was beginning to call': 'The name originated (*Acts* 11.26) in Antioch, some twenty years before this date.'[191] Even from Tacitus' point of view, the Christians were still a fairly novel sect that just began to rise to public consciousness. About half a century after Nero's persecution, his friend, fellow-litterateur, and correspondent Pliny the Younger asked the emperor Trajan what to do with Christians while he was governor of the province of Pontus/Bithynia from 111–113. The most famous letter and Trajan's response (*Letters* 10.96–97) are well worth reading as background information, and are available in English translation here:

http://www.earlychristianwritings.com/text/pliny.html.

44.3 auctor nominis eius Christus Tiberio imperitante per procuratorem Pontium Pilatum supplicio adfectus erat; repressaque in praesens exitiabilis superstitio rursum erumpebat, non modo per Iudaeam, originem eius mali, sed per urbem etiam quo cuncta undique atrocia aut pudenda confluunt celebranturque.

auctor ... adfectus erat: A brief Tacitean digression to explain the sect's origin and growth 'with documentary precision.'[192] This is the earliest reference to the execution of Christ by order of Pilate in pagan literature.

Tiberio imperitante: An ablative absolute.

imperitante per procuratorem Pontium Pilatum supplicio: The alliteration here is very pronounced, adding colour and interest to the Latin and perhaps stressing the lowliness of this religion's founder from

---

190 Lichtenberg (1996) 2170.
191 Miller (1973) 96. Her reference is to the *Acts of the Apostles*, the fifth book of the New Testament. In the Vulgate version of the Bible, the chapter (referring to events in AD 40) reads as follows: *et annum totum conversati sunt in ecclesia et docuerunt turbam multam ita ut cognominarentur primum Antiochiae discipuli Christiani* ('And they conversed there in the church a whole year: and they taught a great multitude, so that at Antioch the disciples were first named Christians'). Text and translation from http://www.latinvulgate.com/.
192 Syme (1958) II 469.

the Romans' point of view – a condemned criminal. The designation *procurator* is an anachronism: as Brunt has shown, the use of this term to refer to provincial governors of equestrian status dates to the reign of Claudius. Pilate's official title was *praefectus*.[193]

Pontium Pilatum: Praefect of Judaea AD 27-37 and in charge of Jesus' crucifixion, which took place in the thirties (but before AD 37). This is the only mention of him by a Roman historian. He is part of the *Apostles' Creed* (*Symbolum Apostolorum/ Symbolum Apostolicum*), a late-antique precis of the key articles of the Christian faith, which remains in use in Christian services today and pegs Christianity to a claim to historicity:

> Credo in Deum Patrem omnipotentem, Creatorem caeli et terrae, et in Iesum Christum, Filium Eius unicum, Dominum nostrum, qui conceptus est de Spiritu Sancto, natus ex Maria Virgine, *passus sub Pontio Pilato*, crucifixus, mortuus, et sepultus, descendit ad inferos, tertia die resurrexit a mortuis, ascendit ad caelos, sedet ad dexteram Patris omnipotentis, inde venturus est iudicare vivos et mortuos. Credo in Spiritum Sanctum, sanctam Ecclesiam catholicam, sanctorum communionem, remissionem peccatorum, carnis resurrectionem, vitam aeternam. Amen.

Different Christian communities use different translations of the creed. In the Church of England there are currently two authorized variants: that of the *Book of Common Prayer* (1662) and that of *Common Worship* (2000). We cite the latter:

> I believe in God, the Father almighty, creator of heaven and earth. I believe in Jesus Christ, his only Son, our Lord, who was conceived by the Holy Spirit, born of the Virgin Mary, *suffered under Pontius Pilate*, was crucified, died, and was buried; he descended to the dead. On the third day he rose again; he ascended into heaven, he is seated at the right hand of the Father, and he will come to judge the living and the dead. I believe in the Holy Spirit, the holy catholic Church, the communion of saints, the forgiveness of sins, the resurrection of the body, and the life everlasting. Amen.

repressaque in praesens exitiabilis superstitio: Although Roman religion was usually tolerant of other religions, Christian monotheism led to mistrust and suppression. As we have seen, Christians refused to recognize official Roman religious practices, including the worship of the emperor in the imperial cult. Other authors contemporary with Tacitus also reject the new creed in no uncertain terms as a pernicious perversion

---

193   Brunt (1966) 463.

of true religion (*superstitio*). See Pliny the Younger, *Epistles* 10.96.8: *nihil aliud inveni quam superstitionem pravam, immodicam* ('But I discovered nothing else but depraved, excessive superstition.'), and Suetonius, who in his biography of Nero notes the emperor's persecution of Christians though without reference to the fire (16.2):

> Multa sub eo et animadversa severe et coercita nec minus instituta: adhibitus sumptibus modus; publicae cenae ad sportulas redactae; interdictum ne quid in popinis cocti praeter legumina aut holera veniret, cum antea nullum non obsonii genus proponeretur; afflicti suppliciis Christiani, *genus hominum superstitionis novae ac maleficae;* vetiti quadrigariorum lusus, quibus inveterata licentia passim vagantibus fallere ac furari per iocum ius erat; pantomimorum factiones cum ipsis simul relegatae.

> [During his reign many abuses were severely punished and put down, and no fewer new laws were made: a limit was set to expenditures; the public banquets were confined to a distribution of food; the sale of any kind of cooked viands in the taverns was forbidden, with the exception of pulse and vegetables, whereas before every sort of dainty was exposed for sale. *Punishment was inflicted on the Christians, a class of men given to a new and mischievous superstition.* He put an end to the diversions of the chariot drivers, who from immunity of long standing claimed the right of ranging at large and amusing themselves by cheating and robbing people. The pantomimic actors and their partisans were banished from the city.]

With supreme economy, Tacitus uses the forceful attribute *exitiabilis* ('deadly', 'bringing death or destruction') to hint at the nature of the charges commonly brought against the Christians, such as the killing of infants (see above). But it suits neither his style nor his purpose to delve into lurid details. Instead, he goes on to generalize on Rome as a cesspool of the world, a place where everything immoral or atrocious (whether to do with religion or otherwise) quasi-naturally converges: see below on *quo ... celebranturque*.

rursum erumpebat, non modo per Iudaeam, originem eius mali, sed per urbem etiam: The vivid verb *erumpebat* ('burst out') conveys the Roman fear of this allegedly dangerous sect, an effect further enhanced by the potent phrase *originem eius mali*. The province of Judaea was the region around Jerusalem in modern Israel/Palestine. *urbem*, as usual, refers to Rome.

quo cuncta undique atrocia aut pudenda confluunt celebranturque: A savage comment on multiculturalism in Rome, with the hard *c*-alliteration conveying Tacitus' bitterness. The hyperbolic *cuncta* and *undique* exaggerate the immorality which Tacitus perceives as seeping into the city, as does the vivid, metaphorical verb *confluunt*: just as all rivers utimately end up flowing into the sea, so Rome naturally attracts anything atrocious and shameful. Tacitus tops the natural metaphor by adding the surprising *celebranturque*: not only does Rome function as a cesspool of global vice; the inhabitants of the city revel in the immorality. In fact, on the lexical level the formulation, which exudes Tacitean disgust, recalls 37.1: *et* celeberrimae *luxu famaque epulae fuere quas a Tigellino paratas ut exemplum referam*: however depraved the imports from all over the world they have a hard time rivalling the degree of depravity achieved by the natives.

44.4 igitur primum correpti qui fatebantur, deinde indicio eorum multitudo ingens haud proinde in crimine incendii quam odio humani generis convicti sunt. et pereuntibus addita ludibria, ut ferarum tergis contecti laniatu canum interirent, aut crucibus adfixi aut flammandi, atque ubi defecisset dies in usum nocturni luminis urerentur.

igitur: Tacitus uses this word to resume his narrative after his digression on Christianity.

primum correpti [sc. *sunt*] **qui fatebantur:** The antecedent of *qui* (and the subject of the main clause) is an elided *ii*. It is (perhaps deliberately?) unclear what the (enforced?) 'confession' of those who were initially apprehended consisted in: admission of guilt for the fire or participation in Christian rites?

indicio eorum: Most of the first group were probably tortured for evidence to denounce their fellow Christians. Roman citizens were immune from torture, but few Christians were likely to have held citizenship.

multitudo ingens: The hyperbole (though it is not perhaps a massive exaggeration) leaves Nero's cruelty in no doubt. There is no way of telling what the actual numbers were.

haud proinde in crimine incendii quam odio humani generis convicti sunt: *convicti* refers back to *correpti*. As Koestermann points out, the two strategically placed verbs mark the beginning and the end of the judicial proceedings against the sect.[194] The Roman people were willing to acquiesce in the Christians' conviction, not because they really believed they had been involved in arson, but because of their anti-social reputation. But the *haud proinde ... quam...* construction makes it clear that Nero's efforts to exculpate himself were in vain.

et pereuntibus addita [sc. *sunt*] **ludibria:** The emphatically placed present participle in the dative *pereuntibus* evokes pathos for the Christians, mocked even as they die: *ludibria* ('humiliations'), from the verb *ludo*, 'to play', seems especially shocking in the context of mass killings: 'They suffered not only death, but a shameful death.'[195]

ut ferarum tergis contecti laniatu canum interirent: Tacitus goes on to detail the kind of indignities that the emperor inflicted on his victims. The scenario he describes first sounds as if Nero staged a contemporary variant of the Actaeon myth: the Christians were covered in animal hides and then torn apart by dogs. The chiasmus (a) *ferarum* (b) *tergis* – (b) *laniatu* (a) *canum*, the first half governed by the participle *contecti*, the second half by *interirent* underscores the careful planning that went into the atrocious spectacle. As in the tale of Actaeon, who was turned into a 'stag-man' by Diana before being torn apart by his own hounds for having seen the nude goddess at her bath (see Ovid, *Metamorphoses* 3 for details), the procedure dehumanizes the victim: a human consciousness continues to reside in what looks like an animal body. According to Suetonius, Nero had a foible for this sort of thing: he reports that the emperor sponsored turns in which dancers brought ancient myths to life (or, as the case may be, death) (*Nero* 12.2):

> Inter pyrricharum argumenta taurus Pasiphaam ligneo iuvencae simulacro abditam iniit, ut multi spectantium crediderunt; Icarus primo statim conatu iuxta cubiculum eius decidit ipsumque cruore respersit.

> [The pyrrhic dances represented various scenes. In one a bull mounted Pasiphae, who was concealed in a wooden image of a heifer; at least many of the spectators thought so. Icarus at his first attempt fell close by the imperial couch and bespattered the emperor with his blood.]

The re-enactment of mythic archetypes fits well with Tacitus' use of *ludibria*.[196]

---

194   Koestermann (1968) 256.
195   Miller (1973) 97.
196   For representations of the Actaeon story at the amphitheatre of Capua, see Bomgardner (2000) 100.

aut crucibus adfixi aut flammandi: After dilaceration, Tacitus lists two further alternatives: crucifixion and burning. The verb continues to be *interirent*. The text of this passage is uncertain throughout and one manuscript reading is *flammati* (instead of *flammandi*). But the correlation of two perfect participles (*contecti*, *adfixi*) with a gerundive is typical of Tacitean *variatio*, and syntactically anticipates what follows. There is clearly an extra element to this humiliation, as the Christians were mockingly subjected to the same punishment as their founder, though Tacitus does not dwell on this. That some were nailed to the cross 'proves that the Christians executed in the Vatican Gardens certainly had no Roman civil rights' since Roman citizens were protected from suffering the *mors turpissima crucis* ('the most humiliating death on the cross'), an atrocious penalty reserved for slaves and other subject people without citizenship.[197] Those sentenced to be burned alive were dressed in the so-called *tunica molesta*, a shirt impregnated with inflammable material (such as pitch).

atque ubi defecisset dies in usum nocturni luminis urerentur: The phrase *in usum nocturni luminis* ('for the purpose of nightly illumination') brings home the appalling use of these human beings as torches: the horribly practical *in usum* ('for the purpose/use of') conveys Nero's callousness. Miller draws attention to the Virgilian echo in *nocturni luminis*.[198] See *Aeneid* 7.13 (when Aeneas and his crew pass by the island of Circe – she who turns human beings into various forms of wildlife): *urit odoratam nocturna in lumina cedrum* ('she burns fragrant cedar-wood to illuminate the night').

44.5 hortos suos ei spectaculo Nero obtulerat et circense ludicrum edebat, habitu aurigae permixtus plebi vel curriculo insistens. unde quamquam adversus sontes et novissima exempla meritos miseratio oriebatur, tamquam non utilitate publica sed in saevitiam unius absumerentur.

hortos suos ei spectaculo Nero obtulerat: Tacitus here steps back in time (note the pluperfect *obtulerat*) to supply information about the setting, in which the appalling executions took place. The sentence unfolds with deliberate relish: we have the chiastic design of *hortos suos – ei spectaculo*, the delayed subject *Nero*, and the placement of the emperor's name right next to *spectaculo*, which generates the mocking rhyme *-lo -ro*. At this stage in the *Annals*, the gardens

197 Lichtenberger (1996) 2171.
198 Miller (1973) 97.

are already notorious: Tacitus has brought them to the attention of his readers beforehand. At 14.14.2, they were the location for some 'private' chariot racing that soon become an attraction in the city: *clausumque valle Vaticana spatium, in quo equos regeret, haud promisco spectaculo. mox ultro vocari populus Romanus laudibusque extollere, ut est vulgus cupiens voluptatum et, se eodem princeps trahat, laetum* ('and an enclosure was made in the Vatican valley, where he could manoeuvre his horses without the spectacle being public. Before long, the Roman people received an invitation in form, and began to hymn his praises, as is the way of the crowd, hungry for amusements, and delighted if the sovereign draws in the same direction'). And at 15.39, Tacitus reports that Nero opened his gardens to those Romans rendered homeless by the fire. As such, though he had decided that they would cramp his own style (33.1), they made an ideal location to put on a show to distract the populace.

et circense ludicrum edebat, habitu aurigae permixtus plebi vel curriculo insistens: In addition to the spectacles provided by the public executions, Nero organized circus games to regain popularity with the inhabitants of Rome. He used the occasion to present himself as a *princeps* of the people, dressing up in the garb of a charioteer, mingling with the common folk in attendance, and presenting himself on a chariot. In the early years of his reign, as 14.14.2 (cited in the previous note) makes clear, this tactic had some measure of success. But it was risky. For one, it could only ever appeal to the *plebs*, and not to the senators (or historiographers of senatorial standing like Tacitus who makes no secret of his disapproval). The upper classes frowned on the emperor, the mightiest man in the word, debasing himself by dressing up like a lowly professional or even slave on the fringes of society (as we saw with the gladiatorial games at 34.1-35.1). The deliberate exposition continues with the chiasmus (a) *permixtus* (b) *plebi* (note the mocking *p*-alliteration, achieved through the use of the intensifying *per-*) (b) *curriculo* (a) *insistens*. It sets up the next sentence, in which Tacitus wryly informs us that Nero's efforts proved futile.

unde quamquam adversus sontes et novissima exempla meritos miseratio oriebatur, tamquam non utilitate publica, sed in saevitiam unius absumerentur: Tacitus here generates a memorable paradox: he stresses the guilt of the Christians and deems them deserving of extreme and unprecedented punishment (*novissima exempla meritos*: note the superlative), and yet records that the Roman populace, despite their hostility, began to feel pity towards them. The juxtaposition of *meritos* and *miseratio* stages the clash at the level of sentence design. Nero achieved the opposite effect to the one he aimed at. Tacitus could almost certainly have had little evidence for this generalisation of the mindset of the Roman spectators at the time. But there are other instances in which the cruelty on display triggered unexpected feelings of pity. Compare, for instance, the sympathy the Roman audience felt towards the elephants that were slaughtered as part of the games staged by Pompey the Great to celebrate his victories in the Eastern Mediterranean.[199]

quamquam adversus sontes: *quamquam* modifies the prepositional phrase ('albeit towards guilty persons'). Focalization is an issue here: who considers the Christians guilty? And of what? Tacitus? He previously cast the Christians as scapegoats, so not responsible for the fire, but could have regarded them as criminals in a more general sense. Or the Roman populace? (If they pitied the Christians despite believing them to be guilty of causing the fire, it would make the *miseratio* even more striking.)

tamquam non utilitate publica sed in saevitiam unius absumerentur: The contrast is once again between public duty and private desire, articulated by the antithesis of *publica* and *unius*. Bestial monarchic power overshadows public need; the contrast between the positive *utilitate* and the highly negative *saevitiam*, is sharp to begin with and further reinforced by the *variatio*: Tacitus moves from an ablative phrase (*utilitate publica*; an ablative of cause) to *in* + acc. + gen. (*in saevitiam unius*), with the change of construction emphasising the second half. Nero did not manage to shed his image as arsonist. Tacitus famously returns to this failure in his account of the conspiracy of Piso when narrating the sentencing of Subrius Flavus (15.67, cited above).

(VIII) 45: Raising of Funds for Buildings

Chapter 45

45.1 Interea conferendis pecuniis pervastata Italia, provinciae eversae sociique populi et quae civitatium liberae vocantur. inque eam praedam etiam dii cessere, spoliatis in urbe templis egestoque auro quod triumphis, quod votis omnis populi Romani aetas prospere aut in metu sacraverat.

Tacitus now focuses attention on the economic consequences of Nero's efforts to rebuild the burnt-out city and his ravaged reputation. The

---

199   Cicero, *ad Familiares* 7.1.

money-raising affected every part of the Roman empire: we move from Italy to the periphery (provinces, allies, supposedly autonomous civic communities within the reach of Roman power) before zooming in on Rome itself and its divinities. As in his stock-taking after the fire, Tacitus here bemoans the loss of treasures in the temples accumulated over centuries of Roman military success. The riches that resulted from close collaboration of Rome's civic community and its supernatural fellow-citizens are now squandered by an irresponsible emperor.

conferendis pecuniis pervastata [sc. *est*] **Italia:** The juxtaposition of these two phrases makes horrifyingly clear again Nero's abuse of the country for his own ends. The strengthened verb *pervastata* ('*thoroughly* ravaged') suggests his ruthless exploitation of Italy. Clearly vast sums of money were needed for the building projects. Cf. Suetonius, *Nero* 38.3: *conlationibusque non receptis modo verum et efflagitatis provincias privatorumque census prope exhausit* ('and from the contributions which he not only received, but even demanded, he nearly bankrupted the provinces and exhausted the resources of individuals'). More generally, as John Henderson points out, this is how capital cities of empires work, and not just Nero's – the exotica and the scum of the earth are scoured and flood in, as we have seen, and the resources of the world are put at the service of beautifying, ennobling, and in case of disaster of putting them back on their feet, back on top, where they presume they belong.

provinciae eversae [sc. *sunt*] **sociique populi et quae civitatium liberae vocantur** [= *et eae civitatium quae liberae vocantur*]: *eversae*, which here refers to financial ruin, takes three subjects: *provinciae, socii populi*, and *civitates liberae*, though Tacitus presents the last item in such a way as to show that Nero and his agents made a mockery of the attribute 'free.' *civitates liberae* were specially privileged states such as Athens that were supposed to be immune from taxation – hence the ironical *vocantur*.

inque eam praedam etiam dii cessere: The polysyndeton continues (-*que*). In addition, the use of the word *praeda* to describe Nero's fundraising is telling: it is used primarily in a military context for the booty stripped from a defeated enemy. Its use here paints Nero's action as ruthless, thieving and hostile to his own subjects – and the gods. Tacitus' use of the gods as subjects unable to withstand the emperor's onslaught dramatically magnifies Nero's greed and sacrilege, an effect helped by the emphasising *etiam*. As often, Tacitus does not leave Nero's crime as simple rapacity, but introduces connotations of sacrilege and brutality as well.

spoliatis in urbe templis: An ablative absolute. *spoliatis* implies military booty seized from a defeated foe, but here is used to convey the savage execution of Nero's fund-raising campaign. The targets of his greed and desperation are the temples of the gods within the city of Rome: *in urbe* makes clear that Nero's abuse of the city did not stop at the building of the *Domus Aurea*. Pliny the Elder, after listing the greatest works of Greek art in Rome in his *Natural History*, finishes by saying (34.84): 'And among the list of works I have referred to all the most celebrated have now been dedicated by the emperor Vespasian in the Temple of Peace and his other public buildings; they had been looted by Nero, who conveyed them all to Rome and arranged them in the sitting-rooms of his Golden House.'

egestoque auro quod triumphis, quod votis omnis populi Romani aetas prospere aut in metu sacraverat: *egesto auro* is another ablative absolute that leads into a *quod*-clause, in which Tacitus details what kind of gold is at issue: the material investment made by successive generations of Roman magistrates in their communication with the divine sphere, either in situations of triumph (*quod triumphis ~ prospere*) or of crisis (*quod votis ~ in metu*; Roman generals vowed gifts to the gods in return for their support on the battlefield; it was often a measure of last resort to avert defeat). The anaphora *quod ... quod...* lays emphasis on the many grand occasions on which these golden statues had been dedicated to the temples. The totalising *omnis ... aetas* makes explicit Nero's abuse of the shared and ancient Roman heritage, emphasised by the formal term *populi Romani*. The polarities *prospere aut in metu*, set off by *variatio* (adverb; *in* + abl.), cover the whole range, suggesting that all precious objects were fair game to Nero. Finally, the verb *sacraverat* reminds us of the holy origin of these items and Nero's irreligiosity.

triumphis: The triumph was the highest honour which could be awarded to a victorious Roman general. Nero perverts this sacred ritual. Far from celebrating public service and dedicating great riches to the Roman people, he steals from the accumulated public treasure for his own uses.

45.2 enimvero per Asiam atque Achaiam non dona tantum, sed simulacra numinum abripiebantur, missis in eas provincias Acrato ac Secundo Carrinate. ille libertus cuicumque flagitio promptus, hic Graeca doctrina ore tenus exercitus animum bonis artibus non induerat.

enimvero: Highly emphatic, denoting the culmination of the list of Nero's victims.

per Asiam atque Achaiam: The provinces of Achaea (mainland Greece) and Asia (Turkey) were the richest in statuary and religious wealth.

non dona tantum sed simulacra numinum abripiebantur: The *non ... tantum, sed ...* construction emphasises Nero's lack of restraint, whilst the violent verb *abripiebantur* underlines his rapacity. And again, Tacitus points to the sacrilegious nature of Nero's plunder. The Greek travel writer Pausanias (writing in the mid-second century) tells us that Nero stole 500 statues from Delphi alone (10.7.1), while also swooping up treasures from other sanctuaries such as Olympia (6.25.9; 6.26.3).

missis in eas provincias Acrato ac Secundo Carrinate: Tacitus uses an ablative absolute to name Nero's agents: Acratus, one of Nero's freedmen, mentioned later in the *Annals* but otherwise unknown, and Secundus Carrinas, who was believed to have been the son of an orator exiled by Caligula. A right pair, this, 'Uncontrollable' Greekling [*akrates* in Greek ethics is someone without command over himself or his passions] plus Roman-*sounding* 'Winner', for the dirty work.

ille [sc. *erat*] libertus cuicumque flagitio promptus: A freedman rather than a senatorial official being sent to collect money was, for Tacitus, a sign of the unhealthy influence of ex-slaves at the imperial court. Almost by definition, such creatures were depraved and Acratus is no exception: Tacitus stresses that his immorality knew no bounds.

hic Graeca doctrina ore tenus exercitus animum bonis artibus non induerat: Secundus Carrinas apparently studied philosophy (*Graeca doctrina*), but only superficially (*ore tenus*: lit. 'as far as his mouth', i.e. he talked the talk but did not bother to walk the walk): his mind (*animus*) remained unaffected by the exposure to the excellent education (cf.

bonis artibus) he received. Tacitus revels in hypocrisy of this sort, and here stresses this with the simple and scathing contrast between *ore* and *animum*: a wonderfully concise and acid description of a hypocrite.

45.3 ferebatur Seneca quo invidiam sacrilegii a semet averteret longinqui ruris secessum oravisse et, postquam non concedebatur, ficta valetudine, quasi aeger nervis cubiculum non egressus. tradidere quidam venenum ei per libertum ipsius, cui nomen Cleonicus, paratum iussu Neronis vitatumque a Seneca proditione liberti seu propria formidine, dum persimplici victu et agrestibus pomis ac, si sitis admoneret, profluente aqua vitam tolerat.

To his account of Nero's sacrilege, Tacitus appends an anecdote about the Stoic philosopher Seneca, Nero's boyhood tutor and chief adviser in the early years of his reign. He last made an appearance in the *Annals* at 15.23, when he congratulated Nero on his reconciliation with Thrasea Paetus. At *Annals* 14.56, Tacitus reported that Seneca put in a request for early retirement and, after Nero refused to grant it, withdrew himself from the centre of power as much as possible. Now he again tries to put suitable distance between himself and Nero, yet again without success. The incident here prefigures his death in the wake of the conspiracy of Piso, which is given pride of place in Tacitus' account of AD 65, at *Annals* 15.48–74. Tacitus makes it clear that he does not wish to vouch for the veracity of the anecdote: with *ferebatur* and *tradidere quidam* he references anonymous sources without endorsing them. But at 15.60.2 Tacitus recounts the attempt to poison Seneca as fact: ... *ut ferro grassaretur* (sc. *Nero*) *quando venenum non processerat* ('... as poison had not worked, he was anxious to proceed by the sword').

quo invidiam sacrilegii a semet averteret: A purpose clause (hence the subjunctive). Tacitus makes Nero's sacrilege explicit, to the point of saying that his close adviser wanted to avoid being tainted by association. The noun *invidiam* is strong, implying real hatred, whilst the emphasised pronoun *semet* (himself) conveys Seneca's fear that he himself might be held in some way responsible.

longinqui ruris secessum oravisse: The emphatically positioned *longinqui* suggests Seneca's desperate wish to be far from the firing line, as does the verb *oravisse*.

ficta valetudine quasi aeger nervis: *ficta* and *quasi* return us to a favourite theme of Tacitus: the gulf between reality and presentation. Here, even the noble Seneca resorts to deceit – such is the nature of Roman political life under Nero. Seneca chose to simulate a muscular disease that restricted his mobility, presumably because it would have been difficult to prove that he faked it; it also offered a good pretext to stay away from court and he kept it going till his number was up (15.61.1). *valetudo* can mean both 'good health' and 'ill health' and here of course means the latter. In the gruesome event, the old valetudinarian bird was so tough he took a great deal of killing to see himself off (15.63.3, 64.3-4).

postquam non concedebatur: The subject is *secessus*. For the tense (*postquam* + imperfect) see Miller's note at 37.3: '*postquam* with the imperfect indicative describes an action which continues up to the time of the main verb. Because of this, it often conveys a causal connection too, "now that".'[200]

cubiculum non egressus [sc. *esse*]: The infinitive *egressus esse*, which here takes an accusative object (*cubiculum*), depends like *oravisse* on *ferebatur*.

tradidere quidam venenum ei per libertum ipsius, cui nomen [sc. *erat*] **Cleonicus, paratum** [sc. *esse*] **iussu Neronis vitatumque** [sc. *esse*] **a Seneca proditione liberti seu propria formidine:** *tradidere* [= *tradiderunt*] introduces an indirect statement with *venenum* as subject accusative and *paratum* (*esse*) and *vitatum* (*esse*) as infinitives. The marked position of *venenum* gives special emphasis to the horrifying fact that Nero tried to poison his old friend and teacher. Note again that it is a freedman involved in this skulduggery, with *ipsius* (his own) emphasising Nero's role.

The detail *cui nomen Cleonicus* may render the story more concrete and hence plausible but, as John Henderson reminds us, the usual point in Tacitus' naming especially Greek 'extras' for walk-on parts is that they tote 'speaking names': so, enter 'Glory-Be-Victory' [from *kleos* = glory and *nike* = victory]. (A favourite is 'Invincible' 'Anicetus', whose persistence finally clinched another staggered sequence of (botched) butchery, when eliminating Nero's mother Agrippina to inaugurate *Annals* 14 and Nero's first break out from the shackles of boyhood (notably Seneca's control)).

---

200   Miller (1973) 87.

paratum iussu Neronis vitatumque a Seneca: The failure of the plan is stressed by the balanced phrases here: 'prepared by Nero's orders, avoided by Seneca.' The hand of the emperor behind this crime is explicit.

proditione liberti seu propria formidine: Again Tacitus gives two possible explanations, linked by the alliteration and paronomasia *proditione ~ propria* and with emphasis on the second. The crime could have been revealed to Seneca by the crumbling of Cleonicus (*proditione liberti*), with the word *proditio* ('treachery', 'betrayal') used with immense irony – his 'betrayal' was to save the life of Seneca, a cutting comment on the perversity of Nero's reign. Or the crime could have been foiled by Seneca's own fear (*propria formidine*): this is the more incriminating explanation because it implies that Seneca was already expecting an assassination attempt from his one-time supervisee. There is *variatio* in constructions (noun + subjective genitive (*proditione liberti*) followed by attribute + noun), which generates a chiasmus that helps to stress the second option, as does the following *dum*-clause.

dum persimplici victu et agrestibus pomis ac, si sitis admoneret, profluente aqua vitam tolerat: Seneca managed to prolong his life by only consuming non-processed food and running water, which pre-empted any possibility of adding poison – though the anecdote brings to mind Livia's murder of Augustus by poisoning figs still on the tree. See Cassius Dio 56.30: 'So Augustus fell sick and died. Livia incurred some suspicion in connexion with his death... she smeared with poison some figs that were still on trees from which Augustus was wont to gather the fruit with his own hands; then she ate those that had not been smeared, offering the poisoned ones to him.' (Tacitus, at *Annals* 1.5, mentions the rumour that Livia tried to poison Augustus, but without going into details.) *et agrestibus pomis* explicates *persimplici victu*. Koestermann points out that the indicative *tolerat* within indirect speech is designed to convey Tacitus' admiration for the Spartan simplicity of Seneca's chosen way of life,[201] but it may just as well cash out as sage precaution against the risk of poison at court (cf. 15.60.3). The subjunctive *admoneret* in the *si*-clause expresses repeated action (and thus has affinity with the generic use of the subjunctive).[202]

---

201 Koestermann (1968) 262.
202 Miller (1973) 99.

5. Bibliography

5.1 Critical Editions

Fisher, C. D. (ed.) (1906), *Cornelii Taciti Annalium Ab Excessu Divi Augusti Libri,* Oxford.

Koestermann, E. (ed.) (1965), *Cornelii Taciti Libri Qui Supersunt, Tom. I: Ab Excessu Divi Augusti,* Leipzig.

Heubner, H. (ed.) (1994), *P. Cornelii Taciti Libri Qui Supersunt, Tom. I: Ab Excessu Divi Augusti,* Stuttgart [2nd, corrected edition; first edition 1983].

Wellesley, K. (ed.) (1986), *Cornelii Taciti Libri Qui Supersunt, Tomus I, Pars Secunda: Ab Excessu Divi Augusti Libri XI–XVI,* Leipzig.

5.2 Commentaries

Furneaux, H. (1907), *Cornelii Taciti Annalium Ab Excessu Divi Augusti Libri/ The Annals of Tacitus edited with introduction and notes, vol. II. Books XI–XVI,* 2nd edn, revised by H. F. Pelham and C. D. Fisher, Oxford.

Koestermann, E. (1968), *Cornelius Tacitus, Annalen, erläutert und mit einer Einleitung versehen, Band IV: Buch 14–16,* Heidelberg.

Miller, N. P. (1973), *Cornelii Taciti Annalium Liber XV,* Basingstoke and London.

5.3 Translations

Jackson, J. (1937), *Tacitus, Annals, Books XIII–XVI,* Loeb Classical Library, London and Cambridge, Mass.

Woodman, A. J. (2004), *Tacitus, The Annals,* translated, with introduction and notes, Indianapolis and Cambridge.

5.4 Secondary Literature

Adams, J. N. (1972), 'The Language of the Later Books of Tacitus' *Annals', Classical Quarterly* 22, 350–73. DOI: 10.1017/S0009838800042130

— (1983), 'Words for "Prostitute" in Latin', *Rheinisches Museum* 126, 321–58.

Allen, W. (1962), 'Nero's Eccentricities Before the Fire (Tac. Ann. xv, 37)', *Numen* 9, 99–109. DOI: 10.2307/3269398

Ash, R. (2006), *Tacitus*, Bristol.

—. (ed.) (2012), *Oxford Readings in Tacitus*, Oxford.

Austin, R. G. (1964), *P. Vergili Maronis, Aeneidos Liber Secundus, with a commentary*, Oxford.

Ball, L. F. (1994), 'A Reappraisal of Nero's *Domus Aurea*', *JRA*, Supplementary Series II, *Rome Papers*, 182–254.

Bartera, S. (2011), 'Year-beginnings in the Neronian Books of Tacitus' *Annals*', *Museum Helveticum* 68, 161–81.

Barton, C. (1989), 'The Scandal of the Arena', *Representations* 27, 1–36. DOI: 10.2307/2928482

Bartsch, S. (1994), *Actors in the Audience: Theatricality and Doublespeak from Nero to Hadrian*, Cambridge, Mass. and London.

Beacham, R. C. (1999), *Spectacle Entertainments of Early Imperial Rome*, New Haven and London.

Bert Lott, J. (2012), *Death and Dynasty in Early Imperial Rome: Key Sources, with Text, Translation, and Commentary*, Cambridge and New York. DOI: 10.1017/CBO9781139046565

Betensky, A. (1975), 'Neronian Style, Tacitean Content: The Use of Ambiguous Confrontations in the *Annals*', *Latomus* 37, 419–35.

Birley, A. R. (2000), 'The Life and Death of Cornelius Tacitus', *Historia* 49, 230–47.

Blösel, W. and Hölkeskamp, K.-J. (eds.) (2011), *Von der militia equestris zur militia urbana. Prominenzrollen und Karrierefelder im antiken Rom*, Stuttgart.

Bomgardner, D. L. (2000), *The Story of the Roman Amphitheatre*, London and New York.

Brunt, P. A. (1961), 'Charges of Provincial Maladministration under the Early Principate', *Historia* 10.2, 189–227.

—. (1966), 'Procuratorial Jurisdiction', *Latomus* 25, 461–89.

Burnand, C. (2012), *Tacitus and the Principate: From Augustus to Domitian*, Cambridge.

Campbell, J. B. (1993), 'War and Diplomacy: Rome and Parthia 31 BC – AD 235', in J. Rich and G. Shipley (eds.), *War and Society in the Roman World*, London and New York, 213–40.

Champlin, E. (2003), *Nero*, Cambridge, Mass. and London.

Cooley, M. G. L. (ed.) (2003), *The Age of Augustus* (= LACTOR 17), London.

Deininger, J. (1965), *Die Provinziallandtage der römischen Kaiserzeit von Augustus bis zum Ende des dritten Jahrhunderts n. Chr.*, Munich.

Develin, R. (1983), 'Tacitus and Techniques of Insidious Suggestion', *Antichthon* 17, 64–95.

Dominik, W. J., Garthwaite, J., Roche, P. A. (eds.) (2009), *Writing Politics in Imperial Rome*, Leiden etc.

Dyson, S. L. (1970), 'The Portrait of Seneca in Tacitus', *Arethusa* 3, 71–83.

Eck, W. (2009), 'The Administrative Reforms of Augustus: Pragmatism or Systematic Planning?', in J. Edmondson (ed.), *Augustus*, Edinburgh, 229–49.

—. (2010), *Monument und Inschrift. Gesammelte Aufsätze zur senatorischen Repräsentation in der Kaiserzeit*, ed. by W. Ameling and J. Heinrichs, Berlin etc.

Eck, W. and Heil, M. (eds.) (2005), *Senatores populi romani. Realität und mediale Präsentation einer Führungsschicht*, Stuttgart.

Edmundson, J. (2006), 'Cities and Urban Life in the Western Provinces of the Roman Empire, 30BC–250AD', in D. S. Potter (ed.), *A Companion to the Roman Empire*, Malden, Mass., 250–80. DOI: 10.1002/9780470996942.ch14

Edwards, C. (1993), *The Politics of Immorality in Ancient Rome*, Cambridge.

Elsner, J. and Masters, J. (eds.) (1994), *Reflections of Nero: Culture, History and Representation*, London.

Feldherr, A. (2009), *The Cambridge Companion to the Roman Historians*, Cambridge. DOI: 10.1017/CCOL9780521854535

Flaig, E. (1992), *Den Kaiser herausfordern: Die Usurpation im römischen Reich*, Frankfurt a. M.

—. (2003), 'Wie Kaiser Nero die Akzeptanz bei der *Plebs urbana* verlor', *Historia* 42, 351–72.

—. (2010a), 'How the emperor Nero lost acceptance in Rome', in B. C. Ewald and C. F. Noreña (eds.), *The Emperor and Rome: Space, Representation, and Ritual*, Cambridge, 275–88.

—. (2010b), 'The Transition from Republic to Principate: Loss of Legitimacy, Revolution, and Acceptance', in J. Arnason and K. Raaflaub (eds.), *The Roman Empire in Context: Historical and Comparative Perspectives*, London, 67–84. DOI: 10.1002/9781444390186.ch03

Frazer, R. M. (1966/67), 'Nero the Artist-Criminal', *Classical Journal* 62, 17–20.

—. (1971), 'Nero, the Singing Animal', *Arethusa* 4, 215–18.

French, V. (1986), 'Midwives and Maternity Care in the Roman World', *Helios*, new series 13.2, 69–84.

Gallia, A. B. (2012), *Remembering the Roman Republic. Culture, Politics, and History under the Principate*, Cambridge.

Garnsey, P. (1988), *Famine and Food-Supply in the Greco-Roman World*, Cambridge.

Gladhill, B. (2012), 'The Emperor's No Clothes: Suetonius and the Dynamics of Corporeal Ecphrasis', *Classical Antiquity* 31, 315–48. DOI: 10.1525/CA.2012.31.2.315

Goodyear, F. R. D. (2012), 'Development of Language and Style in the *Annals* of Tacitus', in R. Ash (ed.), *Tacitus*, Oxford Readings in Classical Studies, Oxford, 357–75 [first published in the *Journal of Roman Studies* 58, 1968, 22–31. DOI: 10.2307/299692].

Gotter, U. and Luraghi, N. (2003), 'Einleitung, Teil I und III', in U. Eigler et al. (eds.), *Formen römischer Geschichtsschreibung von den Anfängen bis Livius. Gattungen – Autoren – Kontexte*, Darmstadt, 9–15 and 31–38.

Gradel, I. (2002), *Emperor Worship and Roman Religion*, Oxford.

Griffin, M. T. (1976), *Seneca: A Philosopher in Politics*, Oxford.

—. (1984), *Nero: The End of a Dynasty*, London.

—. (2009), 'Tacitus as historian', in A. J. Woodman (ed.), *The Cambridge Companion to Tacitus*, Cambridge, 168–83. DOI: 10.1017/CCOL9780521874601.013

Gyles, M. F. (1946/47), 'Nero Fiddled While Rome Burned', *Classical Journal* 42, 211–17.

—. (1961/62), 'Nero, qualis artifex?', *Classical Journal* 57, 193–200.

Gwyn, W. B. (1991), 'Cruel Nero: The Concept of the Tyrant and the Image of Nero in Western Political Thought', *History of Political Thought* 12, 421–55.

Hardie, P. R. (2012), *Rumour and Renown: Representations of Fama in Western Literature*, Cambridge.

Heinze, R. (1915/1993), *Virgil's Epic Technique*, trans. H. Harvey, D. Harvey, and F. Robertson, Bristol [originally published as *Virgils epische Technik*, 3rd edn, Leipzig 1915].

Hemsoll, D. (1990), 'The Architecture of Nero's Golden House', in M. Henig (ed.), *Architecture and Architectural Sculpture in the Roman Empire*, Oxford, 10–38.

Henderson, J. (1998), 'Tacitus: The World in Pieces', in *Fighting for Rome: Poets & Caesars, History & Civil War*, Cambridge, 257–300.

—. (2004), *Morals and Villas in Seneca's Letters: Places to Dwell*, Cambridge. DOI: 10.1017/CBO9780511482229

Hersch, K. K. (2010), *The Roman Wedding: Ritual and Meaning in Antiquity*, Cambridge.

Hickson Hahn, F. (2007), 'Performing the Sacred: Prayers and Hymns', in J. Rüpke (ed.), *A Companion to Roman Religion*, Malden etc., 235–48.

Hind, J. G. F. (1970), 'The Middle Years of Nero's Reign', *Historia* 20, 488–505.

Hölkeskamp, K.-J. (2004), '*Fides – deditio in fidem – dextra data et accepta*', in *Senatus Populusque Romanus. Die politische Kultur der Republik – Dimensionen und Deutungen*, Stuttgart, 105–35.

Humphrey, J. H. (1986), *Roman Circuses: Arenas for Chariot Racing*, London.

Hutchinson, G. O. (1993), *Latin Literature from Seneca to Juvenal*, Oxford.

Jones, C. (2000), 'Nero Speaking', *Harvard Studies in Classical Philology* 100, 453–62. DOI: 10.2307/3185231

Kaufmann, M. (c. 1915), *Das Sexualleben des Kaisers Nero*, Leipzig.

Klauck, H.-J. (2003), 'Do They Never Come Back? *Nero redivivus* and the Apocalypse of John', in *Religion und Gesellschaft im frühen Christentum: Neutestamentliche Studien*, Tübingen, 268-89.

Kleijwegt, M. (2000), 'Nero's Helpers: The Role of the Neronian Courtier in Tacitus' Annals', *Classics Ireland* 7, 72–98. DOI: 10.2307/25528361

Klingenberg, A. (2011), *Sozialer Abstieg in der römischen Kaiserzeit. Risiken der Oberschicht in der Zeit von Augustus bis zum Ende der Severer*, Paderborn etc.

Klingner, F. (1955), 'Beobachtungen über Sprache und Stil des Tacitus am Anfang des 13. Annalenbuches', *Hermes* 83, 187–200.

Koestermann, E. (1968), *Cornelius Tacitus, Annalen Band IV, Buch 14–16*, Heidelberg.

Kraus, C. S. (1994), '"No Second Troy": Topoi and Refoundation in Livy, Book V', *Transactions of the American Philological Association* 124, 267–89.

Kraus, C. S. and Woodman, A. J. (1997), *Latin Historians* (= Greece & Rome New Surveys in the Classics 27), Oxford.

Krebs, C. B. (2012), *A Most Dangerous Book: Tacitus's Germania from the Roman Empire to the Third Reich*, New York.

Kolb, A. (2000), *Transport und Nachrichtentransfer im römischen Reich*, vol. 2, Berlin.

Leppin, H. (1992), *Histrionen. Untersuchungen zur sozialen Stellung von Bühnenkünstlern im Westen des Römischen Reiches zur Zeit der Republik und des Principats*, Bonn.

Lichtenberger, H. (1996), 'Jews and Christians in Rome in the Time of Nero: Josephus and Paul in Rome', *Aufstieg und Niedergang der römischen Welt* 26.3, 2142–76.

Linderski, J. (1996), 'Sellisternium', in S. Hornblower and A. Spawforth (eds.), *The Oxford Classical Dictionary*, 3rd edn, Oxford, 1382.

Lintott, A. W. (2001–2003), '"Delator" and "index". Informers and Accusers at Rome from the Republic to the Early Principate', *The Accordia Research Papers* 9, 105–22.

Luce, T. J. and Woodman, A. J. (eds.) (1993), *Tacitus and the Tacitean Tradition*, Princeton.

Maltby, R. (1991), *A Lexicon of Ancient Latin Etymologies* (= ARCA 25), Leeds.

Marincola, J. (1997), 'Tacitus' Prefaces and the Decline of Imperial Historiography', *Latomus* 58, 391–404.

—. (2003), 'Beyond Pity and Fear: The Emotions of History', *Ancient Society* 33, 285–315. DOI: 10.2143/AS.33.0.503603

—. (ed.) (2007), *A Companion to Greek and Roman Historiography*, 2 vols, Malden etc.

Martin, R. H. (1969), 'Tacitus and his Predecessors', in T. A. Dorey (ed.), *Tacitus*, London, 117–47.

—. (1981), *Tacitus*, London.

—. (1990), 'Structure and Interpretation in the *Annals* of Tacitus', *Aufstieg und Niedergang der römischen Welt* 2.33.2, Berlin, 1500–81.

—. (2001), *Tacitus: Annals V & VI*, Warminster.

Martin, R. H. and Woodman, A. J. (1989), *Tacitus Annals Book IV*, Cambridge.

—. (2012), 'Tacitus (1), Roman Historian', *Oxford Classical Dictionary*, 4th edn, 1426–28.

Mattern, S. P. (1999), *Rome and the Enemy: Imperial Strategy in the Principate*, Berkeley, Los Angeles, London.

Mayer, R. (1982), 'What Caused Poppaea's Death?', *Historia* 31, 248–49.

—. (2010), 'Oratory in Tacitus' *Annals*', in D. Berry and A. Erskine (eds.), *Form and Function in Roman Oratory*, Cambridge, 281-93.

Morford, M. P. O. (1985), 'Nero's Patronage and Participation in Literature and the Arts', *Aufstieg und Niedergang der römischen Welt* 2.32.3, Berlin and New York, 2003–31.

Morgan, T. (2007), *Popular Morality in the Early Roman Empire*, Cambridge. DOI: 10.1017/CBO9780511597398

Murray, O. (1965), 'The Quinquennium Neronis and the Stoics', *Historia* 14, 41–61.

Noreña, C. F. (2011), *Imperial Ideals in the Roman West: Representation, Circulation, Power*, Cambridge.

Oakley, S. P. (2009a), 'Res olim dissociabiles: Emperors, Senators and Liberty', in A. J. Woodman (ed.), The Cambridge Companion to Tacitus, Cambridge, 184–94. DOI: 10.1017/CCOL9780521874601.014

—. (2009b), 'Style and Language', in A. J. Woodman (ed.), The Cambridge Companion to Tacitus, Cambridge, 195–211. DOI: 10.1017/CCOL9780521874601.015

O'Gorman, E. (2000), Irony and Misreading in the Annals of Tacitus, Cambridge. DOI: 10.1017/CBO9780511482335

Oliver, R. P. (1977), 'The Praenomen of Tacitus', American Journal of Philology 98, 64–70. DOI: 10.2307/294003

Pagán, V. E. (ed.) (2012), A Companion to Tacitus, Malden etc.

Paul, G. M. (1982), 'Urbs Capta: Sketch of an Ancient Literary Motif', Phoenix 36, 144–55. DOI: 10.2307/1087673

Phillips, E. J. (1978), 'Nero's New City', RFIC 106, 300–7.

Plass, P. (1988), Wit and the Writing of History: The Rhetoric of Historiography in Imperial Rome, Madison.

Rawson, E. (1987), 'Discrimina Ordinum: the Lex Julia Theatralis', Papers of the British School in Rome 55, 83–114 [= Roman Culture and Society: Collected Papers, Oxford 1991, 508–45]

Rives, J. B. (2007), Religion in the Roman Empire, Malden etc.

Roller, M. (2001), Constructing Autocracy. Aristocrats and Emperors in Julio-Claudian Rome, Princeton.

—. (2009), 'The Exemplary Past in Roman Historiography', in A. Feldherr (ed.), The Cambridge Companion to the Roman Historians, Cambridge, 214–30. DOI: 10.1017/CCOL9780521854535.014

Rudich, V. (1993), Political Dissidence under Nero: The Price of Dissimulation, London and New York.

Rüpke, J. (2008), Fasti Sacerdotum: A Prosopography of Pagan, Jewish, and Christian Religious Officials in the City of Rome, 300 BC to AD 499, Oxford.

Rutledge, S. H. (2001), Imperial Inquisitions. Prosecutors and Informants from Tiberius to Domitian, New York and London.

Sailor, D. (2008), Writing and Empire in Tacitus, Cambridge. DOI: 10.1017/CBO9780511482366

Santoro-l'Hoir, F. (2006), Tragedy, Rhetoric and the Historiography of Tacitus' Annales, Ann Arbor.

Scheid, J. (ed.) (1998), Comentarii Fratrum Arvalium Qui Supersunt (Ecole Francaise de Rome and Soprintendenza Archeologica di Roma), Rome.

Schofield, M. (2009), 'Republican Virtues', in R. Balot (ed.), A Companion to Greek and Roman Political Thought, Malden etc., 199–213.

Seelentag, G. (2004), Taten und Tugenden Trajans. Herrschaftsdarstellung im Principat, Stuttgart.

Shatzman, I. (1974), 'Tacitean Rumours', Latomus 33, 549–78.

Smallwood, E. M. (1967), Documents Illustrating the Principates of Gaius, Claudius and Nero, Cambridge.

Sumi, G. S. (2005), *Ceremony and Power. Performing Politics in Rome between Republic and Empire*, Ann Arbor.

Swain, S. et al. (2007), *Seeing the Face, Seeing the Soul: Polemon's Physiognomy from Classical Antiquity to Medieval Islam*, Oxford.

Syme, R. (1958), *Tacitus*, 2 vols, Oxford.

—. (1970), *Ten Studies in Tacitus*, Oxford.

Varner, E. (2005), 'Execution in Effigy: Severed Heads and Decapitated Statues in Imperial Rome', in A. Hopkins and M. Wyke (eds.), *Roman Bodies: Antiquity to the Eighteenth Century*, London, 66–81.

Vout, C. (2007), *Power and Eroticism in Imperial Rome*, Cambridge.

Wallace-Hadrill, A. (1982), '*Civilis Princeps*: Between Citizen and King', *Journal of Roman Studies* 72, 32–48. DOI: 10.2307/299114

Wildfang, R. L. (2006), *Rome's Vestal Virgins: A Study of Rome's Vestal Priestesses in the Late Republic and Early Empire*, New York.

Winterling, A. (2003/2011), *Caligula: A Biography*, trans. D. L. Schneider, G. W. Most, and P. Psoinos, Berkeley and London [originally published in German by C. H. Beck with title *Caligula: eine Biographie*, Munich 2003].

Woodman, A. J. (1992), 'Nero's Alien Capital. Tacitus as Paradoxographer (*Annals* 15. 36–7)', in T. Woodman and J. Powell (eds.), *Author and Audience in Latin Literature*, Cambridge, 173–88, 251–55 [= *Tacitus Reviewed*, Oxford 1998, 168–89]. DOI: 10.1017/CBO9780511659188.012

—. (2004), *Tacitus, The Annals*, translated, with introduction and notes, Indianapolis and Cambridge.

—. (ed.) (2009a), *The Cambridge Companion to Tacitus*, Cambridge. DOI: 10.1017/CCOL9780521874601

—. (2009b), 'Introduction', in id. (ed.), *The Cambridge Companion to Tacitus*, Cambridge, 1–14. DOI: 10.1017/CCOL9780521874601.001

—. (2012), 'The Preface to Tacitus' *Agricola*', in *From Poetry to History: Selected Papers*, Oxford, 257–90.

Ziolkowski, A. (1993), '*Urbs direpta*, or How the Romans Sacked Cities', in J. Rich and G. Shipley (eds.), *War and Society in the Roman World*, London.

6. Visual aids

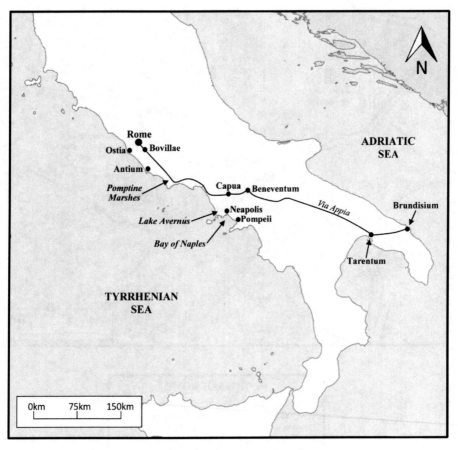

6.1 Map of Italy by Mathew Owen.

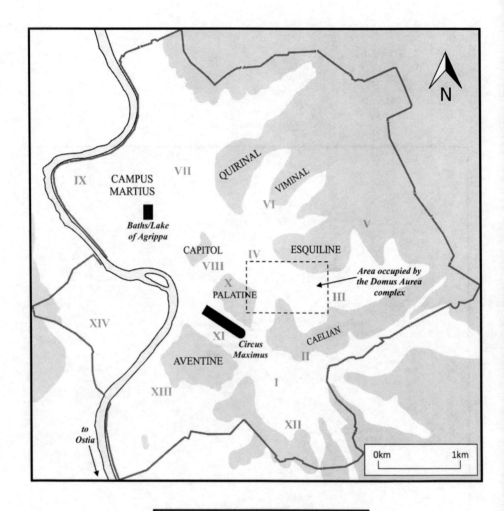

6.2 Map of Rome. By Mathew Owen, design based on 'Map of Ancient
Rome' by Richardprints @ Wikimedia.com.

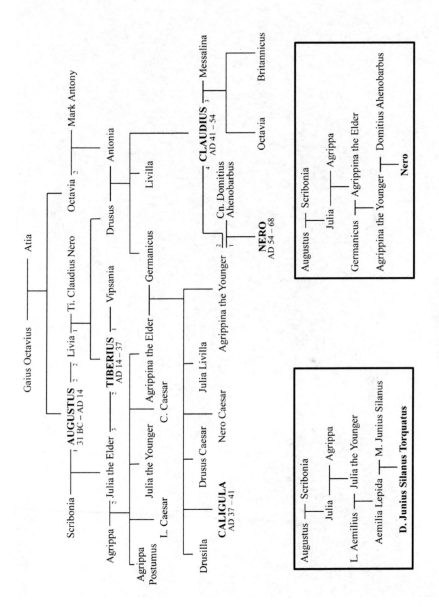

6.3 Family Tree of Nero and Junius Silanus, by Mathew Owen.

6.4 Inside the *Domus Aurea*.
A photograph of part of the interior of Nero's *Domus Aurea*, now open to the public.
The recently-excavated chambers and lavish frescos make it one of Rome's great
tourist magnets. Photo by Kristin Burns, 2007 (CC BY-3.0 license).

This book does not end here...

At Open Book Publishers, we are changing the nature of the traditional academic book. The title you have just read will not be left on a library shelf, but will be accessed online by hundreds of readers each month across the globe. We make all our books free to read online so that students, researchers and members of the public who can't afford a printed edition can still have access to the same ideas as you.

Our digital publishing model also allows us to produce online supplementary material, including extra chapters, reviews, links and other digital resources. Find *Tacitus, Annals, 15.20-23, 33-45* on our website to access its online extras. Please check this page regularly for ongoing updates, and join the conversation by leaving your own comments:

http://www.openbookpublishers.com/isbn/9781783740000

If you enjoyed the book you have just read, and feel that research like this should be available to all readers, regardless of their income, please think about donating to us. Our company is run entirely by academics, and our publishing decisions are based on intellectual merit and public value rather than on commercial viability. We do not operate for profit and all donations, as with all other revenue we generate, will be used to finance new Open Access publications.

For further information about what we do, how to donate to OBP, additional digital material related to our titles or to order our books, please visit our website.

OpenBook Publishers

Knowledge is for sharing